D0710769

POLITICS,
POWER,
and the
CHURCH

BOOKS BY LAWRENCE LADER

1955
Margaret Sanger and the Fight for Birth Control

1961
The Bold Brahmins: New England's War Against Slavery (1831–1863)

1966
Abortion

1969
Margaret Sanger: Pioneer of Birth Control
(with Milton Meltzer)

1971
Breeding Ourselves to Death

1972
Foolproof Birth Control: Male and Female Sterilization

1973
Abortion II: Making the Revolution

1979
Power on the Left: American Radical Movements Since 1946

1987
Politics, Power, and the Church

POLITICS, POWER, and the CHURCH

The Catholic Crisis and Its Challenge to American Pluralism

·

LAWRENCE LADER

Macmillan Publishing Company

NEW YORK

Macmillan Publishing Company
866 Third Avenue, New York, N.Y. 10022
Collier Macmillan Canada, Inc.

Library of Congress Cataloging-in-Publication Data
Lader, Lawrence.
Politics, power, and the church.
Includes bibliographies and index.
1. Catholic Church—United States—History—20th
century. 2. Church and social problems—Catholic Church—
History—20th century. 3. Church and social problems—
United States—History—20th century. 5. Catholic
Church—Doctrines—History—20th century. I. Title.
BX1406.2.L29   1987   322'.1'0973   87-11024

ISBN 0-02-567210-x

Special Sales Director
Macmillan Publishing Company
866 Third Avenue
New York, N.Y. 10022

10 9 8 7 6 5 4 3 2 1

Designed by Jack Meserole

Printed in the United States of America

For

JOAN SUMMERS LADER

CONTENTS

POLITICS,
POWER,
and the
CHURCH

I

Designs for Power

T HE DEVELOPMENT of Catholic power—the influence of its religious morality and political aims on American society—has followed a careful design. Once an immigrant religion so oppressed that the anti-Catholic American party virtually controlled Congress by 1856, the church had ascended to the first stage of power—local, urban power—by 1900. This was accomplished partly by numerical strength: the Catholic population rose from around 10 million to almost 18 million between 1900 and 1920. But it was equally due to the skill of Catholic politicians, mainly Irish, who welded their constituents into urban machines as much at the service of the hierarchy as the political bosses.[1]

By 1980, with the election of President Ronald Reagan, the Catholic church achieved what it had only grasped for before: national power that gave the bishops more access to the White House than any other religion, and made them one of the most awesome lobbying blocs on Capitol Hill. Again, numbers were a factor, as Catholics now constituted a quarter of the population. But the emergence of an alliance between the Catholic church, the Protestant Fundamentalists, and the White House was even more critical. Reagan's triumphs in 1980 and 1984 can be largely attributed to this alliance. "Reagan has used religion aggressively as a weapon, a tool," complained New York's Governor Mario Cuomo, himself a Catholic.[2] And on a whole range of issues, from school prayer to federal funding of parochial schools, Catholics and Fundamentalists, of course, collaborated with Reagan. It was a convenient confluence of interests that thrust religion into politics more brazenly than at any time in the nation's history, and threatened the "wall of separation" between church and state that had been a constitutional tenet since Thomas Jefferson used the phrase in 1802 in analyzing the meaning of the First Amendment.[3]

The first stage of the hierarchy's rise to power—and of its pressure on the wall of separation—can be measured by the reverberations of a single command issued by Archbishop Patrick J. Hayes of New York City on Sunday, November 13, 1921. At Town Hall on West Forty-third Street that evening, Margaret Sanger had called a meeting. Its topic was: "Birth Control—Is It Moral?" A silvery-voiced orator whose auburn hair and delicate beauty cloaked her fanatical dedication, Sanger had put together an international panel that included a former member of the British Parliament and Dr. Royal S. Copeland, health commissioner of New York. Since 1913 she had built a movement of radical outcasts into an organization now supported by many of the city's most prestigious families.

It was such blue-chip names as Mrs. Pierre Jay and Mrs. Lewis L. Delafield who now accompanied Sanger to the hall. A block away, their taxi was halted by a milling crowd. They alighted and pushed towards the entrance, but a policeman told them that the meeting had been canceled. Slipping under the arms of the police at a side door, Sanger struggled into the packed lobby. Recognized immediately, she was boosted onto a man's shoulders and shoved to the stage where her assistant, Anne Kennedy, told her that twenty minutes ago, with the hall half filled, a police officer with an unidentified priest had ordered, "This meeting must be closed."

Presenting a contract and paid receipt for the hall, Kennedy had asked the reason. "An indecent, immoral subject is to be discussed," replied the priest, who introduced himself as Monsignor Joseph Dineen, secretary to Archbishop Hayes. The officer was a Captain Donohue of the local station house.

Sanger now shouted to the audience, "We're going to hold this meeting," but two policemen grabbed her. "Where's your warrant? What's the charge?" she demanded.

Mary Winsor, president of the Pennsylvania Equal Suffrage Association, started to speak, but was pushed aside by the police. Sanger kept shouting to the audience to hold their seats, but was quickly enveloped by policemen. "The stage was in tumult," *The New York Times* reported the next morning. "Mrs. Sanger was still the storm center."

As the police forced the audience out of the hall, Monsignor Dineen ordered Captain Donohue to arrest Sanger and Winsor. They were led down the aisle amid catcalls and hisses. People began to sing, "My country 'tis of thee," and soon everyone joined this ironic paean to liberty. When the two women refused to ride in the patrol wagon, they were followed through the streets by singing, jeering protestors.

Next morning Sanger appeared in court, but Captain Donohue never showed up to press charges. After an assistant district attorney admitted there was no evidence on which to draw a complaint, the judge dismissed the case.

Its real significance, however, was pinpointed by the *Times* reporter who reached Monsignor Dineen at his office late that evening of the meeting. Yes, the monsignor admitted, I ordered the meeting to be closed. In a front-page story the next morning, the *Times* stated, "The police suppression of the birth control meeting at Town Hall Sunday night . . . was brought about at the instance of Archbishop Patrick J. Hayes of this Roman Catholic Archdiocese."

"It was arbitrary and Prussian to the last degree," admonished a *New York Tribune* editorial. "If people cannot come together in a perfectly orderly and open way to debate whether or not a matter is moral," a *New York Post* editorial warned, "then our boasted freedom of speech is a mockery."

The order from Archbishop Hayes, of course, had deeper implications. Beyond the obvious First Amendment violations of speech and assembly, it raised the question of how a church official could seek to force his religious dogma on a city. It raised the further question of who in the city government approved this alliance between church and state and made the police carry it out.

The Town Hall meeting, in fact, was the first open proof that power in New York City had been wrested from the old Protestant establishment and taken over by the Catholic church. The political process ostensibly was in the hands of Mayor John J. Hylan, a Catholic, and the Catholic-dominated Tammany machine under boss Charles Murphy, also a Catholic. Now it had been demonstrated that the "Powerhouse" on Fiftieth Street, as the archdiocese office came to be dubbed, was the ultimate ruler. And for decades thereafter, it would be an accepted axiom that no piece of state or city legislation was even worth bringing to a vote until it had been cleared by the Powerhouse.

Such pillars of Protestant banking and law as Herbert L. Satterlee and Paul D. Cravath still had the prestige to make city hall set up an investigation. But it was all window dressing. After dragging on for three years, no final report was ever made. No one was punished. Politics and religion had been unshakably fused.[4]

It would take many years for the Catholic church to solidify the second stage of power: national power. The event could be measured by its impact on separation of church and state. When President Reagan appointed a U.S. ambassador to the Vatican on January 10, 1984, it was not only a demonstration of the church's national influence, but of its ability to erase a principle seemingly embedded in the First Amendment for almost two centuries.

The United States had never had an ambassador to the Vatican, only a consul until 1848, when the rank was changed to chargé d'affaires and, a few years later, to minister. After Pope Pius IX ordered all Protestant churches to move outside Rome in 1867, Congress even eliminated this small mission by cutting off its funds.

The constitutional block had always been the Establishment Clause of the First Amendment, which prohibits the preference of one religion over another. If an ambassador were sent to the State of the City of the Vatican (terminology adopted by the Lateran Treaty of 1929), the United States would be recognizing the religious ruler of a civil territory. This would open up the possibility that the Anglican church could ask Washington for an ambassador to its seat at Canterbury, England, or that Islam would want an ambassador at Mecca. A government like Iran, with a religious base, presents different conditions. It is a state in every definition of internationl law. The Vatican's 108 acres give it only the slightest resemblance to a state.

This dilemma has been resolved for other countries—most of them lacking the strict, church-state separation of the United States—by accrediting their diplomats to the Holy See, the church's spiritual entity. "Papal diplomacy rests essentially upon the spiritual sovereignty of the Holy See and not upon dominion over a few acres in the heart of Rome," Archbishop Pio Laghi, Apostolic Pro-Nuncio to Washington, insisted during the senatorial debate in 1984. But there seems little difference between spiritual sovereignty and the pope's authority as head of a world religion, and herein lies the crux of the constitutional problem.

"To give one church a preferential status in relation to the American government," the National Council of Churches, a coalition of most Protestant bodies, concluded in 1952, "would set aside the principle of according all religious bodies the same status in the eyes of our government."[5]

Under the pressure of war in 1939, the Catholic church saw the chance to bend constitutional obstacles, and Cardinal George Mundelein of Chicago, Archbishop Francis Spellman of New York, and even Cardinal Eugenio Pacelli, shortly elected Pope Pius XII, lobbied the White House hard. But while President Franklin D. Roosevelt needed a listening post in Rome, he adhered to the separation principle by appointing Myron C. Taylor not as an ambassador but as his "personal representative." And Taylor was forbidden to use a penny of government funds or even write on State Department stationery.[6]

The Vatican pushed even harder for an ambassador after the war. Fearing the rising strength of the Communist party, bolstered by its record in the underground, the pope poured money and organizers into the Christian Democratic party. President Harry S. Truman's anti-Communist containment policy jibed with these needs, and American funds to Italy went not only for foreign aid and to labor organizations, but to the Vatican election fund. Cardinal Spellman frequently handled arrangements, a questionable intrusion by a church official into foreign policy. Under instructions from Monsignor Amleto Cicognani, apostolic delegate to the United States, Spellman lobbied James F. Byrnes, former secretary of state and newly elected governor of South Carolina.[7] As a result of these and other pressures, Truman became the first president to nominate an ambassador to the Holy See, General Mark Clark, on October 20, 1951.

The reaction was instantaneous and sharp. The National Association of Evangelicals, a moderate Fundamentalist group, called on its 8,000 pastors to oppose the appointment and spent $500,000 on a radio campaign. The National Council of Churches, representing 40 million Protestants, produced a barrage of letters and telegrams to Congress. Most Jewish groups joined them. "It was the biggest campaign we ever staged—we even enlisted the janitors," recalled the Reverend Dean Kelley of the National Council. Truman shortly backed down and Clark withdrew his name.[8]

Only when the Catholic–Fundamentalist–White House alliance was cemented in 1984 would the Catholic church secure the symbolic distinction of national power with an ambassador to the Vatican. Its main conduit, in addition to President Reagan, was U.S. Congressman Clement Zablocki (D-Wisconsin), a Catholic whose longtime political aid to the church had been rewarded with the papal title of Knight Commander, and who held the critical post of chairman of the House Committee on Foreign Affairs.

Again, the interests of the White House and the church abetted each other. The president saw the chance to increase his Catholic votes. In Latin America, Pope John Paul II's growing antagonism to the radical Liberation Theology movement would complement the president's efforts to undermine leftist governments. The web of mutual interests went further, of course, including potential Central Intelligence Agency links to Vatican diplomatic channels as a worldwide intelligence source. President Kennedy had scoffed at this possibility. Dr. James Draper, president of the Southern Baptist Convention, warned: "The implication that our government might use religious organizations for information, if not espionage, endangers not only the credibility of the message they deliver but, in some war-torn countries, their very lives."[9]

President Reagan first had to repeal the 1867 ban on federal funds for a Vatican mission. Zablocki introduced a bill into the House, Richard Lugar (R-Indiana) into the Senate. It was passed without hearings and at sessions with few legislators attending. Nor were any hearings held on a subsequent bill to fund the mission. Not till Reagan appointed his close friend William A. Wilson, a California real-estate developer and convert to Catholicism, as his ambassador in January 1984, would the opposition realize that this breach in the wall of separation had almost been accomplished.

Catholic power as part of the three-pronged alliance was not the only factor. The coalition long opposing a Vatican ambassador was now fragmented and diluted. The National Council of Churches and other groups made routine appearances before congressional committees, but there was no follow-up of letters and telegrams similar to the campaign that had inundated Truman. Although the National Association of Evangelicals spoke out against the Wilson nomination, the Fundamentalists (with a few dissenters like the Reverend Jerry Falwell) supported their Catholic allies. Jewish groups were mainly quiet, the assumption being that they were so eager to get Vatican recognition of Israel that they couldn't antagonize the pope. "It just wasn't a front-burner issue for us," the Reverend Dean Kelley admitted.[10]

This tepid defense of a ban that had stood for almost two centuries stemmed in part from the humanity infused in the church by Pope John XXIII and a growing acceptance of the anti-Communist strategies of the pope and the White House. It also came from a burst of ecumenism after Vatican II. Reagan's own personal influence was equally important. In a confidential memo during the debates, obtained by the *Chicago Sun-Times*, the Reverend Billy Graham concluded: "If anyone can do it and get away with it, it is President Reagan."[11] The Senate vote on March 6, 1984, approving Wilson's nomination by 81 to 13, confirmed the impact of the three-pronged alliance.

Americans United for Separation of Church and State, joined by the National Council of Churches and twenty other religious organizations, immediately went into federal court to have the Vatican appointment declared unconstitutional. But on May 7, 1985, Judge John P. Fullam of the U.S. District Court for the Eastern District of Pennsylvania dismissed the suit. His ruling held that the Constitution gave the president and Congress exclusive authority in foreign policy, and that the plaintiffs lacked "standing" to sue because they were not directly harmed by this link between the government and the Vatican. The plaintiffs, consequently, appealed to the U.S. Court of Appeals and to the U.S. Supreme Court, both of which refused to hear the case.[12]

Ironically, during a period of great political power, the Catholic church was rent by crisis. It was confident of its strength. "We Catholics, you know, have a marvellous organizational network, as ideal as any politician would want," a bishop told Mary Hanna, the author of a study on the church and government.[13] Still, the church, as well as Fundamentalists, now found their religious image damaged by political intervention. "I'm frankly sick and tired of the political preachers across the country telling me as a citizen that if I want to be a moral person, I must believe in A, B, C or D," complained U.S. Senator Barry Goldwater of Arizona, a conservative Republican and former presidential candidate. "I am even more angry as a legislator who must endure the threats of every religious group who [sic] thinks it has some God-given right to control my vote on every roll call in the Senate."[14]

The Catholic church increasingly suffered from a blurred identity. Was its spiritual purpose being overtaken by political involvement? For almost two millennia it had drawn millions with its blend of mystery and faith. It preached a vision always just beyond human capability. It promised a sure road to salvation. It drew people from their daily struggle and pain to seek an ideal that few could reach, but that all at least believed was within their grasp.

Yet, with its emphasis on morality and the afterlife, the church often resembled a political machine. It had a clear obligation under the First Amendment, like all religions, to educate its followers on political issues. The pastoral letter of the U.S. Conference of Bishops in 1983, striving to deal with the threat of nuclear disaster, was an extraordinary fulfillment of this purpose. But how could Cardinal Humberto Medeiros of Boston castigate a candidate for Congress and another up for reelection without soiling his office by violating a federal law against religious intervention? How could Cardinal John O'Connor of New York lacerate Geraldine Ferraro's candidacy for vice president by charging that no candidate could be a true Catholic and tolerate the religious beliefs of others on abortion?

These are disturbing questions that go to the meaning of the church today. If we are to understand it, we must examine its dual identity. The church no longer remains monolithic. It is a church divided, groping in different directions. Essentially, it remains rooted in the past, an autocratic structure through which the pope and bishops make all decisions, and their constituents follow them without question. Pope John Paul II, too, often turns the Vatican into a political machine, putting money and workers into Italian elections. He has tried to bend

Liberation Theology in Latin America from its radical course, punishing a Brazilian theologian with "penitential silence" and harassing the "People's Church" through his local bishops.

But part of the U.S. church—a small part still—has revolted against its autocratic structure. The decisive event was Pope Paul VI's encyclical in 1968, *Humanae Vitae*, which maintained the church's ban against birth control. The vast majority of U.S. Catholics refused to obey it. Increasing numbers ignored similar prohibitions against divorce, intermarriage with other faiths, and premarital sex. A "new Catholic" was staking out a sphere of independence that claimed personal responsibility on social issues beyond the control of the pope or the hierarchy.

The revolt eventually challenged the very authority of the church. Evolving from the women's movement, it sought to destroy male domination and admit women to the priesthood. Radical nuns, and even a few bishops, campaigned for the Equal Rights Amendment against the neutral position of the hierarchy. Nuns and priests, again in conflict with most of the hierarchy, gave sanctuary to political refugees from Central America and defied federal law; some were even arrested and tried by the U.S. government. Radical nuns, risking expulsion from their orders, insisted that abortion was a legitimate Catholic choice in the broader demand for women's control of their own procreation. What these rebels wanted was to revolutionize the system and create a community-based "People's Church" whose outlines were already being shaped in Latin America.

All these patterns of change must be examined against a hierarchy which, in the main, refuses to accept separation of church and state under the First Amendment. Pluralism has always been basic to the social stability of the nation. It involves acceptance by all society of the importance of its parts. For Catholics, the election of John F. Kennedy to the presidency ensured their place in the pluralist tradition, proving that the Protestant majority no longer monopolized the political process.

Yet, the Catholic hierarchy still rejects pluralism when many of its moral beliefs and dogma are in dispute. Through legislation on divorce, school prayer, abortion, and a host of issues, it has sought to legalize its moral codes. The precedent set by Archbishop Hayes in blocking the Sanger meeting on birth control has become a national practice. While Catholic bishops and Fundamentalists certainly have the right under the First Amendment to preach and educate on any issue, the question is whether their power should be used to push their beliefs on the majority through legislation without a national consensus.

The use of power must be explored. Is it used responsibly or dangerously? The nuclear letter of the bishops, seeking only to educate and stir debate, seems eminently responsible. The attack on the U.S. Supreme Court decision legalizing abortion, both through federal and state legislation—and often blown so out of proportion that Cardinal Bernard Law of Boston called it the number-one issue of the 1984 campaign—seems to threaten our whole pluralist tradition and could damage our social cohesiveness.

In an appeal to responsibility a few decades back, generally un-heeded, Cardinal Richard Cushing of Boston urged: "Catholics do not need the support of civil law to be faithful to their own religious convictions and they do not seek to impose by law their moral views on other members of society."[15]

Since the hierarchy can control its constituents only to varying degrees on varying issues, Catholic power depends on the strategy of focusing the votes of a hard-core, and often fanatical, faction on "swing" legislators. Unless they were elected by large margins from safe districts, legislators dread the possibility of losing a race by a thousand votes and are particularly vulnerable to compact pressure groups. The special skill of the church is that it can put together busloads of lobbyists through the parish machinery and concentrate a mass of phone calls, letters, and telegrams on a necessary target.

Such pressure may be part of democracy. But when it represents only a minority faction, and when it involves highly sensitive, moral issues, the spiraling of force and counterforce can bring ominous results. Senator Goldwater has called the joint pressure of the church and the Moral Majority "a divisive element that could tear apart the very spirit of our representative system, if they gain sufficient strength."[16]

Paradoxically, the Catholic alliance with the Fundamentalists, as-suring the hierarchy's rise to power, is the source of its greatest em-barrassment, for Fundamentalism had always been an enemy of the church, a key factor in the defeat of Al Smith, a Catholic, for the presidency in 1928. Even today, the alliance is based mainly on moral and sexual issues and areas of self-interest, such as federal funding of parochial schools. On the nuclear letter, among other cases, the church has come into direct conflict with its Fudamentalist allies. With this constant shift in alignments, Catholic power may be subject to increasing strains both from its rebels within and its allies without.

This problem particularly disturbs the liberal wing of the church. "Whoever is responsible, the image of the Catholic church which has been created in the American mind, is not the Church of Christ," pointed out John Cogley, a Catholic author, a few years back. "It is the image of a power structure." The problem also disturbs many in the hierarchy. "I thought the Powerhouse was a terrible thing to call a church office, the worst thing imaginable," Bishop Joseph Sullivan of Brooklyn lamented.[17]

If power corrupts, the increasing power of the Vatican has not only corrupted its religious mission but produced a rebellious constituency. Catholic power, allied with Fundamentalism, has threatened the American tenet of church-state separation and shaken the fragile balance of our pluralistic society. The next decades may decide whether the internal conflicts of Catholicism will turn an autocratic church into a people's church, in tune with both ecumenism and constitutional principles.

II

The Upward Leap:
1900–1960

THE OBJECTIVES of the American Catholic church were delineated as early as 1850 by a confident prelate. In a book titled *The Decline of Protestantism and Its Causes*, Archbishop John Hughes of New York City declared: "Everybody should know that we have for our mission to convert the world—including the inhabitants of the United States . . . the Senate, the Cabinet, the President and all."[1]

Hughes's ambitions peaked at a time of anti-Catholic oppression. In the 1840s employment ads in Northeast cities carried the warning, "No Catholics Need Apply." Catholic churches had been burned down in Philadelphia, and parishioners killed in anti-Catholic riots. As waves of immigrants, mainly Irish, flooded the job market, native-born Americans in the Know-Nothing party attempted to block immigration through legislation. Nothing fazed Hughes, however. Determined to get a share of public money to expand his parochial school system, he set up a Catholic party to pressure legislators. Although he drew few votes and the attempt failed, it was a precedent for increasingly bitter campaigns in the next century to finance religious education with tax money.[2]

It was not till the 1920s, after a new tide of immigration from Italy and Eastern Europe, that the Catholic population became large enough to dominate many cities. Political bosses such as Charles Murphy in New York, mayors such as Edward Kelly and Richard J. Daley in Chicago, and even mayors in smaller cities, such as Frank Hague of Jersey City, completed the fusion between their machines and their church. The Irish in Boston foretold the decline of Protestant control—fulfilling Hughes's prediction—when John F. Fitzgerald, President John F. Kennedy's grandfather, was elected mayor in 1905, and was succeeded by James M. Curley in 1913.

The building blocks of these urban machines were jobs, favors, the appointment of commissioners, election to city councils and state legislatures, and a favored position in police and fire departments. By 1964, for example, the Irish in Chicago filled at least forty-one of seventy-two of the highest administrative ranks in the police department. The electoral base was strengthened by a high Catholic birthrate as well as immigration. From 1936 to 1968 the Catholic population soared 139 per cent while the population as a whole rose only 56 per cent.[3]

Still, national power remained unobtainable while Catholics were limited by language, education, and working-class status. Only a handful, including John J. Raskob, chairman of the finance committee of General Motors, reached real wealth and influence. The rate of illiteracy from 1899 to 1910 was 54 per cent for Southern Italians and 35 per cent for Poles in the fourteen years and older age group. Forty-five per cent of Catholics considered their parents "working-class" compared to 32 per cent of Jews in a 1969 study of 60,000 faculty members at higher institutions. Among all U.S. Catholic bishops in 1957, only 5 per cent of their fathers had graduated from college, and the same percentage had some college education.[4]

Except in certain urban areas, the Protestant ethic still ruled the country, as was convincingly demonstrated by the Volstead amendment in 1919, prohibiting alcoholic beverages. Backed by most Protestant clergy and the Protestant rural vote, it failed ratification in only two heavily Catholic states, Connecticut and Rhode Island.

The limitations on Catholic national power were further demonstrated by the rancor and prejudice that swept the 1928 campaign of Governor Al Smith of New York, a Democrat and first Catholic candidate for president. Elected governor four times, Smith was responsible for a large body of progressive legislation. He announced immediately: "I believe in the absolute separation of church and state."[5] The Federal Council of Churches of Christ in America and other responsible clergymen tried to forestall an anti-Catholic campaign. But the depth of prejudice, particularly in the South and border states, was too great.

"The ambition of the Romanists is to make America Catholic," charged the Reverend I. M. Haldeman, a New York Baptist minister. Another toured the country branding Smith the "nominee of the worst forces of hell." Former Governor Sidney J. Catts of Florida claimed that Catholic churches were stocked with guns and dynamite in a plot to take over the country. At frequent railroad stops on his campaign train, Smith was pelted with eggs and tomatoes, and the Ku Klux Klan burned crosses on nearby hilltops.

Smith, of course, had other obstacles besides religion. His rasping New York accent, his ever-present brown derby tipped at a rakish angle, and his stand for modification of the Volstead Act hardly appealed to the Fundamentalist vote. Furthermore, in a tide of prosperity that many considered the by-product of Republicanism, it is doubtful any candidate could have beaten Herbert Hoover in 1928. Smith received only 15 million votes to Hoover's 21.4 million, and even lost New York State by 110,000 while Franklin D. Roosevelt, a Protestant, won the governorship by 26,000.[6]

The Catholic hierarchy had always hesitated to leave its urban base and take on national issues. It ignored the abolitionist movement before the Civil War, although Protestant clergy crowded its ranks, and some, like the Reverend Thomas Wentworth Higginson, risked their lives in attempts to rescue fugitive slaves. It stayed aloof from the Prohibition debates. Only in 1936, when General Francisco Franco revolted against the freely elected Republican government of Spain, would the hierarchy see the advantage of exploiting anti-Communist passions and enter a national conflict.

Even as Nazi Germany and fascist Italy poured their troops and armaments into Franco's armies, almost every U.S. bishop branded the war a choice between "God and anti-God," in the words of Archbishop John T. McNicholas of Cincinnati. Archbishop Joseph Schrembs of Cleveland rated Franco another George Washington. "As liberty-loving Americans, we want nothing of either fascism or communism in our country," declared Monsignor Frank A. Hall of the Cincinnati archdiocese. "But if we must make a choice, we should unhesitatingly choose fascism as the lesser of two evils."[7]

When Claude Bowers, the U.S. ambassador to Spain, and many of President Roosevelt's inner circle decided that Adolf Hitler and Benito Mussolini were more a threat to peace than the Soviet Union and lobbied to lift the embargo that outlawed arms for the Spanish Republicans, the Catholic hierarchy countered with a "Keep the Spanish Embargo Committee." It operated from the same Washington address as the National Catholic Welfare Conference. Father Charles E. Coughlin, a Michigan priest whose popular radio program bristled with anti–New Deal and anti-Semitic tirades, aided the campaign. Together they roused almost 100,000 letters to Congress against Republican Spain. When sixty members of Congress drew up a declaration sympathetic to the Republican armies, an outburst of Catholic mail forced half to revoke their endorsements.

Roosevelt leaned towards lifting the embargo, but feared, according to his secretary of the interior, Harold Ickes, it would "mean the loss of every Catholic vote next fall. . . ." After Republican Spain was defeated, Ickes portrayed the president as admitting that his failure to lift the embargo had been a disastrous mistake.[8]

The impact of the hierarchy may have been a critical factor, but the country's isolationist and pacifist mood, and particularly the anti-Soviet sentiment against a government with a large Communist bloc, weighed heavily for neutrality. In addition, the hierarchy never fully swayed its constituents. In a December 1938 Gallup poll, 58 per cent of Catholic voters supported Franco and 42 per cent were for the Republicans, contrasted with 17 and 83 per cent among Protestants, respectively. But even if the bishops fell short of unanimity in their first show of national power, they had already learned how to create the illusion of power, and that convinced Congress.[9]

After World War II the Catholic church was ready to test its strength on one of the most volatile of all issues: federal funding of parochial schools. Since Archbishop Hughes's first attempts, almost every state constitution had prohibited public money for religious schools, and the U.S. Supreme Court had interpreted the First Amendment's Establishment Clause to apply as well to federal money. Religious groups could set up their own educational system, but tax revenues could be used only for public schools, which law and tradition considered the bulwark of equality and a guarantee that immigrant children would have the same chance as the native born.

When Congressman Graham Barden (D-North Carolina) introduced a bill into the House in 1949 to aid public education, Cardinal Francis Spellman of New York City, the dominant political manipulator among U.S. bishops, angrily denounced it and demanded an equal share for parochial schools. He had his statement posted on the doors of all diocesan churches and read at masses, asking that Catholics flood Congress with letters and telegrams. Shortly, he would provoke a vehement confrontation with Eleanor Roosevelt, widow of the president.

In her nationally syndicated column, "My Day," on June 23, Mrs. Roosevelt had defended the principle of church-state separation, only mentioning tangentially Spellman's attack on Barden. The cardinal, however, was no booster of separation. He backed the National Catholic Welfare Conference in calling it a "shibboleth of doctrinaire secularism." He was also piqued at Mrs. Roosevelt for supporting a resolution against Franco at the United Nations, and at her and New York's Governor Herbert H. Lehman as well for protesting a ban on *The Nation* magazine in New York City public schools. The ban had followed Paul Blanshard's exposé series on the church, and had probably been instigated by the Powerhouse.

The cardinal wrote Mrs. Roosevelt caustically on July 21. "For, whatever you may say in the future," he charged, "your record of anti-Catholicism stands for all to see—a record which you yourself wrote on the pages of history which cannot be recalled—documents of discrimination unworthy of an American mother."[10]

In answer, Mrs. Roosevelt cited her long campaigning for Catholic candidates, Al Smith at the head of the list. But her crucial sentence stressed the separation principle: "Spiritual leadership should remain spiritual leadership, and the temporal power should not become too important in any church."

Most bishops backed Spellman's demands for federal funds, and the Vatican seemingly added its support when a semi-official source called Spellman's statements "necessary and therefore approved." Fearing a concentrated assault on separation of church and state, Mrs. Roosevelt wrote a friend, "I think they felt the time had come to form a Catholic party in this country. . . ."[11]

The confrontation between Mrs. Roosevelt and Spellman sent shock waves through the Democratic party, which foresaw a Catholic boycott of Governor Lehman's upcoming race for the U.S. Senate. Ed Flynn, a Catholic and New York State's most potent Democrat, flew to Rome for a Vatican meeting, where he was assured that the cardinal would be ordered to patch things up. Spellman thereupon sent an aide to Hyde Park with a statement of reconciliation, and soon appeared in person at her house.[12]

"My feeling is that if the figures show that the Catholic vote has gone appreciably against Lehman," Mrs. Roosevelt told Spellman bluntly, "it will make it impossible for any Catholic to get elected in this state for many years to come. Because a lot of liberals, Jews and Protestants will be very resentful."

"Oh, Mrs. Roosevelt," the cardinal protested, "I'm not opposed to Governor Lehman! I'll get in touch with Ed Flynn as soon as he returns to town." The message was passed from the Powerhouse to Democratic leaders throughout the state, and Lehman went on to win the election. Although Spellman's subsequent statements on federal funding for parochial schools muted his demands, he was only biding his time. The campaign for "parochiaid" would shortly be renewed by the church.[13]

An important form of Catholic power—moral censorship—claimed for one religion the right to force its standards on all others. Margaret Sanger's birth control meeting had been closed in 1921 because "an indecent, immoral subject is to be discussed." Cardinal Spellman decided that *The Miracle*, a film opening in New York in 1951, not only threatened the morals of his diocese but of all the nation's Catholics. Directed by Roberto Rossellini, it had just been chosen the best foreign picture of the year by the New York Film Critics. Spellman had not seen the film, but assumed that its story of a demented woman who is seduced by a stranger, and then believes she has conceived miraculously, paralleled the virgin birth. On Sunday, January 7, at St. Patrick's Cathedral, Spellman denounced it as a "despicable affront to every Christian," and had his indictment read at mass in every diocesan parish.

The Catholic War Veterans and other Catholic groups immediately picketed the theater. The city's fire commissioner, a Catholic, issued violations against it, although it had been inspected monthly since its opening two years earlier. Claiming bomb scares, the police raided the theater repeatedly. The New York Board of Regents, which was responsible for the licensing of films, called a hearing to remove *The Miracle*'s license.

While Spellman's indictment from the pulpit was certainly a legitimate form of moral guidance for his diocese, the harnessing of political forces behind church policy raises a deeper question of church-state separation. No matter what the righteousness of a religious position from its own viewpoint, can a church use its influence over the governmental process to enforce it? Church policy can be translated one step further into picket lines, which still allow the possibility of counter-picketing. But when it uses political power over the police and fire departments and Regents, hasn't religion overstepped its constitutional limits? Ephraim London, the civil liberties lawyer retained by *The Miracle*'s distributor, was startled to find that Charles Tobin, state lobbyist for the Catholic church, sat beside the Regents at the licensing hearing. "His influence was considerable," London noted. "Everything had to be cleared with him."

After the Regents removed the film's license, London went to court and eventually carried the case to the U.S. Supreme Court. In May 1952, with a landmark decision affecting freedom of speech for the media and entertainment industry, the Court overturned the Regents' ban. The Court ruled: "It is not the business of government in our nation to suppress real or imagined attacks upon a particular religious doctrine, whether they appear in publications, speeches, or motion pictures."[14]

Determined to carry the American church into Italian politics, Cardinal Spellman would possibly violate the nationality laws of the United States. The Vatican had little understanding of separation. In fact, when a postwar treaty of friendship was being drawn up between Italy and the United States in 1947, the Vatican protested the inclusion of "freedom of conscience and freedom of worship." But with Spellman and other bishops teamed with the Vatican in influencing the

Italian elections of 1948, they could hardly be unaware of the law that bound American citizens to "absolutely and entirely renounce and abjure all allegiance and fidelity to any foreign prince, potentate, state or sovereignty. . . ."

Yet Spellman acted as an agent for the Vatican and for the Italian Christian Democratic party—possibly showing allegiance to a foreign state—against the Italian Communists and Socialists. Along with Cardinal Amleto Cicognani, the apostolic delegate to Washington, he organized American dioceses in turning out thousands of letters from Italian-Americans to relatives in the old country urging votes for the Christian Democrats. Along with Enrico Galeazzi, a confidant of Pope Pius XII and Roman representative of the Knights of Columbus, he raised money for Vatican support of the Christian Democrats among American industrialists and his brother bishops.

"No one knows how much money Spellman funneled directly to the Vatican, but it must have been considerable," observed John Cooney, Spellman's biographer. In fact, this secret alliance between the Vatican, the U.S. government and Spellman was critical in producing the election sweep by the Christian Democrats, and Spellman continued financing Vatican involvement in the general elections of 1953 and 1958 and the Sicilian elections of 1955.[15]

By 1948, the church was equally influential in the political policy of the Congress of Industrial Organizations (CIO). In contrast to the craft-oriented American Federation of Labor, the CIO—which organized total industries—had grown up overnight in the turbulent 1930s by signing up millions of auto, steel, and electrical workers through sit-down strikes and other bloody confrontations. It had, to be sure, a number of Communist party members in key offices, but Philip Murray, the CIO president and a devout Catholic, had always praised their contributions. Ostensibly, this left-wing faction gave a rationale for the church's intervention, but the reasons went deeper. In accordance with papal encyclicals on labor, the church had decided to push the CIO towards safe, conservative ground.

The guidelines were Pope Leo XIII's *Rerum Novarum* in 1891, which ruled that not only communism but socialism "must be utterly rejected," and Pius XI's *Quadragesimo Anno* in 1931, which called for a conservative structure for economic and social life remarkably akin to the guilds of the Middle Ages. Pius declared that "strikes and lockouts are forbidden." Anything that could lead to violence, such as the sit-down strikes so crucial to CIO success, was condemned. To bring harmony to the working class through a hierarchal system, Pius wanted "those who follow the same industry or profession—whether in the economic or other field—[to] form guilds or associations. . . ."[16]

Determined that "American economic life will be reconstructed (not merely reformed) according to the program of the social encyclicals," as Father George Higgins put it, the bishops established the Association of Catholic Trade Unions (ACTU). All members—only Catholics could join—pledged to work for the papal objectives. Catholic chaplains were assigned to each chapter; chaplains held half the seats on the ACTU governing board. At least 7,500 union members were recruited and trained each year at over 100 ACTU schools, paid for by the church with all tuition free.

While any religion had the right to work within the union movement, the question is whether ACTU as an instrument of the church had not become virtually a political faction by 1948. Spurred by the anti-Communist passions of the period and particularly by the presidential candidacy of Henry Wallace, Roosevelt's former vice president now running as a Progressive with broad radical and Communist party support, ACTU concentrated on the Transport Workers Union. Its membership in New York's Local 100 was 80 per cent Catholic. Its head was "Red Mike" Quill, who flaunted his Irish brogue and shillelagh as well as his radicalism. He damned ACTU as a "strikebreaking outfit" and said "no decent Catholic would belong to it."

Quill at first supported Wallace. But by 1948, ACTU had made such inroads into Local 100 that all officers were graduates of the Xavier labor school, and a poll showed the local was supporting the reelection of President Harry S. Truman. As evidence of the church's political effectiveness, Quill abandoned Wallace and came out for Truman.

Similarly, ACTU was instrumental in gaining control of Local 60 of the United Auto Workers in Detroit, the largest local in the world, and aligning it with Walter Reuther in his successful bid for the international union's presidency. But ACTU's main target was the United Electrical Workers, whose 650,000 members were the base of the CIO left. Father (later Monsignor) Charles O. Rice was put in charge of the campaign, first taking over the giant Local 601 in Pittsburgh. As Phil Murray's confessor, Rice was able to draw on both church and CIO funds. Priests in Pittsburgh and other cities were ordered to preach against the union. "They announced it would be a mortal sin to vote UE—the nuts took over," Rice said later. In 1949 he arranged for the local's officers to be subpoenaed before the House Un-American Activities Committee, and the resulting headlines, tarring them with Communist links, enabled ACTU to win six of the eight top offices. Eventually, Rice would acknowledge, "Many UE members I attacked as Communists turned out to be FBI plants."

After Truman's victory, Phil Murray forced the UE out of the CIO. Working with ACTU, he helped decimate the UE by establishing a rival union under James Carey, a Catholic and instrumental in ACTU policy. Once it had accomplished its mission of swinging the CIO to a centrist position and abetting the Truman campaign, ACTU faded away. Monsignor Rice would always regret his role. "The CIO became part of the McCarthy hysteria," he concluded.[17]

The church's intervention into politics was now becoming shaped by a new force—the growing independence of the constituency from the hierarchy. It was an independence nourished by the surge of Catholics into professional and monied classes as a result of higher education under the G.I. Bill of Rights. By 1961, Catholics made up 18 per cent of all college graduates; by 1969, 29 per cent, higher than the Catholic proportion of the country's population. Although still underrepresented at leading universities, they made up almost 19 per cent of college faculties nationwide.

Similarly, while only 21.6 per cent of Catholics were classified as "upper class" in 1943 (as pollsters used this generalized term), compared to 50 per cent of Jews and 26.3 per cent of Protestants, a Gallup survey between 1963 and 1965 showed the Catholic upper class had almost doubled to 41 per cent, compared to 58 per cent of Jews and 35.9 per cent of Protestants. The Protestant figures, of course, reflected the lack of educational opportunity among rural whites in the South, Appalachia, and elsewhere.[18]

Catholic politicians had also broken from the limitations of city hall machines. In 1958 ninety Catholics were elected to the U.S. House of Representatives and twelve to the U.S. Senate. While many continued to follow the hierarchy's positions, Catholics in Congress responded to the same secular pressures as other members. The most independent Catholic of all, of course, was John F. Kennedy, so independent that Cardinal Spellman and other bishops quickly shunned him. His record as president proved his dedication to separation of church and state. He turned down all federal aid to parochial schools. When asked to appoint an ambassador to the Vatican in order to give the White House an advantageous listening post, he commented tartly, "I do not think there is any lack of information or communication back and forth."

Still, the Kennedy campaign in 1960 was haunted by the same specter of anti-Catholicism as Al Smith's. Many Protestant denominations, particularly Fundamentalists, hammered at the old fear that a Catholic president would become a tool of the Vatican. The Southern Baptist Convention, the largest Protestant group in the country, claimed that Kennedy was "under control" of the Catholic church. A meeting of one hundred fifty ministers on September 7, called together by Dr. Norman Vincent Peale, a nationally known preacher and best-selling author, attacked the "very nature of the Roman Catholic Church which is, in a very real sense, both a church and a temporal state."[19]

Kennedy knew the issue had to be met head-on. The setting he chose was his Houston speech on September 12 before an assemblage of seemingly unsympathetic Southern and Fundamentalist ministers. In the pink-and-green carpeted ballroom of the Rice Hotel, speaking slowly and emphatically, Kennedy told his audience: "I believe in an America where the separation of Church and State is absolute—where no Catholic prelate would tell the President (should he be a Catholic) how to act, and no Protestant minister would tell his parishioners for whom to vote—where no church or church school is granted any public funds or political preference. . . ."[20]

The speech made a favorable impression across the country, and a number of Protestant and Jewish clergy defended Kennedy's commitment to church-state separation. But just two weeks before the elections, an incident occurred in Puerto Rico that could have brought disaster to the Kennedy campaign. Governor Luis Muñoz Marín of the ruling Popular Democratic party was up for reelection. He had always stood for the law providing birth control at public health clinics and had recently blocked an attempt to repeal it. The Christian Action party opposed both Muñoz Marín and the law. Now the archbishop of San Juan and two other bishops on the island, all born on the U.S.

mainland, forbade Catholics to vote for the governor or any candidates running with him. The punitive power of the church was thrown behind this ban, as the archbishop warned in a pastoral letter that "those who knowingly violate the injunction commit sin—the sin of disobedience."

The church's intervention in Puerto Rican politics created an uproar, final proof for many Protestants that the Vatican still controlled Catholic candidates, including Kennedy. "They said it couldn't happen in America, but it did," declared the *Baptist Standard*. Many Fundamentalist clergy used Reformation Sunday on October 30 to link Kennedy with the church's manipulations in Puerto Rico. Some implied that Cardinal Spellman, who had met with the Puerto Rican bishops a few weeks before, had engineered the church's injunction.[21]

Governor Muñoz Marín, as it turned out, won handily, but Kennedy just squeaked past Richard M. Nixon. Kennedy took an impressive majority of the Catholic vote, 78 per cent according to the Gallup poll, but 61 per cent in other estimates. Although he fared reasonably well among Protestants, with polls showing a range of 38 to 46 per cent, he was hurt among normally Democratic, Protestant voters in the South and in border states, where an estimated 17 per cent defected to Nixon. Balancing his gains among Catholics with his losses among Protestants, the religious issue probably cost Kennedy one million votes.

The election of the first Catholic president would cleave the immigrant Catholic past from its upwardly mobile progress. It was the culmination of a long route to respectability and status. For the hierarchy, however, it required a shift in strategy. As the Catholic base moved to the suburbs, the bishops could no longer count wholly on urban political machines, except in cities with increasing Hispanic groups. By intervening in national issues that affected the nation at large, the hierarchy's power had to adjust to the secularization of the church. Not just the Kennedy presidency, but a surge in Catholic legislators—124 elected to the House of Representatives, 18 to the U.S. Senate by 1984—meant that the bishops had to deal with a constituency growing more independent and more integrated into mainstream America.[22]

On some issues, such as parochiaid, the hierarchy still controlled a reasonable share of the Catholic constituency. On other issues, such as birth control, it was mainly ignored. Consequently, the church needed new alliances to bolster its lobbying in national politics. It would achieve real power only when its interests began to converge with the Fundamentalists in the 1970s, and when conservative Catholics allied themselves with Ronald Reagan in 1980. The path to power may produce strange bedfellows, but few have been more effective.

III

Catholic Schools: The Church's "Essential Instrument"

HE DEMAND for federal and state funding of parochial schools has long dominated Catholic issues. U.S. Senator Ernest Hollings (D-South Carolina) described Catholic bishops, lobbying Congress for parochiaid, as "running around in the hallways like a bunch of kids looking for votes. . . . It is a disgrace." In 1983 alone, the Knights of Columbus flooded Congress with 9 million postcards on the issue. U.S. Congressman John N. Erlenborn (R-Illinois), pressured by Catholic lobbyists, smilingly told an official of the U.S. Conference of Catholic Bishops that "if he would stay out of politics, I wouldn't insist that priests remain celibate."[1]

Catholic schools have always been pivotal in the molding of children toward the church's objectives—"an essential instrument for the spreading and deepening of faith," Pope John Paul II called them in 1984. The Code of Canon Law of 1918 ruled that, "From childhood on all faithful must be so educated that not only are they taught nothing contrary to faith and morals, but that religious and moral training takes the chief place." Pope Pius XI in his 1929 encyclical, *Rappresentanti in Terra*, ordered that "all the teaching and the whole organization of the school, and its teachers, syllabus and textbooks in every branch, be regulated by the Christian spirit, under the direction and maternal supervision of the Church." Aware that public schools were becoming an increasing temptation, he decreed that they were "forbidden for Catholic children, and can at most be tolerated" with the approval of the local bishop "with special precautions."[2]

From the time of Archbishop Hughes in 1850, the Catholic church has wanted public money to support its schools. This demand, of course, collides with the principle of separation of church and state. Defining Catholic education as the "rock on which the whole structure rests," U.S. Supreme Court Justice Robert Jackson in 1947 argued that "to render tax aid to its church school is indistinguishable to me from rendering the same aid to the Church itself."

The separation principle was so revered in the nineteenth century that President Ulysses S. Grant wanted it maintained not just for school funding, but applied as well to other areas of religious tax exemption. "Declare Church and State for ever separate and distinct," he urged in an 1875 address, "but each free within [its] proper sphere, and that all Church property shall bear its own proportion of taxation." Grant wanted most religious tax exemption eliminated, or specifically confined to exemption for the "last resting place of the dead and possibly, with proper restrictions, church edifices."

Grant's sweeping policy was turned into a constitutional amendment in 1876 by U.S. Congressman James G. Blaine (R-Maine), speaker of the House and Republican candidate for president. The Blaine amendment, prohibiting tax money from coming under the "control" of any religious sect or being "divided between" any sects, passed the House by 180 to 7. A slightly different version passed the Senate 28 to 16, failing the necessary two-thirds majority. Those senators and House members who failed to vote were not only influenced by religious pressures, Protestant as well as Catholic, but by the conviction that the ground had already been covered by the First Amendment.

But despite the rejection of a reinforced separation principle on a federal level, almost every state has incorporated similar language in state constitutions. The Arizona statute of 1912, for example, reads: "No tax shall be laid or appropriation of money made in aid of any church, or private or sectarian school, or any public service corporation."[3]

Catholic demands for public money for its schools, consequently, have sharpened the clash between parochial and public systems. Public schools were conceived before the Civil War as the fulcrum of American egalitarianism, teaching immigrants the American vision and producing unity in a chaos of conflicting cultures. "The greater the proportion of our youth who fail to attend public schools and who receive their education elsewhere, the greater the threat to our democratic unity," insisted James Bryant Conant, former president of Harvard University, in 1953.[4]

U.S. Supreme Court Justice William Brennan in 1963 attributed to public education a "uniquely public function: the training of American citizens in an atmosphere free of parochial, divisive or separatist influences of any sort—an atmosphere in which children may assimilate a heritage neither theistic nor atheistic, but simply civic and patriotic."[5]

The recent migration of Catholics from the core cities to the suburbs has only intensified the church's demands for parochiaid. With parochial schools few and hard to reach in many areas, and public schools not only free but generally of high standard, the increasing Catholic preference for public schools hit the parochial system hard. From 1975 to 1985, 251 of its high schools and 582 of its elementary schools had to be closed. From 1975 to 1985 enrollment at elementary and secondary schools dropped by 562,760.

The system was hit further by the sharp decline in the number of teaching priests and nuns who had always been the inexpensive backbone of the faculty. Sixty-nine per cent of teachers came from religious orders in 1969, only 23 per cent in 1985. Forced to recruit lay teachers, often unionized and demanding salaries equal to those of public schools, the Catholic system had to raise its tuition costs from a few hundred dollars in New York City twenty years ago, for example, to an average of $1,200 in 1984. As a result, low-income parents increasingly switched to public schools.[6]

Daunted in its attempts at federal funding, the Catholic church tried a new tack in the 1940s. It concentrated on states with sizable Catholic populations, seeking legislation for specific services such as school busing and textbooks. One of its first successes was in New Jersey, where the legislature passed a bill allowing Catholic children who had previously paid for using public school buses to ride for free. Instead of the parochial school being reimbursed, public money would be paid directly to the students under the "child benefit" concept. When separationist groups challenged the law in court, *Everson* v. *Board of Education* was carried to the Supreme Court in 1947, and henceforth the Court would become a battleground in the parochiaid conflict.

In a 5 to 4 decision upholding the constitutionality of the New Jersey busing law, the Supreme Court opened a crack in the wall of separation. The majority ruled that only the child would benefit. By funding the parochial school rider, students would be spared the hazards of traffic and public transportation, and their safety would be assured.

But if the state could provide busing for child safety, Justice Wiley B. Rutledge asked in his dissent, why shouldn't it finance the repair of fire hazards or unsafe walls at parochial schools? "How can it be proper for the public to pay for transportation to religious instruction and worship from Monday through Friday," demanded Thomas Reed Powell, a Harvard Law School professor, "if it could not provide for rides to Saturday or Sunday worship?"[7]

Insisting that the First Amendment "requires the state to be neutral" in regard to religion, Justice Hugo Black summed up the Court's interpretation of the separation principle. Neither state nor federal government "can pass laws which aid one religion, aid all religions, or prefer one religion over another," he declared. "No tax in any amount, large or small, can be levied to support any religious activities or institutions, whatever they may be called, or whatever form they may adopt to teach or practice religion."

As a result of *Everson*, at least thirty states have provided publicly funded transportation for parochial students, sometimes used flagrantly as in a Pennsylvania county where taxis carried two students at $48 a day, or $64,000, for the school year. In Louisiana, parents received $375 annually. A state constitutional prohibition against payments has often been circumvented in Kentucky, and a state supreme court ruling has been circumvented in Idaho. Still, eighteen states have made no provision at all for transportation payments of parochial students.[8]

In its next case a year later, *McCollum* v. *Board of Education*, the Supreme Court swung back to the separation principle. The case dealt with a "released time" plan at Champaign, Illinois, public schools, which allowed students to leave their classes during school hours to take religious instruction on school property. Busing had been treated as child-safety convenience. Here the issue went far deeper: a compulsory education system was taking part in the promotion of religion on publicly owned property. The Court's 8 to 1 vote, declaring Champaign's "released time" plan unconstitutional, reflected the justices' objections to the divisive intrusion of religion. "The unifying objective of our educational system," stressed Justice Felix Frankfurter, "is undermined by the divisive specification of children as Catholics, Jews, Protestants or the offspring of stubborn misfits."[9]

In 1952, in *Zorach* vs. *Clauson*, the Supreme Court hedged on *McCollum* without repudiating it. The Catholic lobby in New York State had been strong enough to pass a different type of "released time" law. Students could leave classes for an hour a week for religious instruction, not at school as in Illinois, but off the premises. Administrators and teachers were ostensibly banned from using any pressure, but as one child testified in describing how pupils had to line up separately in class, "I could sense the hostility between these two groups." Furthermore, there were no safeguards for those who didn't participate at all and suffered the prejudice of dissidents cast adrift in the school building.

In a challenge brought by the children of Tessim Zorach, an Episcopalian, and other public school pupils, the Supreme Court by 6 to 3 ruled the New York plan constitutional. Father Robert Drinan, a constitutional scholar and former congressman, considered it a step towards "cooperation" rather than a breakdown of separation. But the plan cooperated, above all, with Catholics, Fundamentalist Protestants, and Orthodox Jews who favored weekday religious instruction. "The state also affords sectarian groups an invaluable aid," Justice Black pointed out in his dissent, "in that it helps to provide pupils for their religious classes through the use of the state's compulsory school machinery."[10]

Once the "child benefit" theory opened a crack in the wall in *Everson*, it became the device for a range of parochial funding, first under military pressures. When the Soviet Union launched *Sputnik* into space, the American people panicked at the possible deficiency of scientific education. President Dwight D. Eisenhower, as a result, had no trouble rushing through the National Defense Education Act of 1958, which granted equipment for science, math, and foreign language teaching to parochial as well as public schools.

President Kennedy refused to sanction any parochial funding. Therefore, his aid to education bill was buried in the House Rules Committee in 1961 because U.S. Congressman James Delaney (D-New York), the principal Catholic spokesman in Congress, would not let anything through that ignored parochial schools. President Lyndon B. Johnson had a subtler approach. His parochial grants were hidden under the umbrella of anti-poverty programs. The poor, in parochial as well as public schools, would profit from the "child benefit" theory with an outpouring of funds for teachers, textbooks, visual equipment, guidance counseling, and remedial instruction.

Shrewdly, Johnson put forward his Higher Education Facilities Act first. Since no one was forced to attend a college or university, higher education circumvented the compulsory character of the school system. The bill passed in 1963. The Elementary and Secondary Education Act passed in 1965, providing everything from instructional services to libraries and visual aids. In the first eight years, almost $1 billion went to religious colleges. In the early 1980s, an estimated $190 to $300 million a year was going to parochial and private school students under Chapter I of the act for instructional services, and an estimated 10 per cent of that amount for equipment under Chapter II.[11]

Buoyed by the success of the "child benefit" approach in both the Supreme Court and Congress, Cardinal Spellman decided on a frontal assault on New York's "wall" of separation in 1967. Parochial school funding had been prohibited by state law since 1842; the prohibition was embedded in the state constitution since 1894 (called the Blaine amendment after James G. Blaine). Now, with the cooperation of the state's preeminent Catholic politicians—Anthony Travia, Democratic speaker of the state assembly, and Earl Brydges, Republican majority leader of the senate—the cardinal had assembled a seemingly unbeatable package.

During the constitutional convention that spring and summer, called to rewrite the state constitution, Travia and Brydges had agreed to insert a clause that would eliminate the Blaine prohibition and allow parochial school funding. They were so confident the clause would pass that they insisted the constitution be approved as a single unit, with parochial funding indivisible from other changes. After all, Travia and Brydges controlled the selection of convention delegates. Travia would be convention chairman. Cardinal Spellman would even give the opening invocation.

The cardinal thought he had lined up every political and religious faction. Frank O'Connor, a Catholic, president of the New York City Council and Democratic candidate for governor in 1966, supported repeal of the Blaine amendment. U.S. Senator Jacob Javits, a Republican and a Jew, backed it also. U.S. Senator Robert F. Kennedy, a Democrat and a Catholic, remained silent at first, but Spellman was sure he could win him over. He also expected he had Governor Nelson A. Rockefeller, a Republican and a Protestant, under control. When Rockefeller divorced his wife of thirty years and was criticized by some Protestant ministers, Spellman embraced him publicly—undoubtedly to stress his friendship—despite his long condemnation of divorce. The cardinal solidified the alliance by contributing to the governor's reelection in 1966.[12]

Setting the tone for his campaign by calling it the "gravest crisis in the history of the Catholic Church in America," Spellman showed his financial muscle with a budget estimated at $2 million. Still, this was hardly exorbitant since parochial funding could bring church schools $700 million a year in tax dollars. The cardinal established a quota for each diocese—the bishop of Ogdensburg, for example, wanted $25 from all his priests. Even Brooklyn schoolchildren were asked to give a dollar apiece. Spellman exhorted his parishioners with a letter read at mass in the city's 402 churches, and other bishops issued their own pronouncements. Although Citizens for Educational Freedom (CEF) was ostensibly the church's political arm, the campaign was run from the Powerhouse, and Spellman assigned Monsignor George Kelly to coordinate it.[13]

With Catholics constituting 40 per cent of the state's population, and Spellman's campaign exerting continued pressure on the convention, Travia and Brydges had no trouble lining up every Catholic delegate, and many of the Protestants and Jews. In fact, Assemblyman Percy Sutton and William Haddad, who headed a recently formed committee to stop the Blaine amendment repeal, complained that the "delegates to the Constitutional Convention are so frightened that here is a kind of gentleman's agreement not to discuss the question." On August 16, 1967, the convention voted by 132 to 49 for a new constitution that would remove the ban on parochial school funding.

Spellman's "Fairness to Children" rally at Madison Square Garden on September 26 had all the trappings of a final celebration. A constant flow of notables trooped to the rostrum: Jim Farley, the masterful campaign manager of President Roosevelt's early victories; George Meany, president of the AFL-CIO, who was expected to deliver the union vote; U.S. Senator Eugene McCarthy (D-Minnesota), whose anti–Vietnam War candidacy for president gave a liberal tinge to the proceedings; Monsignor Fulton J. Sheen, the spellbinding television preacher; and U.S. Congressman Hugh Carey, soon to be governor of New York. Still, the night belonged to Spellman. When he mounted the rostrum at the climax, the band played thunderously and the audience leaped to its feet and "accorded His Eminence an ovation not soon to be forgotten," reported *The Tablet*, a Catholic journal.

The pro-Blaine coalition, by contrast, started slowly. By election day in November, it had to convince the public to vote against the new constitution as a whole, with its numerous advantages, in order to defeat parochial funding. The League of Women Voters, United Federation of Teachers, Americans for Democratic Action, Citizens Union, New York Association of Reform Rabbis, and most Protestant groups organized the coalition. Money dribbled in, and the New York State Council of Churches gave about $15,000 to set up headquarters. The media paid so little attention to the coalition that the discovery of a spy at headquarters, paid $50 a week by the Citizens for Educational Freedom's executive director, provided one of its few newsbreaks.[14]

Cardinal Spellman gradually realized that the electorate was balking. The Knights of Columbus, with 128,000 members in the state, turned to scare tactics and accused the Blaine coalition of "totalitarian, thought-control systems of education devised by the communists in the Soviet Union or Nazis in Hitlerite Germany." CEF launched an expensive advertising campaign that showed a mentally disturbed nine-year-old presumably denied psychological counseling by the Blaine amendment and a five-year-old with a speech defect who had been denied therapy. Actually, such services were not affected by Blaine. The Blaine coalition countered with a New York City Board of Education letter stating that Blaine had no bearing on the speech therapy, remedial reading and counseling, which had been supplied to 29,000 parochial and private students the previous year.

Cardinal Spellman was troubled by other ominous signs. A Catholic Laymen's Association in Brooklyn and Queens criticized the church's fund-raising pressure tactics. When a Bronx truck driver, William Crist, Jr., passed out leaflets opposing the Blaine repeal in front of St. Helena's Church, he was beaten to the ground by parishioners. Instead of arresting his attackers, the police arrested Crist. Then he spent $3,000 of his own money for a newspaper ad stating: "I uphold my fellow man's basic right not to be forced to support my five Roman Catholic children going to Roman Catholic school, directly or indirectly."

Spellman's carefully wrought alliance was crumbling. Perry Duryea, the Republican minority leader of the assembly and a Protestant, warned that Blaine repeal would threaten the state's economy. Rockefeller's budget director, Norman Hurd, estimated the cost of parochial funding at $23 billion over ten years, which would necessitate an 80 per cent rise in taxes. The Conservative party, overwhelmingly Catholic in membership, labeled repeal a "prescription for fiscal disaster."

As these fiscal omens seeped into the electorate, Governor Rockefeller started backing away. The Al Smith dinner in October, always presided over like a fiefdom by New York's cardinal, was an obligatory function for state, and even national, politicians. Rockefeller, however, found some excuse to decline the invitation. Mayor John V. Lindsay of New York City was conveniently away on vacation, but on his return he came out flatly against the Blaine repeal.

The election returns on November 7, 1967, were one more proof that the bishops could no longer dominate the Catholic voter on issues that conflicted with his personal interests. Even with the city's solid Catholic base, the vote went against Spellman by 1,103,034 to 638,352. Upstate, the margin was greater: 1,794,082 to 532,820. Blaine repeal was defeated in every county, and even in overwhelming Catholic districts, such as Parkchester and Throgs Neck in the Bronx.[15]

The fear of higher taxes, of course, disturbed Catholics as well as the general electorate. But suburban and rural Catholics, too, were strongly influenced by the free tuition and often high status of local public schools. "Catholic support for Catholic schools is declining because Catholics now realize that in the suburbs where they now live, the public schools are better," concluded Father Andrew Greeley from a National Opinion Research Center study at the University of Chicago.

Catholics had also become disillusioned with the merits of parochial education. One of Spellman's own priests, Father Gerald Collins, branded the parochiaid campaign an "unjustified attempt to get state funds to help the ailing parochial school system—a system which is antiquated in much of its religious attitudes, and has an administrative setup that is woebegone, and is in itself of questionable necessity in the United States today."[16]

The standards of Catholic education had been criticized for at least a decade. Of 845 National Science Foundation fellowships in 1957, only 19 had gone to students at Catholic colleges. "The 35 million Catholics in this country and our Catholic educational system are not producing anywhere near their proportion of leaders," the Reverend John J. Cavanaugh, former president of Notre Dame University, asserted in 1958.

Mary Perkins Ryan, a Catholic specialist in education, analyzed the deficiencies of religious separatism. "What half a century ago still seemed to be its great advantage—getting the children together in a Catholic atmosphere and keeping them apart from the non-Catholics—now appears to be a serious disadvantage," she wrote in 1964.

Daniel Callahan, a former Catholic editor and director of New York's nonsectarian Hastings Center, questioned the argument that parochial schools produced a unique brand of student. "To my knowledge no studies have demonstrated that parochial schools—Protestant or Roman Catholic—produce value systems, behavioral patterns, personality structures, or even church loyalties in pupils consistently distinguishable from those produced in public schools," he claimed.[17]

The Catholic bishops ignored such arguments which, after all, represented only a minority faction at the time. Even if they had lost the referendum in New York, they were chipping away at the wall of separation in the U.S. Supreme Court. The New York State legislature, with Rockefeller's blessing, presumably to shore up political ties with the hierarchy, had already passed a law providing free textbooks to parochial as well as public school students under the pretense that these books were only "loaned" and would eventually be returned by parochial administrators. In *Board of Education* v. *Allen* in 1968, the Supreme Court ruled that the law was constitutional. Continuing the "child benefit" theory of *Everson*, it considered the children, not the schools, the primary beneficiaries.

Again in *Tilton* v. *Richardson* in 1971, five justices upheld the Higher Education Facilities Act and allowed federal money for construction at Catholic colleges and universities of such buildings as chemistry labs and gyms that had no religious purpose. Although four justices objected to the decision that college students were less impressionable to religious influence than high school students, and that the buildings could be easily monitored to prevent religious use, the majority ruled that no "entanglement" with religion was involved. Entanglement was one of the tests adopted by the Court to interpret whether separation of church and state under the First Amendment had been violated.

But as Catholic strategists pushed laws through state legislatures that went beyond construction and textbooks, the Supreme Court drew the line in two cases that were decided jointly in 1971. *Earley* v. *DiCenso* involved the Rhode Island Salary Supplement Act, authorizing the state to supplement the salaries of teachers of secular subjects in elementary parochial schools as long as they taught only courses offered in public schools, used only public school texts and materials, and agreed in writing not to teach religious courses while on supplementary pay. *Lemon* v. *Kurtzman* involved a Pennsylvania law that allowed the state to finance secular subjects in parochial schools, such as math, science and languages, by reimbursing the schools for teacher salaries, textbooks and instructional materials.[18]

In a decision concurred in by all justices and written by Chief

Justice Warren Burger, the Court ruled both laws unconstitutional. They had failed the "entanglement" test. Both required constant state supervision to prevent a teacher under religious control from straying into religious instruction. The law would produce further entanglement when state officials examined school records to separate public funding from prohibited religious courses. Burger's opinion stressed the danger to the First Amendment from legislation that allowed divisiveness along religious lines, a danger already warned of in the *McCollum* "released time" case.

Catholic strategy now turned to a device—tuition reimbursement for parochial students—that henceforth would become the core of the parochiaid drive. The Catholic lobby had pushed through a New York State law providing partial tuition reimbursement to parents of parochial students with taxable income under $5,000 a year and some tax benefits to parents who earned up to $25,000. When the Committee for Public Education and Religious Liberty (PEARL), established after the Blaine referendum to defend public education, challenged the law, the Supreme Court in *PEARL* v. *Nyquist* in 1973 ruled it unconstitutional.

With three judges dissenting, the decision found that tuition reimbursements were illegal whether they went to the parents or directly to the schools, or whether the income tax benefit was called a "credit" or given any other label. The Court depended on two tests: the "primary effect" of the law on the First Amendment, and possible "entanglement" between church and state. The law failed to meet both tests.

Another potent Catholic lobby in Pennsylvania passed a law giving an extensive range of state-financed aid to parochial schools. But in *Meek* v. *Pittenger* in 1975, the Court banned instructional materials except for textbooks. Similarly, counseling, speech and learning therapy, and other remedial services were declared unconstitutional.

Since state law made school attendance compulsory, the church claimed that First Amendment religious freedom would be violated for a parent whose conscience required him to send a child to parochial school, but was denied that choice by lack of public funding. This argument was blunted by the fact that Catholic schools charged tuition, and real choice, therefore, applied only to those who could afford it, and not to the majority of parents dependent on free public schools.

The Catholic position also insists that since all parents are taxed to support public schools, those choosing parochial or private schools are subject to the inequity of double taxation. The weakness of this position is that many citizens are taxed for public services they do not or cannot use: Christian Scientists refuse certain treatment at municipal hospitals, the Amish pay for highway upkeep although refusing to drive, childless couples and the unmarried still pay school taxes. Everyone pays for services needed by the community as a whole.

Another flaw in the double-taxation claim is that parents of students in public schools, where all must be admitted, would be forced to pay for an elite parochial or private system which can accept or reject applicants according to its own standards. A specific religion, color, or ethnic background can be preferred over another. Whereas public schools are controlled by local boards which can be replaced by the vote of their constituents, the elite parochial or private system would be supported by public tax money taken from citizens with absolutely no decision over what they are paying for.[19]

As the parochiaid drive concentrated on tax reimbursements for tuition, particularly after the election of President Reagan in 1980, the Catholic hierarchy soon took on new partners. The Fundamentalist alliance added a powerful, new lobbying bloc: there were one million children in 20,000 Fundamentalist private schools, concentrating on biblical teaching as the basis of Christian education. But they were an embarrassment as well, bringing a jarring hypocrisy to the Catholic position. Many Catholic priests had marched and risked their lives in the confrontations for black equality in the South, and the church had finally taken an unalterable stance against segregation of any sort. Yet that same church was allied with a Fundamentalist school system that was defiantly racist.

Almost without exception, Fundamentalist and Christian schools in the South, Midwest, and border states barred black students from admission. Their primary purpose was to circumvent the integration laws with an all-white system that cordoned off their clientele from mixed public schools. In addition, their philosophy conflicted with Catholic schools that had worked hard to raise educational standards, and meet the special needs of black and Hispanic children in the poverty-stricken inner cities. The Fundamentalist schools generally emphasized conservative religion over education. Many of them used a prepackaged study curriculum that was supplied by a central source, Accelerated Christian Education of Lewisville, Texas. "Those of us involved in Christian education place the Christian first and education second," concluded William Russell, principal of the Faith Bible Church Academy in Elkridge, Maryland.[20]

The rapid growth of these Fundamentalist schools intensified the threat of parochial tax-funding, which could bring a total fragmentation of education. If tax-funding became available to every religious sect, even shoestring cults, public schools would soon be drained of their financial base. A flood of new religious schools could drive many public school boards, already hard-pressed to meet their budgets, to the edge of bankruptcy.

With his administration bill in 1983 for tuition tax credits, President Reagan not only solidified his political base, but the Catholic–Fundamentalist–White House campaign to bolster parochial education as well. Calling a meeting of the Catholic bishops, the Knights of Columbus, the Moral Majority, and Agudath Israel, which runs private Hebrew schools, the president assured them that tax credits and vouchers were "flagship issues" for his secretary of education, William J. Bennett, and that "Secretary Bennett and I intend to see [tax credits] through to their enactment."[21]

Although budget-cutting had been basic to his agenda, Reagan's tax-credit bill, called the Educational Opportunity and Equality Act, would cost the federal treasury $1.5 billion in 1986, according to the administration's own estimates, and twice that according to its critics. The bill would provide a tax credit—deducted from final taxes owed— to parents of parochial and private school students earning less than $40,000, and partial credit for those earning up to $60,000. "It certainly makes no sense," protested U.S. Congressman Tim Wirth (D-Colorado), "when public education programs have borne damaging cuts already. . . ." James M. Dunn, executive director of the Baptist Joint Committee on Public Affairs, pointed out that tax credits could destroy public education by placing a "bounty on the head of school children to withdraw from the public schools."[22]

Although the president's bill had still not passed Congress by 1986, the Catholic church lobbied and passed a tax-credit bill in Minnesota that allowed parents of parochial and private school students to deduct

$700 per child in high school and $500 in elementary school from their state income tax for *tuition* as well as textbook and transportation expenses. The Supreme Court upheld the constitutionality of the law in 1983 in *Mueller* v. *Allen*, which seemed to undercut the Court's previous decisions in the *Lemon*, *DiCenso*, and *Nyquist* cases.

Justice William Rehnquist, for the 5 to 4 majority, disposed of the First Amendment's Establishment Clause by asserting that the Minnesota law "neutrally provides state assistance to a broad spectrum of citizens." But how broad was this spectrum? Only one in ten children in Minnesota attended parochial or private schools, and 75 per cent of the law's benefits would go to them. The law, consequently, was an invitation to middle-class parents to abandon the public schools and leave them to those too poor to get any advantage from a tax deduction.

With a more conservative Court than a decade earlier, the decision marked a drastic shift from *Nyquist.* "The Minnesota statute violates the Establishment Clause," protested Justice Thurgood Marshall, "for precisely the same reason as the statute struck down in *Nyquist:* it has a direct and immediate effect of advancing religion." But the five-member majority surmounted this conflict in a mere footnote, which inferentially distinguished between a direct payment of money in *Nyquist* and tax deduction in the present case. Skirting the separation issue, the majority equated school deductions with other tax deductions, such as medical expenses and charitable contributions, that were available to Minnesota residents.

The Court also skirted "political divisiveness," a test for maintaining neutrality between church and state that went back almost forty years. Now the Court insisted this test must "be confined to cases where direct financial subsidies are paid to parochial schools or to teachers in parochial schools," and not be applied to tax benefits given parents.

The most drastic section of *Mueller* was its minimalization of the Establishment Clause and of the wall of separation. "At this point in the 20th century we are quite far removed from the dangers that prompted the Framers to include the Establishment Clause in the Bill of Rights," Justice Rehnquist declared, quoting a previous decision.[23]

Justice Rehnquist, of course, ignored a decade of bitter religious conflict over school prayer and abortion, to cite just two issues. The majority's sanguine assessment of the religious threat to the democratic process put the separation principle in jeopardy. The Court was obviously moving towards conservatism, and fundamental issues from parochial school aid to school prayer and abortion could soon be affected.

IV

Birth Control

I

PAUL VI, an aging pope mired in indecisiveness, brought the church to a crisis in 1968. His encyclical, *Humanae Vitae*, reinforced the church's ban on birth control, which most Catholic authorities had expected to be tempered or revoked.

The issue had dominated the Second Vatican Council, organized by Paul's humane predecessor, Pope John XXIII. It had split the church for decades, with Catholics in Western Europe and the United States increasingly adopting birth control despite the Vatican prohibition. By 1963 a study at the University of Chicago's National Opinion Research Center showed that 45 per cent of American Catholics approved of contraception. The official commission of Vatican Council II, made up of cardinals, theologians, scientists, and marriage experts—appointed by John and continued by Paul—had already voted 64 to 4 to reverse the birth control ban. Cardinal Leo Josef Suenens of Malines-Brussels had pleaded: "I beg you, my brothers, let us avoid a new Galileo case, one is enough for the Church."[1]

But Pope Paul, convinced that the church's hold on sexuality was crucial to his authority, dreaded any loss of Vatican power. His whole career had been spent in curial intrigues. The changes unleashed by

Vatican II frightened him. Starting off as a reformer, he retreated behind a bureaucratic fortress as his health crumbled. All he could do now was to delay. All he wanted in his last years was to maintain the unity of the church. And *Humanae Vitae*, ruling that "every conjugal act must be open to the transmission of life," gave him the illusion that unity was preserved.

Instead, of course, it was a disaster, condemning Catholic couples worldwide to bear child after child even if they were crushed by poverty or in a marriage that was disintegrating, or one of the partners was crippled by alcoholism. "I ask my Pope if he knows he is tearing homes apart," a former priest commented. With famine in Africa and elsewhere, the impact of *Humanae Vitae* affected not just Catholics but the problems of hunger, health, and survival internationally. World population had already doubled from 2.5 billion people in 1953 to an expected 5 billion in 1987, and demographers projected 6.25 billion by the year 2000 at present birthrates. The Vatican ban on contraception obviously intensified the threat of population growth.[2]

Catholics who obeyed the ban had only one alternative to avoid incessant childbearing: the Ogino-Knaus method, known as rhythm, which had been approved by Pope Pius XII in 1951. Requiring the complex ritual of a woman's charting her daily temperature to determine the period of the month when intercourse would not produce conception, rhythm had proved so risky in studies that it had been dubbed "Vatican roulette." The pope believed that rhythm conformed to "natural law." But Dr. André Helligers, a Catholic obstetrician-gynecologist and member of the Vatican II commission, complained, "I cannot see that salvation is based on contraception by temperature and damnation is based on rubber."

Rhythm was difficult enough for a sophisticated woman. "To imagine being able to teach the Ogino-Knaus method to 250 million illiterates," protested Father James Tong, director of the Association of Catholic Hospitals of India, "seems morally impossible to me."[3]

Nor could the personal damage be minimized. From his study of 2,300 rhythm-users, Dr. John Cavanagh, a Washington, D.C., psychiatrist, told the Vatican commission that the method had left his Catholic patients "insecure, rebellious and frustrated. Serious psychiatric disorders have arisen as a result." The Christian Family Movement of Chicago gathered hundreds of questionnaires from rhythm-users to present to the commission. One husband wrote: "It makes necessary my complete avoidance of all affection toward my wife for three weeks at a time. I have watched a magnificent spiritual and physical union dissipate. . . . Rhythm seems to be immoral and deeply unnatural. It seems to me diabolical."

Ironically, the church's ban had almost no roots in early canon law. The New Testament makes no mention of birth control, and references to it were ambiguous until the mid-nineteenth century. Only when contraception became accepted in the United States, Britain and other industrialized nations did Pope Pius XI in 1930 rule in *Casti Connubii* that "human interference" is an "offense against the law of God and of nature, and those who commit it are guilty of a grave sin."[4]

The church's "natural law" tradition stems, in part, from its aversion to sex and its denigration of women. Paul, who disliked women, preached, "It is good for a man not to touch a woman." Yet he tolerated marriage for those who "cannot contain . . . for it is better to marry than to burn" (I Cor. 7:1,9). Saint Augustine (354–430), the consummate misogynist who fathered one son by a concubine and took a second concubine, may have reacted to his debauchery by establishing the church's attitude towards sex and women. Sex was only acceptable to produce children, he wrote, and women, condemned by the sin of Eve to the sorrow of childbearing, were to be ruled by men.

Saint Jerome (c. 340–420) developed virginity into an ideal of the church. Determined to establish the perpetual virginity of Mary, mother of Jesus, he reinterpreted three Gospel references to Jesus' brethren and made them relatives instead (Matt. 12:46–50; Mark 3:31–35; Luke 8:19–21). The Lateran Council of 649 turned the perpetual virginity of Mary into church doctrine. Jerome also wanted to dispose of sex eternally and taught that although "we rise from the dead in our own sex, we shall not perform the functions of sex" in heaven.[5]

Saint Thomas Aquinas (1225–74) wrote that women were only recipients, not active participants, in the conjugal act. Any genital stimulation, except for procreation, was immoral.

Although the Bible makes no direct reference to masturbation, its condemnation was ordered in 1054 by Pope Leo IX, who forbade masturbators from entering sacred orders. The basis of this condemnation was the church's twisted interpretation of the Genesis story of Onan, second son of Judah, who was told by his father to marry his brother's widow in order to "raise up seed to thy brother." Onan, not wanting to give his brother official credit for paternity under Jewish law, spilled his seed on the ground, and God "slew him also." Onan was actually being punished for defying traditional property law rather than for masturbation (Gen. 38:8–10).

The most disturbing issue in the conflict over birth control during the Second Vatican Council was whether the papal ban of 1930 had to be considered infallible. The doctrine of infallibility stems from *Pastor Aeternus*, which had been pushed through the First Vatican Council in 1870 by Pope Pius IX. Most American bishops then opposed it: the Southern bishops particularly could see the furor it would raise among Protestant Fundamentalists. Lord Acton, Britain's foremost Catholic, considered it a "soul-destroying error."[6]

When the pope speaks *ex cathedra* (from the chair of Peter), infallibility means he has "full and supreme power over the universal church in matters pertaining to faith and morals (teaching authority), discipline and government (jurisdictional authority)," according to the *Catholic Almanac*. Such a "definitive act," the Second Vatican Council's "Dogmatic Constitution of the Church" stated, was "performed with the assistance of the Holy Spirit." Infallibility thus made the pope errorless and virtually divine.

Even when the pope is not speaking *ex cathedra*, the Second Vatican Council ruled that the "authentic teaching authority of the Roman Pontiff" requires "religious submission of will and mind," and Pope Paul VI in 1967 declared the magisterium, or teaching authority, a "subordinate and faithful echo of the divine word."

The crux of the conflict was that the Vatican's own special commission of theologians had voted during the Second Council that the 1930 ban on birth control was not infallible and, therefore, could be reversed. This position was affirmed later by Paul VI himself. The theologians also agreed that contraception was not intrinsically evil.[7]

"Doesn't it follow that a non-infallible magisterium can make a mistake?" asked Cardinal Julius Doepfner of Munich during the council. "Or that the church could not learn something in this matter from the separated brethren [Protestants]—as it has done in a number of other questions during the council?" These questions, attempting to define the scope of dissent permitted under a non-infallible magisterium, would plague the church increasingly and provoke a bitter debate after the condemnation of the Reverend Charles Curran, a prominent theologian, in 1986.

By October 1966, three commission reports, all published in the *National Catholic Reporter*, had come out for acceptance of birth control. Discussing *Schema* 13, Cardinal Paul Emile Leger of Montreal said, "We have a pessimistic, negative attitude toward love. This *schema* is intended to amend these conceptions and clarify love and its purposes." But even with a majority of 64 to 4 favoring the final report in 1967, Pope Paul VI cringed at revoking his predecessor's encyclical. The principle of collegiality and consensus came to the fore during Vatican Council II, but Paul had trouble accepting it. In the end, by keeping the birth control ban, Paul brought chaos to the church instead of unity. Patriarch Maximos IV Saigh called on the Vatican Council to see things "as they are, not as we would like them to be." But Dr. Franz Saes, president of the Association of Dutch Catholic Physicians, concluded: "In Rome the sun still rotates around the earth."[8]

The impact of *Humanae Vitae* on the American clergy was bitter. Forty Baltimore priests rebelled openly. Seventy-seven theologians at Catholic University in Washington, D.C., accused the pope of enforcing the theory that the "church is identical with the hierarchal office," and Cardinal Patrick O'Boyle could only stop the revolt by threatening canonical penalties. Eventually, most priests dealt with the problem by simply ignoring the birth control ban in the pulpit and confessional. From studies at the National Opinion Research Center, Father Andrew M. Greeley, the Catholic sociologist, concluded that four-fifths of the clergy "would not insist on acceptance of the official birth control teaching in the confessional."

Although American bishops ostensibly obeyed the Vatican, James P. Shannon, auxiliary bishop of St. Paul–Minneapolis, wrote the pope bluntly that the encyclical was "bad theology, bad psychology" and, in addition, was not an "honest reflection of my own inner conviction." Paul VI offered him a minor assignment outside the United States, which was tantamount to exile without responsibility. Instead, Shannon resigned his office, still insisting that the church was his "spiritual home." He became a college vice president and married a year later.

But the most drastic effect of *Humanae Vitae* was on the Catholic constituency. Father Greeley from his National Opinion Research Center studies called it a "disaster for the church." Catholics increasingly considered birth control a social problem outside Vatican authority. By 1974, NORC studies found that Catholic use of birth control had risen to 73 per cent. Almost 90 per cent did not consider birth control a sin. By 1984 only 13 per cent thought that birth control information should not be made available to teenagers. A study of young adults in 1979 showed that 77 per cent believed that for a couple to live together before marriage was "sometimes or never wrong."

The negative reaction to *Humanae Vitae* damaged all Catholic practices. Between 1963 and 1974 NORC studies found that attendance at weekly mass dropped from 71 to 50 per cent. Catholics going to confession "practically never" or "never at all" rose from 18 to 30 per cent. Contributions of family income to the church declined 31 per cent. At a synod of the National Conference of Catholic Bishops in 1980, Archbishop John Quinn of San Francisco begged his fellow bishops to come to terms with these statistics.[9]

But even with Catholics in Western industrialized nations as well as in the United States ignoring *Humanae Vitae*, Pope John Paul II became more obsessed than Paul VI with enforcing it. Authoritarian in style, his toughness honed as a Polish priest and primate during years of confrontation with Nazi and Communist regimes, he was determined to stamp his personal domination on the church. Not just on contraception, but on every sexual issue, he acted as though the slightest concession could destroy the Vatican.

Going to the core of Catholic faith, he proclaimed in 1983 that "those who practice contraception or even believe it to be lawful are refusing objectively to acknowledge God." A year later he insisted that when couples use contraception, their relations "cease to be an act of love."

These statements could be attributed to momentary fanaticism if he did not repeat them so often. Even on the pope's tour of Africa in 1985, surrounded by famine, poverty, and overpopulation (for example, the population of Kenya soared from 6 million in 1968 to 20 million), he hammered away at enforcing the Vatican ban. In the Netherlands that year, where the church has long been at loggerheads with the Vatican, and the pope was greeted with violent demonstrations, bottle throwers and signs urging "Kill the pope," he still insisted that Vatican encyclicals on birth control and other sexual issues would "remain the standard for the church for all time."[10]

Obviously committed to an ideal that a large portion of the church ignored, John Paul may have been convinced that his personal magnetism and power would eventually influence his listeners. More likely, he had more pragmatic motives. The refusal of Catholics in France, Italy, Spain, and other Western Catholic countries to obey the birth control ban may have already been discounted. Their populations had stabilized. They were no longer considered the bedrock of the church. Instead, the church's future in numerical terms lay in Latin America, Africa, and the Far East, where soaring populations partly stemmed from a ban on birth control or minimal contraceptive facilities.

The Vatican's strategy on population could be detected at the United Nations International Conference on Population in Mexico City in August 1984. On the U.N.'s official listing, the Holy See, in its religious function, is called a "permanent observer mission." Yet despite its insistence on "spiritual sovereignty" rather than territorial statehood during the debates over a U.S. ambassador to the Vatican, the Holy See at the population conference claimed the right to propose an amendment, a right seemingly limited to states.

Teamed up with the Reagan administration, the Holy See's delegation pushed hard on both the abortion and population issues. It proposed a strongly anti-abortion amendment that stated: "In population programs, abortion should be excluded as a method of family planning." Although the amendment was supported only by Ireland, Peru, and a few others, the Holy See's links to the United States gave it special power. President Reagan had threatened to cut off government funds from International Planned Parenthood unless member countries removed abortion from their services. With this combination of religious and political pressure, the conference had to find a compromise, settling on, "Governments are urged . . . to take appropriate steps to help women avoid abortion, which in no case should be promoted as a method of family planning. . . ."

At the conference, the Holy See joined the Reagan administration again in espousing a policy that conformed to Pope John Paul II's aims. As outlined by the U.S. chief delegate, James Buckley, soon to be appointed a federal circuit court judge by Reagan, runaway population growth "in itself presents no problems." It was a natural phenomenon, neither good nor bad. All that was needed to improve living standards, Buckley insisted, was free market economics and entrepreneurial initiative. Then a soaring birthrate would become immaterial even in the poorest countries.

This policy, which came to be called "voodoo demographics" at the conference, was a sharp reversal of all previous congressional positions on population control as well as public opinion. In a Gallup poll taken a month before, 90 per cent of the American people had agreed that economic development is damaged by high rates of population growth. A. W. Clausen, president of the World Bank, told the conference that the "evidence is overwhelming that rapid population growth impedes efforts to raise living standards in most of the developing world." The Vatican, however, was determined to push the White House approach. *L'Osservatore Romano*, almost always the Vatican's mouthpiece, called it a "historic step." But of all the delegations, only North Yemen supported the White House approach that Buckley had enunciated.[11]

Pope John Paul II was relentless in his efforts to enforce *Humanae Vitae*. If he could not discipline U.S. Catholics, whose use of contraception had lowered the Catholic birthrate to the same level as other faiths, he could make a symbolic target of one of the church's rebels. In 1986 the Vatican ordered the Reverend Charles E. Curran, a professor of moral theology at Catholic University in Washington, D.C., to retract his views on birth control and other sexual issues or resign from the theology department. Curran was an obvious mark. In 1968 he had emerged as the leader of at least six hundred Catholic theologians and academics who opposed *Humanae Vitae*. Now John Paul not only wanted to muzzle him, but to prove once and for all that Rome could not be challenged, or that "issues of truth are settled by actions of power," as Sister Margaret Farley, a professor at Yale Divinity School, put it.

The clash was abstract to an extent: "whether a theologian may legitimately dissent from authoritative non-infallible teachings of the papal magisterium," explained Father William H. Shannon, an emeritus professor at Nazareth College, in Rochester, New York. It went to the meaning of what was non-infallible. Should the church's teaching on Galileo have been challenged? Or its decision in the nineteenth century that slavery was not intrinsically evil when many theologians disagreed? The clash also involved the meaning of dissent. During Vatican Council II in 1965, the Pastoral Constitution said in *Gaudium et Spes:* "Let it be recognized that all the faithful, clerical and lay, possess a lawful freedom of inquiry and of thought, and the freedom to express their minds humbly and courageously about those matters in which they enjoy competence."[12]

At the same time, the clash was decidedly specific in its effect on the American church. If by dissenting from Vatican teaching on birth control a theologian loses his right to teach theology, asked Francis Schüssler Fiorenza, president of the Catholic Theological Society of America, does that mean that 85 per cent of American Catholics, who dissent as well, cease to be Catholics? "Is Curran being made a scapegoat because the Vatican thinks, as Cardinal Joseph Ratzinger apparently thinks," asked the *National Catholic Reporter*, "that it is possible either to be an American or a Catholic, but not both?"[13]

2

The constant Vatican assault on birth control has severely limited the church in dealing with a critical national problem: the rate of teenage pregnancies. One million teenagers had undesired pregnancies in 1985, the highest rate among industrialized nations. The pregnancy rate for fifteen- to nineteen-year-olds reached 96 per thousand, according to 1981 statistics analyzed by the Alan Guttmacher Institute, in contrast to 14 per thousand in the Netherlands, 35 in Sweden, and 45 in England and Wales.

The low teenage rates in other countries cannot be attributed to abortion since the United States has a far higher abortion rate at each age. Nor can it be attributed to greater U.S. sexual activity since the median age at first intercourse is similar for teenagers in all countries studied. Nor does welfare seem to be an incentive. Welfare support is higher in countries with lower birthrates than in America.

Two factors, above all, have caused the American teenage problem: the lack of available contraceptive services, and the lack of sex education in the schools. "Teen-age pregnancy rates are *lower* in countries with *greater* availability of birth control and sex education," the Guttmacher study concluded. While the U.S. clinic network is reasonably accessible in cities, but less so in rural areas, it suffers not just from weaker geographic coverage than European countries, but from the stigma that these clinics are really for welfare clients.[14]

And it suffers particularly from a virtual boycott by the Catholic church and the Fundamentalist churches. For both, the principle bastion against pregnancy is the preservation of chastity, or as a leading Fundamentalist journal calls it, "the validity of virginity, the management of masturbation." Joseph Scheidler, head of Chicago's Pro-Life Action League, brands contraception as "disgusting, people using each other for pleasure." Phyllis Schlafly, the Catholic head of the Eagle Forum with strong influence among Fundamentalists, opposes any sex education in schools. "Teachers are authority figures," she says, "and when they discuss contraception, they are giving students permission to engage in sexual intercourse." The Fundamentalist, and to some extent the Catholic, position is that parents are "their children's prime sex educators," as *Christianity Today*, a Fundamentalist journal, stresses. Consequently, only six out of 20,000 Fundamentalist and evangelical schools had courses in sexuality in 1983. In areas where the Catholic-Fundamentalist alliance controls school boards, public schools have trouble establishing sex education programs.[15]

Despite the highest teenage pregnancy rate in New York State, the Suffolk County legislature, many members of which were elected with right-to-life backing, turned down a federal grant that would have provided nurses for teenage counseling. The county executive of Erie County, New York, elected with similar backing, also rejected a $350,000 federal grant.

Even in New York City, with a 50 per cent increase in the pregnancy rate of ten- to fifteen-year-olds in the last decade, the Board of Education has struggled interminably to get Catholic approval for sex education. The Reverend John Woolsey, head of the archdiocese's Christian and Family Development Office, insisted that "teaching a child about contraception is not the answer to promiscuity." The archdiocese, said Woolsey, would prefer a curriculum that stresses "chastity and saying no."

The opposition of the church intensified in 1986 after the New York State Department of Health had financed clinics at nine New York City schools—two dispensing contraceptives to students with parental permission, seven writing prescriptions that had to be filled elsewhere. When the chancellor of the city's Board of Education asked for continuation of the program, pressure from Cardinal O'Connor on the board—one black Protestant voting the Catholic position—forced the elimination of contraceptive distribution at two schools, but allowed the clinics to operate for another six-month trial period.

Similarly, in Boston, Cardinal Bernard Law branded a program for dispensing contraception at schools "morally unacceptable," and claimed it would imply school approval of sex and would increase pregnancy rates. But Loretta Roach, member of the State Board of Education and a Catholic, saw "something insidious about white Catholic leaders telling blacks and Hispanics that it's morally wrong to dispense birth control. It smacks of colonialism, like we're a bunch of natives." State Assemblyman Thomas M. Gallagher, a Catholic, pointed out that "The church's problem is that it refuses to admit that not everyone adheres to its point of view."[16]

The effectiveness of sex education has been increasingly shown in U.S. studies. At two St. Paul, Minnesota, high schools, with sex education in the curriculum and an evening clinic for contraception set up at a nearby hospital, the fertility rate was cut from 60 to 46 per thousand between 1976 and 1979. Another study of four high schools with a similar program found that a rate of 59 births per thousand was cut to 37 per thousand between 1976 and 1977 and 1984 and 1985. A Johns Hopkins University study at Baltimore schools, starting in 1981 and lasting three years, showed that students exposed to a sex education program for twenty months had 22.5 per cent fewer pregnancies than at the time of the baseline survey. Students at non-program schools, by contrast, had 39.5 per cent more pregnancies in that period.

The American public has recognized the value of these programs. In a Gallup/Phi Delta Kappa poll in 1985, 75 per cent approved sex education in high schools, 52 per cent for grades four to six. A Lou

Harris poll reported that 67 per cent favored laws which would require public schools to be linked to family planning clinics. Still, school boards continue to resist public opinion. Dr. Sol Gordon of Syracuse University claims that "less than 10 per cent of school kids get anything approaching sex education." The U.S. House of Representatives Select Committee on Children, Youth and Families found that the "efforts that do exist are too few" and "uncoordinated."[17]

Despite its ban on contraception, the Catholic church began to advocate a "positive and prudent sexual education" during Vatican II. For the first time in papal history, its "Declaration on Sexual Morality" in 1976 recognized sex as a determining factor in human personality and essential, not just for procreation, but for the spiritual and physical unity of marriage. More and more clergy are being trained in sexual psychology. One of the Catholic pioneers, the Reverend Matthew Kawiak of Rochester, New York, has developed a sixteen-hour workshop for parochial educators that seeks to foster in children "healthy attitudes and positive moral values," and to teach parents ways to begin to talk about sex and understand how parental behavior supports these talks.

The ultimate hypocrisy, of course, is for the Catholic church to ban contraception and abortion, and yet do little to alleviate their need through comprehensive sex education programs at parochial schools. Although the groundwork has been laid in Milwaukee, Jacksonville, Florida, and a few other cities, Kawiak himself admits that "few dioceses provide sex education programs." The Reverend Thomas Lynch, director of the project at the National Conference of Catholic Bishops, insists that "we're letting it come up from the grass roots so there are no protests from parents. We're trying not to come down from on high."

State law mandates sex education in all school systems in New Jersey, Maryland, and the District of Columbia, but only in New Jersey has the Catholic church established a widespread curriculum. In 1980, New Jersey's bishops called knowledge of human sexuality "an important priority of Christian education." Unlike most Catholic and Fundamentalist officials, who consider any contraceptive information inherently dangerous, the Reverend Robert Harrington, director of Newark's project, claims that a "young person's knowing that contraception exists does not automatically lead to sexual activity." Harrington also contends that "ignoring the misuse of sexuality will not make it disappear." Newark's parochial system, consequently, instituted courses in sexuality in all of its forty-two high schools and 60 per cent of its two hundred elementary schools by 1985.[18]

But the dominant approach for Catholics and Fundamentalists remains chastity, and the influence of this alliance on Congress was vividly demonstrated with the passage in 1981 of the Adolescent Family Life Act (AFLA). Promoting "self-discipline and other prudent approaches to the problems of adolescent, pre-marital sexual relations," the legislation represents a bizarre attempt to control youthful morality by the imposition of the standards from a limited religious viewpoint. It prohibits any funding for abortion, even for counseling. Ostensibly, it aims to preserve the "integrity of the American family," but its implications go deeper. U.S. Senator Roger W. Jepsen (R-Iowa) has called it a bulwark against the "wave of humanism which has swept the country." Jeffrey Hart, a syndicated columnist usually in the conservative camp, considers it part of a "secret agenda, which is nothing less than to counter-revolutionize contemporary sexual behavior."

Certainly, the thrust of the bill goes against majority attitudes. A Gallup poll in 1985 found that only 39 per cent of the public thought that premarital sex was wrong, and just 18 per cent in the eighteen-to twenty-nine-year-old age group. Among Catholics, 33 per cent thought it was wrong; and in the South, where Fundamentalism flourishes, the figure was 48 per cent, lower than might be expected.

Introduced into the Senate by two Catholics and a Mormon, AFLA passed the Labor committee with neither hearings nor a vote. Since it was attached to the Omnibus Budget Reconciliation Act of 1981, there was no separate vote on the Senate floor. Similarly, the House accepted it in conference without hearings or vote. Constantly embattled with family planning and abortion bills, Congress may have considered chastity too close to mom and apple pie to fuss with.[19]

But as it turned out, AFLA quickly came into conflict with the principle of separation of church and state. Federal grants under it went to six Catholic organizations, to one affiliated with the Lutheran Church–Missouri Synod and to Brigham Young University run by the Mormons. All used the funding to promote their particular religious morality. Marjory Mecklenburg, the project's conservative administrator for the U.S. Department of Health and Human Services, later conceded "troublesome issues of potential federal funding of religious activity."

As a result, the American Civil Liberties Union charged in federal court that AFLA had produced "serious violations" of the Constitution. Referring to the Supreme Court's *Kurtzman* decision in 1971, ACLU's lawyer testified that "if the government may not give money to parochial school teachers to teach math, then certainly the government should not give financial aid to religious groups for teaching chastity or sexuality."

St. Margaret's Hospital in Dorchester, Massachusetts, a Catholic institution, was funded by AFLA for $446,806 in 1982 and $235,000 in 1983 to run sex education courses. The curriculum covered only Vatican doctrine on contraception, sterilization, and abortion, and the teachers paid by AFLA also taught religion at parochial schools.

Catholic Charities of Arlington, Virginia, operated by the diocese, received $75,000 in both 1982 and 1983 for sex education courses that were held solely in Catholic churches and were often addressed by priests. St. Ann's Infant and Maternity Home in Maryland, also funded by AFLA, taught only "Billings Ovulation," a variation of the rhythm method, which its director called the "Christian alternative."

Mecklenburg chose the grant recipients herself, generally ignoring outside evaluators, according to the testimony of Patrick J. Sheeran of the Office of Adolescent Pregnancy Programs. Sheeran said Mecklenburg ordered that no grant should go to "left-leaning" organizations listed in the *Conservative Digest*. Although the Urban Institute applied, it was never funded. The University of Arkansas was funded once and rated highly, but was passed over later for the fifth-ranked Family of the American Foundation, the center for Billings Ovulation teaching in Louisiana.[20]

ACLU's federal lawsuit against the bill gained a strong ruling on April 15, 1987, from a U.S. District Court judge, who declared that federal funds have been used for "education and counseling that amounts to the teaching of religion" and that violates First Amendment separation of church and state. But the irony is that Catholic influence on Congress through the Fundamentalist alliance has proved more effective than among the church's own constituents. The hierarchy can push through a constitutionally dubious "chastity" bill, although only 13 per cent of Catholics opposed birth control information going to teenagers. The Vatican can bend President Reagan's population policy to its ends. Obviously, church lobbying power has reached a peak at the same time as its influence among the parishes is diminishing.

V

Abortion: Cutting Edge of the Religious Right

EW ISSUES have touched a more sensitive nerve in the American people, or disturbed their religious or ethical beliefs, more than abortion. Few other issues in this century have torn the country apart so dangerously, for the right to an abortion is fundamental to women, allowing them to control their childbearing if contraception fails, and consequently their health and family stability, their opportunity for education and jobs, their very lives.

By making abortion the "critical issue of this campaign," as Cardinal Bernard Law of Boston called it in 1984, the Catholic church was attempting to force its moral teaching on all others. It is natural for one religion or one pressure group to try to educate and persuade the public on its positions from the pulpit or through the media. But when that religion remains a minority and fails to achieve anything like a national consensus, and when it still insists on translating its morality into legislation, then the highly sensitive balance of a pluralistic society can be threatened seriously.

The Catholic teaching on abortion (followed by the Fundamentalists) is based on the belief that a fetus is a human life, endowed

56

with all the rights of personhood, virtually from the moment of conception. Therefore, it concludes that abortion at any point is the equivalent of murder. Orthodox Jewish congregations, in general, condemn abortion from the standpoint of their own teachings.

Almost all Protestant and other Jewish denominations, by contrast, reject the belief that a fetus is already a human life endowed with personhood, and that it has any legal or moral rights superseding those of the pregnant woman. The majority of Americans believe in the position of the U.S. Supreme Court legalizing abortion in 1973: "We need not resolve the difficult question of when life begins. When those trained in the respective disciplines of medicine, philosophy, and theology are unable to arrive at any consensus, the judiciary, at this point in the development of man's knowledge, is not in a position to speculate as to the answer."[1]

Since both sides in the conflict have formed their opinions solely on the basis of their religious and moral beliefs, neither side in a pluralistic society should attempt to stamp its beliefs on others through punitive legislation. Every woman has the choice, under the Supreme Court decision, to follow her own conscience and her doctor's counsel.

Still, after the Catholic hierarchy forged a new alliance in 1980 with the Fundamentalists and President Reagan, the campaign of religious conservatives provoked a fury that strained the traditional concept of separation of church and state.

Never before, in fact, on any national issue of importance, has the Catholic hierarchy focused its whole apparatus of money and clergy on an exhaustive and lasting political campaign. Starting in 1970, the archdiocese of Washington, D.C., ordered its parishes to distribute a letter backing Congressman Lawrence J. Hogan, an anti-abortion Republican from Maryland, and opposing a list of pro-choice candidates for the state legislature. Even after abortion was legalized nationwide in 1973 by the U.S. Supreme Court decision, the church attempted to use religious discipline against Catholic members of the Maryland legislature. James Shaneman, executive secretary of the Maryland Catholic Conference, presumably speaking for the hierarchy, warned legislators that they would be excommunicated if they voted for a bill conforming state law to the Court's decision. The Catholic Conference backed down after Catholic officeholders protested this attempt to subjugate their responsibilities to Vatican dogma.

The archdiocese of Seattle, Washington, organized and ran a state-wide anti-abortion campaign from its offices in 1970. The state legislature had already passed a bill legalizing abortion in the first seventeen weeks of pregnancy, which would become law if voters approved it by referendum. In a letter on his official stationery in April, Archbishop Thomas A. Connolly ordered that "we must 'tool up' for the Catholic effort." Other letters ordered all priests to attend an organizing and training session, distributed a booklet on how to coordinate the campaign, and apealed for funds to finance it. The abortion rights bill was confirmed in the November referendum by 56 per cent of the voters.

The National Conference of Catholic Bishops expanded the campaign nationwide with its Pastoral Plan for Pro-Life Activities in 1975. This blueprint made every diocese and parish a political machine, harnessing every priest, Catholic school, and church-sponsored organization to the passage of legislation outlawing abortion. Each parish must form its own unit, ordered the National Conference, and "its task is essentially political, that is, to *organize people* to help persuade the elected representatives. . . ."[2]

The pastoral plan was rashly applied in New York State in 1976. In a letter on Diocese of Buffalo stationery on September 6, Bishop Edward D. Head ordered all priests to collect money at masses on November 6 and 7 that would be turned over to the state Right to Life Committee (NYSRTL). For James Buckley's reelection race for the United States Senate, NYSRTL raised $200,000, part of it coming from such church fund-raising held in cooperation with the New York State Bishops' Conference. The New York City diocese gave $44,000 and Buffalo $11,000, among others. The *Village Voice*, a New York weekly, concluded: "Secret minutes of more than a half-dozen NYSRTL board meetings, and a three-inch stack of internal private documents indicate that NYSRTL, with fundraising assistance from the church, has directly intervened in scores of New York political races, both local and state-wide."

In one race, R. Bradley Boal, Republican candidate for the Westchester County legislature, was attacked for his abortion stand in the bulletin of St. Joseph's Church, Croton Falls, and from the pulpit at many masses at St. Patrick's Church, Bedford Village.

The funneling of money collected in church into a political campaign, or supporting or attacking political candidates through church newspapers or any facility, is strictly forbidden by the United States Tax Code. Since contributions to all religious organizations are tax-exempt, the law prohibits direct political intervention in return for this exemption which may be worth hundreds of millions of dollars annually to the major faiths. Churches and synagogues, of course, can debate or take sides on any political issue and lobby for legislation. But by supporting and attacking candidates, Catholic dioceses have risked losing their tax exemption.

Aware of potential violations of the tax code, Helen Greene, chair of NYSRTL, reported their lawyer's warning "not to attack any candidate in print" at the June 5, 1976, board meeting. Marge Fitton, the treasurer, was less cautious in her September guidelines, saying "unless the pastor objects, volunteers (for NYSRTL collections) should stand in the vestibule or foyer of the church." Political money, of course, must be raised outside church property to stay within the law. Greene was equally concerned about "washing" money at the September 11 board meeting, saying: "If a church insists on making out a church check, the local group should deposit it in their account and write a check to NYSRTL in that amount."[3]

As the church became politicized, it seemed as though Archbishop John O'Connor of New York had been specially appointed to raise the abortion issue in the 1984 campaign to a divisive level. He had hardly been invested when he announced he would make abortion "my No. 1 priority." Shortly afterwards he added, "I always compare the killing of 4,000 babies a day in the United States, unborn babies, with the Holocaust." This point was bound to offend not only Jews but anyone sensitive to the immeasurable atrocities of the Nazi regime. Rabbi Balfour Brickner of New York's Stephen Wise Free Synagogue retorted: "The two are not comparable and should not be linked even by casual innuendo. The Holocaust stands alone. . . . There are no legitimate or acceptable analogies."

Then O'Connor took on his own constituents. "I don't see how a Catholic in good conscience can vote for a candidate who explicitly supports abortion," he announced on June 24 in the heat of the election campaign. He was targeting not only Catholic members of Congress who voted for abortion rights, but specifically two important Catholics in his own state—Mario Cuomo, the Democratic governor, and Congresswoman Geraldine Ferraro, Democratic candidate for vice president.

Both had repeatedly stated they were devout Catholics and against abortion, but had to respect the constitutional rights of others in a pluralistic society as a result of the Supreme Court decision. Cuomo, however, realized that O'Connor's confrontation with Catholic officeholders had thrown the debate into a dangerous new area. O'Connor was bludgeoning politicians into following the dogma of their faith rather than the law of the land. Challenging O'Connor head-on, he pointed out: "Now you have the Archbishop of New York saying that no Catholic can vote for Ed Koch, no Catholic can vote for Jay Goldin, for Carol Bellamy, nor for Pat Moynihan or Mario Cuomo—anybody who disagrees with him on abortion."[4]

In the space of a few months, O'Connor had made himself the battering ram of conservative Catholicism. It was obviously the role the Vatican had picked for him. "He was the boss. There was no opposition allowed," recalled a rabbi who had served with O'Connor when he was chief of chaplains for the armed forces.

A Protestant minister, who also served with O'Connor, remembers a meeting when the subject of abortion came up. "His face got crimson. He was furious. He said, 'It's murder and that's it.' There could be no discussion. The chief had spoken."

When another chaplain disagreed with him at a staff meeting, O'Connor began tearing him to shreds before everyone. "He couldn't stop. He was like a vulture, tearing and tearing for fifteen minutes," the rabbi remembered. "He's cruel and ruthless. Everyone hated him."

By the time O'Connor retired as rear admiral in 1979 after twenty-seven years as a Navy chaplain, Cardinal John Krol was impressed by this six-foot brawler, and was probably instrumental in having a Philadelphia native appointed bishop of Scranton, Pennsylvania.

O'Connor had been born in West Philadelphia in 1920, one of five children in a working-class family. His father's parents came from Ireland, his mother was of German ancestry. She had been blinded by glaucoma, but when her sight was restored in a year this deeply religious family considered it a miracle. At West Catholic High School, John was so frail and small for his age that he was nicknamed Shadow. But he played sandlot football, worked as a Western Union messenger boy, ran his own bicycle repair shop, and grew quickly. At seminary school, he directed musicals and painted, always busy enough to "give another person a nervous breakdown," another seminarian recalled.

After ordination as a priest in 1945, he received his M.A. degree in clinical psychology at Catholic University in Washington and his Ph.D. in political science. By choosing a military career as Navy chaplain in 1952, O'Connor must have recognized a need for command. He served in the Korean War and with Marine ground forces in Vietnam, and had tours of duty on destroyers, submarines, and cruisers. He was chief of chaplains from 1975 to 1979 and was awarded the Legion of Merit and Distinguished Service Medal.

O'Connor's military career made him a logical choice to represent the conservative faction on the Bishops' Committee debating the church's stand on war and peace, leading to its noted position paper in 1983. O'Connor battled constantly to dilute the criticism by liberal bishops of President Reagan's nuclear policy. He opposed a freeze on nuclear weapons and advocated the use of small-scale nuclear arms. He was constantly at loggerheads with Bishop Thomas J. Gumbleton of Detroit, but O'Connor frequently won the dispute by arguing "longer, louder and more insistently," as one observer recalled. Others say he bolstered his arguments by frequent phone calls to officials in the Reagan administration, and that he was responsible for watering down crucial paragraphs of the position paper.[5]

O'Connor's penchant for harsh confrontations was apparent in New York when he raised the homosexual issue almost simultaneously with abortion. The archbishop protested Mayor Edward Koch's executive order barring discrimination because of race, creed, age, or sexual preference either by city agencies or by private or religious charitable groups that receive city money. The Catholic church receives sizable funds from the city for day care and other services. But O'Connor refused to agree to the executive order because homosexuals were included.

His argument was that signing would condone homosexuality and violate Catholic teaching. Like contraception, homosexuality "excludes all possibility of transmission of life," according to the church. Then he expanded his confrontation beyond the executive order to argue that all anti-discrimination machinery involves government encroachment on religion, and that the mayor had "exceeded his authority in setting up his own private [enforcement] army."

The confrontation produced a note of absurdity when a Gay Pride March passed St. Patrick's Cathedral just as a contingent of Catholic War Veterans came the other way, with signs reading "Down with Mondale, Koch, Cuomo and their gay empire!" The archdiocese's lawyer demanded that the mayor apologize to O'Connor and church-run charities "for damage done to their reputation."[6]

It seems hardly accidental that another hard-liner, Bernard F. Law, became archbishop of Boston, the country's third largest Catholic diocese, within a few days of O'Connor's investiture. By rating abortion as the "critical issue" in the presidential race, Law not only cemented the conservative bloc, but raised doubts about his judgment in those months when nuclear arms control and turbulence in Central America might have rated equal priority. Inviting almost a hundred Protestant and Jewish leaders to his investiture on March 23, 1984, Law ignored their diverse views on the subject and lashed out at abortion as the "primordial darkness of our time." "Many of us were offended that he would confront us at such a portentous moment," remarked the Reverend James Nash, executive director of the Massachusetts Council of Churches, a Protestant group.

"Archbishop Law is obsessed with abortion," noted William V. Shannon, a Boston University professor, former ambassador to Ireland, and a Catholic. "He's dealing in moral absolutes. He's afraid that if you don't draw the line here, then everything becomes permissible. He is anti-woman in the Marian tradition. Women for him are removed from a competitive world. They must be placed on a pedestal, the ultimate figure."

Law, consequently, represents the most vehement sector of the hierarchy opposing the ordination of women. His investiture at Holy Cross Cathedral was a media event with television coverage, and five cardinals and 165 archbishops and bishops, as well as Senators Edward M. Kennedy and Paul Tsongas and Governor Michael S. Dukakis, were in the procession. But Catholic nuns were furious that they were virtually excluded. "Law is downright anti-woman," said one nun. "It was an almost all white, all male ceremony."

At the public investiture, blocs of tickets were given each bishop and Catholic colleges and faculties. But although the chair and executive director of Boston Theological Institute are both women, neither was invited, nor was anyone from that influential center with

Catholic women on the faculty. At a special mass for religious women on the third day, Law made it clear he wouldn't discuss sensitive issues like female ordination. "He just doesn't grasp that many nuns are saying I'm a woman first, then a Catholic," Nash observed.[7]

With his mellifluous voice, blue eyes, and wavy white hair, Law presents a dazzling image on television. "All the women reporters were crowding around him and hugging him at his investiture," a Boston newspaperman recalled. Almost six feet tall, large-chested, and portly, Law has heavy features that dominate his face. He talks and smiles easily. He plays the piano and boasts a rich baritone which he shows off occasionally at meetings.

"Bristling with ambition," as Shannon describes him, he has harnessed public relations to the needs of the church. He makes appearances everywhere, at the Boston Symphony, at a Red Sox baseball game, speaking at Harvard Law School. Many observers think he has a "Harvard style"—"bright, sophisticated, smooth," a Boston minister described it. One nun called him "slippery, a clerical Barbie doll."

Law, in fact, graduated with the class of 1953 at Harvard, possibly the only archbishop in history to attend an Ivy League college. Except for majoring in medieval history, his classbook lists few activities. He was a member of the Democratic Club and vice president of the Catholic Club, whose occasional parties were described as "proof that dogma and dances do mix . . . that parties do not have to be immoral."

The son of an Army colonel whose assignments changed constantly, Law was born in 1931 in Mexico. He attended school in the Virgin Islands and at college gave his home address as Panama's Canal Zone. He studied for the church at a Benedictine abbey near New Orleans and was ordained in 1961. But in his ascent to the bishopric of the Springfield–Cape Girardeau diocese in Missouri in 1975, there is a striking difference between Law's career and O'Connor's. An inflexible conservative on most issues, Law quickly became involved in racial justice. He served in Vicksburg and Jackson, Mississippi, working with Office of Economic Opportunity programs and with the black rebels of the tumultuous 1960s. Charles Evers, Medgar's brother, praised him for his dedication to "justice and what is right." In his Harvard twenty-fifth reunion book, Law wrote: "To have been part of that significant moment of our history is in itself a grace, a gift."

Law's constant shift of cultures obviously gave him a cosmopolitanism beyond most bishops. During his high school years in the Virgin Islands, he was one of the few whites in his class. Unlike other bishops, too, his education was primarily secular, at Harvard particularly, immersed in a freewheeling, almost anti-religious intellectualism. In Washington as an administrator with the National Conference of Bishops, he came to oppose the Vietnam War, and often arranged for food and lodging for protestors flooding the capital.

"Once he was appointed bishop," a friend observed, "he changed drastically. He became rigid and harder. The position does that to you. He was talking about some of the dissident theologians and nuns one day, and his face flushed, and he muttered, 'Those people have got to straighten up. Straighten up or get out.' "8

The politicization of the church, even before O'Connor and Law, revoled to a large extent around violations of the United States Tax Code, which grants a religion tax exemption as long as it "does not participate in, or intervene in (including the publishing or distributing of statements), any political campaign on behalf of any candidate for public office." But by 1978, Catholic intervention for and against political candidates had spread from Maryland and New York to Minnesota, Michigan, and across the country. Churches in Pittsburgh became notorious for their barrage against Congressman William S. Moorhead and "his consistent record of votes in favor of abortion and of votes against any form of aid to nonpublic schools."

With the presidential race of Ronald Reagan in 1980, Fundamentalists, particularly in the South, began supporting candidates. One candidate in Jacksonville, Florida, was backed by the First Baptist Church and the Blessed Trinity Catholic Church. The pastor of West Hillsborough Baptist Church in Tampa told a reporter, "I filled out a ballot, printed it and handed it out to my congregation."

The sharpest confrontation with the tax code occurred in San Antonio, Texas. In an editorial on May 2, 1980, with a blazing headline, "To the IRS—'NUTS!!!,' " the official diocese newspaper, *Today's Catholic*, supported Reagan and a list of candidates for the U.S. Senate and House under the stamp of Archbishop Patrick F. Flores. The Reverend Brian Wallace, the editor, admitted the Internal Revenue Service had warned of violations "through recent rulings," and that the Catholic Press Association had sent him and all Catholic papers the IRS guidelines. But Wallace retorted, "And as for a fight with the IRS, I dare them." This challenge caused a furor in the press, and Wallace resigned and was assigned elsewhere.[9]

Cardinal Humberto Medeiros of Boston intervened in two congressional campaigns in the fall of 1980. The immediate cause was the vacant House seat left by Congressman Robert Drinan, a priest and former dean of the Boston College Law School. Drinan had infuriated Medeiros by his consistent votes for abortion rights in Congress. The cardinal was determined to get him out, and the Vatican cooperated by ordering that no priest or nun could hold public office. Drinan resigned from the House, but the cardinal became even more disturbed when a new candidate, Barney Frank, a former Massachusetts legislator, supporter of abortion rights and a Jew, ran strongly in the polls taken before the primary election. The cardinal's temper was further jarred by Congressman James Shannon, a Catholic who had voted for abortion rights, now up for reelection and holding his own against a popular conservative backed by the hierarchy.

Egged on by wealthy lay contributors determined to make abortion the nub of these races, Medeiros attacked candidates supporting abortion a few days before the primary in a letter to be read at 410 parishes throughout the state. The letter also appeared in *The Pilot*, the official archdiocese paper. Although the cardinal had not mentioned Shannon and Frank by name, church officials immediately identified them as the target. In another letter "mailed to a number of homes and delivered to several churches in Fourth District communities," according to the Boston *Globe*, Monsignor Leo Battista of the Worcester diocese attacked Barney Frank by name on abortion.

There was an immediate storm in the press. Medeiros had seemingly violated the tax code. "A lot of priests were angry and embarrassed," a Protestant minister reported. "They said to me, 'Let the cardinal stew in his own juice.' " Thirty per cent of the priests in Shannon's district refused to read the letter at mass. Senator Kennedy came out for both Frank and Shannon. Frank's Jewish constituents in Brookline and Newton were incensed the letters had been released on a Jewish holy day when the candidate could not reply.

As a result, the turnout of volunteer workers and voters was far above normal expectations. Pamela Lowry, an aide to Governor Dukakis, drove for Frank on primary day and was assigned to pick up two elderly Irish-Catholic women. "We wouldn't have bothered to vote," they told her, "but we're just furious at the cardinal." Despite earlier predictions of close races, Frank won the primary by 2,000 votes and Shannon by 8,000, and both were elected to the House in November.[10]

In 1982 and 1984, Cardinal Krol in Pennsylvania and Bishop Thomas J. Welsh in Virginia involved their parishes in many campaigns against abortion rights candidates. Congressman Robert Edgar of Pennsylvania was a particular target. When Welsh was assigned to Allentown, Pennsylvania, he had volunteers conduct political registration drives in church vestibules for the first time in the diocese's history. "Politics is the way we do things," Welsh proclaimed.

One of the most peculiar aspects of this politicization is that both the Catholic Press Association and Archbishop James A. Hickey of Washington, D.C., warned of legal violations in 1984. Hickey carefully instructed his parishes not to "endorse, support or oppose any candidate or group of candidates, directly or indirectly; authorize or permit the distribution of partisan campaign material in church through official channels, such as church bulletins." In August the National Conference of Catholic Bishops ordered all dioceses to stop acting "for or against political candidates." Still, violations continued.

The Internal Revenue Service, of course, could have blocked these violations years before if it had moved to take away the tax exemption of any offending diocese. It did nothing. When Abortion Rights Mobilization and twenty other national organizations and individual plaintiffs, such as Protestant and Jewish clergy, brought suit in federal court in 1980 to make the IRS follow the law, the defendants tied up the suit for six years with interminable legal maneuvers. And in 1986 the U.S. District Court declared that the Catholic bishops "have wilfully misled" the plaintiffs and have "made a travesty of the court process."

Strangely, the IRS had acted in 1964 against an offending liberal Protestant journal, *The Christian Century*. After it published editorials endorsing Lyndon B. Johnson for the presidency, the IRS removed its tax exemption for three years. But in the 1980s the IRS was presumably too influenced by the Reagan administration to prosecute its Catholic and Fundamentalist allies.[11]

Archbishop O'Connor's pronouncement in the 1984 campaign that no Catholic "in good conscience" could vote for an abortion rights candidate was aimed at Congresswoman Ferraro, not, significantly, at male candidates. He jabbed at her for weeks, seemingly intent on destroying her. He insisted that she had "said some things about abortion relative to Catholic teaching which are not true."

O'Connor's evidence, it turned out, was a letter sent two years before by Ferraro and other Catholics to all Catholic members of Congress, inviting them to a briefing. The briefing would show that the "Catholic position on abortion is not monolithic and that there can be a range of personal and political responses to the issue." What infuriated O'Connor was that "she has given the world to understand that Catholic teaching is divided. . . ." O'Connor insisted there is "no variance."

Ferraro's position, of course, was hardly unique. It reflected that of fifty-five theologians, twenty-four nuns and four priests and brothers who took out a full-page ad in *The New York Times* a month later headlined: "A Diversity of Opinion Regarding Abortion Exists Among Catholics." Their statement stemmed from "adherence to principles of moral theology, such as probabilism, religious liberty, and the centrality of informed conscience." As a result, the statement concluded, "A large number of Catholic theologians hold that even direct abortion, although tragic, can sometimes be a moral choice."

Catholics for a Free Choice, the organization taking the ad, pointed out that seventy-one other Catholic theologians agreed to its contents but were afraid to sign it for fear of losing their jobs. They also noted that only 11 per cent of Catholics surveyed by the National Opinion Research Center disapproved of abortion in all circumstances. But O'Connor's inflexible position against Catholic "diversity," of course, echoed the Vatican. Dissidents had to be whipped back into line. The twenty-four nuns who had signed the ad were pressured to retract their beliefs. Three of the four priests and brothers recanted.

The pressure came from the top, from the Vatican's Sacred Congregation for Religious and Secular Institutes in Rome. Its letter of November 30, 1984, stressed that any deviation from the church's teaching on abortion is a "flagrant scandal and is sufficient cause for the dismissal of a religious guilty of such conduct." The letter called for a "public retraction" and "an explicit threat of dismissal" to be carried out "if the religious remains obstinately disobedient to the Church and to you, the Superior."[12]

While trumpeting the majesty of canon law, the Sacred Congregation ignored the reality that there had indeed been "diversity" in the church's teachings for almost nineteen centuries until 1869. In the early church, abortion was punished as murder only after the soul became rational or "animated," a thesis probably taken from Aristotle and set at forty days after conception for a male fetus, eighty or ninety days for a female (with no explanation how sex would be determined). The Decretals of Pope Gregory IX (1227–41) confirmed this law. And except for three years after 1588, animation was the church rule until 1869, when Pope Pius IX eliminated all distinction between animated and non-animated, and abortion became murder at the moment of conception.

Archbishop O'Connor's campaign to bludgeon Catholics to vote against abortion rights candidates and the insistence by Catholic dissidents that "diversity" could be applied to dogma after 1869 launched a massive crisis in the relationship of religion to politics. No one questioned the right of the Catholic to call abortion "murder," a religious interpretation opposed by almost all other faiths. But as Senator Edward M. Kennedy pointed out, could not other denominations then try to force their morality on the public? Could not orthodox Jews try to ban business on Saturday? Or Christian Scientists impose their medical beliefs? "Religious leaders may say anything they feel bound in conscience to say," Kennedy asserted, "but they must not ask Government to do something which it cannot do under the Constitution or the social contract of a pluralistic society."

The crux of the problem was that "uncertain area between private and public morality when the vindication of one religious tradition can come only at the expense of another," stressed Henry Siegman of the American Jewish Congress. The Supreme Court decision simply gave women in need a choice; it forced no one to have an abortion. The insistence by the Catholic church and Fundamentalists that their religious position had to be accepted by everyone could force a woman to have an unwanted child, and was "particularly damaging to our pluralistic ethic and destructive of public peace," Siegman added.

Not all members of the hierarchy followed O'Connor and Law in focusing on abortion as the number-one issue. *The Tablet*, official newspaper of the Brooklyn diocese, insisted: "We cannot let one issue—however important and even crucial—bind us. . . ." Cardinal Joseph Bernardin of Chicago called abortion part of a "seamless garment" that included shelter for the homeless, jobs, nuclear arms control, the plight of the "helpless in our nation as well as the poor of the world."[13]

Other members of the hierarchy tried to define the critical line between teaching the church's position on abortion or forcing it on everyone through legislation. Auxiliary Bishop Joseph Sullivan of the Brooklyn diocese pointed out during the 1984 campaign: "As much as I think we're responsible for advocating public policy issues, our primary responsibility is to teach our own people. We haven't done that. We're asking politicians to do what we haven't done effectively ourselves."

The greatest danger of O'Connor's pressure on Catholic office-holders, and attempts to legislate Catholic morality for the country, was that it struck at the foundations of a pluralistic society so carefully maintained by President Kennedy. In a speech at the University of Notre Dame after he had challenged O'Connor, Governor Cuomo pointed out that Catholic officials take an oath to preserve the Constitution in our pluralistic society "because they realize that in guaranteeing freedom for all, they guarantee *our* right to be Catholics. . . . To assure our freedom we must allow others the same freedom, even if it occasionally produces conduct by them which we hold to be sinful." Cuomo concluded: "I protect my right to be a Catholic by preserving your right as a Jew, a Protestant or non-believer, or anything else you choose."

On the practical level of enforcement, Cuomo pointed out that no law could work in a pluralistic society that wasn't supported by a consensus of the people. Prohibition, legislated by Protestant moralists, had not worked in the 1920s. "Given present attitudes [if abortion were outlawed], it would be Prohibition revisited, legislating what couldn't be enforced and in the process creating a disrespect for law in general." Or if the Supreme Court decision were changed to allow control of abortion by each state, as the Hatch Act called for, Cuomo predicted a "checkerboard of permissive and restrictive jurisdictions" that would make women travel long distances to abortion rights states and would mainly penalize the poor.

The further danger of the Catholic hierarchy's position was that no consensus had been achieved even among Catholics. In the National Opinion Research Center's study for 1984, 86 per cent of Catholics favored abortion if the woman's health is seriously endangered; 76 per cent if the woman becomes pregnant as a result of rape; and 34 per cent for any reason. Catholic opinion was virtually the same as the general population: 90, 80 and 39 per cent, respectively, in these categories.

Governor Cuomo's conclusion that the outlawing of abortion would be unenforceable seems to be borne out by 1966 studies, a year when not one state had yet liberalized its law and abortion was banned throughout the country. Although based on partial statistics because abortion was an underground procedure then, Dr. Christopher Tietze, the leading statistician of abortion, estimated that 1.2 million were performed annually. If abortion were outlawed again, the wealthy would have little problem flying to Britain or other countries with legalized abortion. Only the poor would be driven back to kitchen table abortion, leading to the maimings, deaths, and damage to maternal and child health that existed before legalization in the United States.[14]

If we accept the conclusions of President Kennedy, Governor Cuomo, and other Catholic leaders that one religious morality cannot be forced on others, particularly if no consensus would make enforcement workable, how can O'Connor's type of confrontation be explained? Surely the Catholic hierarchy would not go to all the effort and money to outlaw abortion when women, including their own communicants, would undoubtedly seek abortion in other countries, or underground, as they did before legalization.[15]

One explanation is Vatican panic. Pope John Paul II has increasingly dreaded the liberalization of the church in the United States. He has pounded away at holding traditional teaching even on birth control when most bishops, and certainly most Catholics, have ignored him. Consequently, he may have chosen to make abortion a symbol of a line that must be held at any costs in an era when the church's teachings on divorce, premarital continence, and other fundamentals receive diminishing obedience. The Vatican may see abortion as an issue that can build conservatives into a political force capable of combating the liberal trend. It must be a significant part of Vatican strategy that abortion becomes the dominant issue in the United States, while its legalization has been virtually ignored in such Catholic countries as Poland and Italy, which has the highest abortion rate in Western Europe.

Cardinal O'Connor and Cardinal Law have turned abortion into the "cutting edge" of the right-wing assault on separation of church and state. It is the most easily dramatized weapon in their arsenal. A fetus can stir passionate reactions, portrayed as the helpless and innocent victim in movies like *The Silent Scream*, which concentrate total attention on incipient life and ignore the disaster that unwanted pregnancy can wreak on women and families. Abortion, moreover, strikes at the darkest corners of sexual repression among conservatives. It conjures up the threat of rampant sex among the young. It is the path to promiscuity, a means of total license that must be crushed if the country is to be restored to what conservatives consider the moral bedrock of the past.

Abortion has thus become the prime instrument of the assault on First Amendment separation, leading the way for a whole range of issues from sex education to homosexuality. Abortion represents the core of the Catholic–Fundamentalist–White House alliance. It represents the best possibility of a breakthrough for the conservative agenda. If abortion rights can be destroyed, all other objectives can be won more easily.

VI

Catholic Medicine

N^{O ASPECT} of Catholic power involves more fundamental problems than the continued efforts of the church to make accepted medical practices conform to its religious position. It might be expected that a Catholic hospital should bar birth control from its premises. Since the church owns the hospital, it can control its procedures, just as the Christian Science church sets the rules for its adherents. A Catholic hospital might also try to stop a Catholic staff physician from dispensing birth control to his private patients, although this intrusion would seem to depend on the individual's willingness to bend his medical standards to his faith. But when Catholic discipline takes in the non-Catholic doctor and insists on regulating his professional life outside the hospital, the problem invades the area of medical ethics.

St. Francis Hospital in Poughkeepsie, New York, raised this issue in 1952 when it presented an ultimatum to seven non-Catholic doctors on its staff. Following their own medical beliefs and conscience, they had joined the local Planned Parenthood Federation. The hospital gave them a disturbing choice: either resign from Planned Parenthood or from the staff. Rather than abandon their patients, three doctors quit the federation. The others left the hospital.[1]

In addition to harming its medical standing by such censorship and depriving its patients of the services of four doctors, St. Francis provoked a broader issue that may have involved a violation of the Constitution. It had recently accepted federal funds for the construction of a new wing, making it, in effect, a quasi-public rather than a solely religious institution. The question, increasingly pressing as religious hospitals take government money, is whether such a hospital has not infringed the Establishment Clause of the First Amendment by practicing some form of religious medicine in conflict with regular medical standards. The Catholic Theological Society of America, consequently, urged in 1973 that since most Catholic hospitals are quasi-public, they "ought to permit medical procedures forbidden by Catholic doctrine."

The Catholic hierarchy's unfortunate habit of reprisals against the medical profession persisted through the next decade. When six prominent non-Catholic physicians testified against Connecticut's law banning birth control, they were dropped from the staffs of Catholic hospitals. A test of the Connecticut law was then carried to the U.S. Supreme Court. After Dr. Oliver Stringfield, the leading pediatrician in Stamford, submitted an *amicus* brief in favor of revocation, he lost his privileges to practice at a local Catholic hospital. The hierarchy in Parkersburg, West Virginia, organized a public campaign in 1953 against the opening of a Planned Parenthood clinic at the city-owned Camden-Clark Memorial Hospital, but failed. Fifty-three Catholic agencies resigned from New York City's Health and Welfare Council in 1953 to block the admission of Planned Parenthood, and the organization remained in shambles for three years until it was re-created as the Greater New York Community Council, with Planned Parenthood denied voting status.[2]

The punishment of doctors or health groups for not submitting to Catholic medical doctrine was damaging enough. But when this type of pressure was applied to the public hospital system of a huge city, Catholic power endangered medical standards for millions of patients. At New York's Kings County Hospital in 1958, its chief of obstetrics and gynecology, Dr. Louis M. Hellman, prescribed contraception for a Protestant patient, a diabetic with two previous cesarean sections whose health would be seriously threatened by another pregnancy. Under Cardinal Spellman's direction, Catholic organizations immediately initiated a mail and press campaign against Hellman and his boss, Dr. Morris A. Jacobs, the commissioner of hospitals. Although there was no official policy against birth control, few doctors had previously been willing to tangle with the church.

In First Amendment terms, it was a clear-cut case of religious medicine being imposed on publicly funded institutions. In practical terms, the case affected the birth control needs of mainly poor patients at city hospitals. "Inhumane discrimination against the medically indigent," Dr. Nicholson J. Eastman, professor of obstetrics and gynecology at Johns Hopkins University, called it.

Describing the Catholic position as "arbitrary support for one minority view" and "contemptuous treatment of others," a joint statement of the New York City Protestant Council, the American Jewish Congress and other religious groups rebutted Cardinal Spellman and the church. After five months of uproar, Mayor Robert Wagner, himself a Catholic, left the final decision to the hospital board. With Dr. Jacobs abstaining, the board voted 8 to 2 in September that any ban on birth control, official or nonofficial, must be removed.[3]

In rural areas where a Catholic hospital may be the only one available, the imposition of Catholic medicine can do particular harm both to the standards of community health and to the right of a patient to have access to a procedure of his choice. That was the case in Miles City, Montana, in 1972 when Holy Rosary Hospital prohibited local physicians from performing voluntary sterilizations on its premises. Women who wanted this form of birth contol, as a result, had to travel to distant cities, causing patients, especially those with young children to look after, "emotional turmoil, exasperation and inconvenience," according to Dr. Robert K. Scarlett. Branding it "bad medicine, unethical, and horrible," Scarlett and six other doctors went to court to get Holy Rosary to accept standard medical procedures. When that failed, the whole group of doctors moved to cities and towns where they could practice medicine without religious domination. Not only were non-Catholic, as well as Catholic, patients penalized, but six doctors were lost to Miles City and Holy Rosary.[4]

When it can influence local politics, the Catholic hierarchy tries to promote its form of medicine over that required by public policy. This is common in the case of abortion services. Although Margaret Hague Hospital of the Jersey City (New Jersey) Medical Center was a municipal corporation supplying obstetrical-gynecological services to all citizens of Hudson County, it continued to ban abortion (and kept crèches and other religious symbols on its floors). In 1977, Abortion Rights Mobilization, a New York–based group, brought suit against the hospital on the grounds it must practice public medicine in conformity with the 1973 Supreme Court decision. Mayor Paul T. Jordan, a board member, agreed that the hospital was "bound by the laws of the state," and the day before the case was filed in court, the hospital board voted 5 to 2 to allow abortion.

Similarly, Cardinal John O'Connor of New York tried to stop a nonsectarian institution, New York Medical College, from sending its abortion cases to two city hospitals, Lincoln and Metropolitan, with which it was affiliated. If it did not stop abortion services, the Medical College would lose its support from the archdiocese, the cardinal warned. The cardinal had inside clout at the Medical College, since the church had loaned it $10 million a few years before and thus controlled its board of trustees. The Medical College, however, still remained a nonsectarian institution and stood to lose $2.25 million a year in state funds if the separation principle were abridged. The Medical College would also lose $24 million a year if its contract with the two municipal hospitals was broken. This financial blow must have been explained to the cardinal, for a few days later archdiocese officials stated that the "conflict does not exist. . . ."[5]

The imposition of Catholic medicine is hardly restricted to birth control, abortion, and voluntary sterilization. It intrudes on a range of other procedures from organ transplants to artificial insemination, and to the complex issue of donor egg programs. Even if Catholic patients were the only ones affected, the problem would be large enough. But by geographic necessity, non-Catholic patients are also seriously affected since one-third of all Catholic hospitals serve communities lacking any other medical facility. Furthermore, the size of the Catholic hospital system accentuates its impact. Catholic hospitals hold 29 per cent of all beds in the country and make up 731 of 3,267 nonprofit, nongovernmental institutions.

A disturbing question is whether this huge system can adhere first and foremost to the highest medical standards. Enunciating a policy in 1957 that has never been altered, Archbishop Edward F. Hoban of Cleveland stated that the "ultimate and essential purpose of the Catholic hospital is the same as that of the Catholic Church—the sanctification and salvation of souls." Even a non-Catholic doctor must agree that dogma takes priority over medical standards. "When a doctor comes on staff, he signs a statement that he will abide by the Catholic moral code," explains Sister Joan Upjohn, administrator of Salt Lake City's Holy Cross Hospital and former board chair of the Catholic Health Association.[6]

An equally disturbing question, applying to all Catholic and religious hospitals of any faith taking public funds, is whether the imposition of morality on medicine may not violate the Constitution by establishing one religion in preference to others. The question has become critical since Congress passed the Hill-Burton Act in 1946, awarding government funds for construction to religious as well as nonsectarian and public hospitals. From 1946 through 1960, $202.8 million (58.4 per cent) went to Catholic hospitals, $112.5 million (37.2 per cent) to Protestant hospitals, and $14.6 million (3.5 per cent) to Jewish hospitals. Significantly, the Catholic share amounts to over twice its proportion of the population.

The government's 1985 catalogue of hospitals, with the amount each must provide in uncompensated services as a result of Hill-Burton construction grants, indicates the size of federal funds going to Catholic facilities. In New York City, St. Mary's received over $5 million, Calvary and Misericordia over $2.5 million. In Chicago, St. Mary of Nazareth received over $6 million, St. Bernard's and Mercy around $2 million. In Los Angeles, Holy Cross received over $3.6 million and Queen of the Valley over $1.3 million. In Philadelphia, Mercy received almost $5 million, and St. Agnes and Mercy Douglass around $3 million.

Such government funding of religious hospitals would seem to give them public status and require them to follow public health policy. In 1963 the U.S. Court of Appeals for the Fourth Circuit ruled that a hospital receiving Hill-Burton money could not maintain a dual system for whites and blacks, and Congress a year later passed an amendment prohibiting discrimination on the basis of "race, creed or color" at these hospitals.

"Creed" would seem to include discrimination against a Protestant or Jewish patient at a Catholic hospital. One U.S. District Court judge in Oregon, in fact, in a case brought by a woman seeking sterilization at a Catholic hospital, ruled that facilities receiving Hill-Burton funds "cannot engage in racial or other arbitrary forms of discrimination when deciding which patients and physicians to admit to the hospital." The Court of Appeals for the Ninth Circuit, however, called the case moot in 1974 since the woman had secured a sterilization elsewhere before it heard the case.[7]

At least five other federal court cases in 1973 decreed that a hospital with Hill-Burton funding was "acting under the color of state law" or used similar wording. Although Congress in 1973 exempted private voluntary hospitals from performing abortion and sterilization if they went against the religious and moral convictions of the institution, the U.S. Supreme Court by 1986 had still not ruled on the responsibilities of a Hill-Burton hospital in other areas of medical practice.[8]

Catholic medicine presents a thorny problem for the medical profession because of its dependence on what the Vatican likes to call "natural law." The Vatican's interpretation often stems from the conclusions of an ancient theologian, not a treatment that may be best for the patient's health. Many medical decisions, consequently, may be made a priori. Anesthesia in childbirth, for example, was at first condemned as sinful, since Saint Augustine in the fourth century had ruled that pain was a divine punishment meted out to women for Eve's disobedience, and the Bible had declared in Genesis, "In sorrow thou shalt bring forth children."

What the Vatican considers "unnatural" may simply conform to what the Vatican disapproves of. Glanville Williams, professor of law at Cambridge University in England, analyzed the application of natural law in a Catholic question-and-answer column. Question: "My wife is sterile but wants her 'marital rights.' I have a contagious venereal disease. May I wear a prophylactic sheath?" Answer: "No. Even though she could not conceive and you would infect her, contraceptive intercourse is an intrinsically evil act." "Here it is in a nutshell," observes Williams. "The situation makes no difference. The end sought makes no difference. Nothing makes any difference. The act itself is wrong. This is the essence of 'intrinsic' morality."

Similarly, the Catholic archdiocese of Los Angeles in 1986 withdrew from an AIDS education project because it condoned the use of condoms. "In the issue of AIDS, such use implies either heterosexual promiscuity or homosexual activity," Archbishop Roger Mahony stated. "The church approves of neither." Although the end sought—control of a rampant disease that may become a worldwide epidemic—would seem to be of overriding importance, the church had to stick to its interpretation of natural law in its ban on condoms rather than cooperate in a critical health campaign.

Although neither the Bible nor any ecumenical council until this century makes any mention of voluntary sterilization, Pope Pius XI forbade it in the encyclical *Casti Conubii*, in 1930. He ruled that men and women "are not free to destroy or mutilate their members, or in any other way render themselves unfit for their natural functions, except where no other provision can be made for the good of the whole body."

This application of natural law—Cardinal Patrick O'Boyle of Washington, D.C., called it "so profoundly sacred that it may not be taken away from the individual"—often changes at the Vatican's convenience. For centuries until 1870, despite natural law's ban on mutilation, the Sistine Choirs prized their *castrati*, or adult male sopranos whose testicles had been removed at an early age to prevent their voices from changing to the normal masculine pitch.[9]

The demands of Catholic teaching obliterate any consideration of the woman patient. Although a woman has had one or more children by cesarean section and doctors conclude that another cesarean birth could prove fatal, although a woman suffers from renal or cardiac disease and another pregnancy could endanger her life, neither sterilization nor contraception is allowed. A woman who has borne a child with Down's syndrome, Tay-Sachs, or other genetic defects, virtually assuring that future offspring would be defective, still cannot request sterilization.

A woman who has been raped can take no defensive measures. Catholic Medical Directives have ruled that "curettage of the endometrium after rape to prevent implantation of a possible embryo is morally equivalent to abortion."

"The Catholic preference for doing nothing to assist the mother," concludes Glanville Williams, "amounts in fact to a preference of the fetus over its mother, if not a sentence of death for both."

In dealing with an ectopic pregnancy—a fertilized egg lodged in a fallopian tube, or sometimes the ovary, where continued growth could prove fatal to both mother and embryo—Catholic medicine has made a recent exception. In 1902 the Congregation of the Holy Office was questioned about the standard treatment of cutting the fallopian tube (or sterilization) and destroying the embryo through abortion. It answered: "No, it is not lawful. Such a removal is a direct killing of the fetus and is therefore forbidden."

By 1945, however, Catholic theology had developed the "double effect" exception, which followed Saint Thomas Aquinas in concluding that a "part may be sacrificed to save the whole" and that "indirect killing" is not sinful when its primary aim is to preserve the woman's life. As a result, Catholic Medical Directives now state that operations and treatments are "permitted when they cannot be safely postponed until the fetus is viable, even though they may or will result in the death of the fetus." Catholic surgeons may thus perform a hysterectomy of a pregnant uterus for a malignant ovarian tumor. And radical therapy can be done on a cancerous prostate gland to save a man's life, although sterilization may result.

"Meanwhile, we cannot help wondering how many mothers have died uselessly between 1902 and 1945," concludes Joseph Fletcher, a professor of social ethics at Harvard's Theological School, "when moral theologians were sticking fast to their theocratic absolutes. . . ."[10]

2

Artificial insemination—a last-resort medical procedure for a couple who want a child but cannot produce a pregnancy by sexual union—has always been restricted by Vatican teaching. Entailing varying techniques of depositing semen in the vagina, cervical canal, or uterus, it can be done through insemination by the husband (AIH) or through insemination with donor sperm (AID) when the husband's sperm is nonviable.

Since Catholic morality prohibits masturbation based on its twisted interpretation of Onanism in the Old Testament, a husband must not morally produce a sperm sample to inseminate his wife, or even to give to a physician for testing for viability. Some theologians have sanctioned the release of semen through manual exercise of the prostate gland by the doctor. In this case, semen results from medical treatment with no pleasure involved, so the process could be licit. But even this option seems to have been eliminated by Pope Pius XII's pronouncement in 1949 that AIH was "entirely illicit and immoral" unless it served "as an auxiliary to the natural act of union of the spouses." The only moral alternative left is for a husband or wife somehow to collect an adequate amount of semen during coitus.

Donor insemination is absolutely condemned by the Vatican and raises complex issues as well for people of any faith. Catholic theologians—and other clergy—have even labeled it adultery. AID requires a healthy donor whose hair, eyes, and other features reasonably match those of the husband. A physician may mix the husband's sperm with the donor's in the long-shot chance that it could be responsible for impregnation. A physician may also require the husband to press the syringe that injects the donor sperm into his wife's vagina to give him a psychological part in the reproductive process.

Since courts have occasionally held a child resulting from AID to be illegitimate, all parties concerned are generally bound to secrecy. Yet all these obstacles must be weighed against a moral end: a couple's desperation for a child whose genes will be at least half their own. The charge of adultery has little basis when there is no deceit between husband and wife, and no relationship with the anonymous donor. The main legal complication could be a disputed inheritance in case of future divorce and remarriage. AID, in fact, could be said to resemble any medical process with humane objectives, such as an organ transplant, in that semen is transferred from one person to another.

Catholic theology raises further obstacles to the accepted standards guiding organ transplants. It condemns transplants done after the death of a donor. Even with inter vivos transplants—the gift of one unneeded kidney by a living person, for example, to save a second person's life—theologians are split. Most consider them illicit. But the Reverend Charles McFadden, author of a Catholic work on medical ethics, represents the minority in defending them through Aquinas's principle of totality. The donor may give up a kidney because it preserves the renal function—the totality—of another. The whole is more important than the parts.[11]

Catholic medicine differs even more drastically with the new reproductive biology known as in vitro fertilization. This technology, more complex than artificial insemination, was first developed in the birth of Louise Brown at an English hospital in 1978. The mother's ovaries produced eggs, but they could not pass down the fallopian tubes to be fertilized. Dr. Patrick Steptoe, therefore, removed eggs from her ovaries and placed them in a glass dish, where they were fertilized by the husband's sperm. Then he transferred the embryo to the mother's womb, where it developed normally and was born as Louise Brown. In the next five years 184 pregnancies were produced from 1100 in vitro procedures: a 17 per cent rate compared with 45 per cent for normally fertilized ova achieving implantation, but still a remarkable gain for couples who would never have had a biological child otherwise.

Although most Protestant and Jewish groups—"We're 'co-creators' with God," asserted the *Christian Century*—hailed IVF as a moral and medical breakthrough, the Vatican under natural law branded it "immoral and absolutely illicit." "Fecundation must be carried out according to nature and through reciprocal and responsible love between a man and a woman," a Vatican spokesman ruled.

According to the Vatican, IVF not only involved illicit masturbation to produce male sperm, but broke the natural "process by which human life is transmitted." In a pithy analogy from the New York archdiocese, the Reverend William B. Smith protested: "It's the contraception argument backward. Pius XII talked about not wanting to change the home into a laboratory. I call it switching the marital bed into a chemistry set."[12]

Catholic theology clashed further with advancing technology after the development of a "donor egg baby program" in Australia in 1983. In cases of infertile women, scientists at Melbourne's Queen Victoria Hospital extracted an egg group from a fertile donor and preserved them by freezing. When needed, one egg from the bank would be unfrozen and inserted into the womb of an infertile patient after being fertilized by her husband's sperm. There it grew and often became a healthy birth, but its genetic origin, of course, was half from the donor.

One couple involved, Mario and Elsa Rios, was killed in a plane crash. Since he was infertile, eggs extracted from Elsa had previously been fertilized with sperm from an anonymous donor. The embryo implanted in Elsa resulted in a miscarriage, but two other eggs had already been frozen in a bank before she died. Should Elsa's eggs be implanted in other women or be immediately destroyed? If implanted and producing a live birth, should the children have the right to inherit the Rios estate?

Catholic clergy and right-to-life groups in Australia, joined by a few Orthodox Jewish rabbis, insisted that the sanctity of life demanded that the frozen embryos be implanted in other patients. Yet this position seemed to counter the Vatican.

On March 10, 1987, the Vatican issued a sweeping ban on almost every form of biomedicine that interferes with or bypasses coital reproduction. Surrogate motherhood, prenatal diagnosis for the purpose of eliminating fetuses affected by malformations, the freezing of an embryo even when done to prolong its existence, all attempts to influence chromosomic or genetic inheritance not completely therapeutic—these were among many technologies the Vatican prohibited as violations of natural law.

The Vatican's doctrines were as startling to some of its allies among other faiths as they were to much of its constituency. Although Orthodox Jews generally sided with the church against abortion, Dr. Moses Tendler, professor of Jewish medical ethics at New York's Yeshiva University, retorted that "unnatural is not a sin but an opportunity to complete God's work. You cannot commit adultery with a catheter or a hypodermic syringe."

Those Catholics who desperately wanted a child and who had failed at conception through intercourse were liable to ignore the Vatican ban. What then was the pope's purpose in alienating more followers already embittered by *Humanae Vitae*? The church seemed concerned with politics rather than Catholic harmony. It seemed to be bringing its moral imperatives to Congress and state legislatures, determined to impose its will before a consensus had been formed. Its politics were ambitious as always.

The legal issues of reproductive technology had become equally tangled. The American Fertility Society came out for guidelines that would make it compulsory for the disposition of unneeded eggs to be decided beforehand, and would limit frozen egg banks to the reproductive years of the woman donor. To bring some resolution to the medico-legal complexities that may continue to involve church and state, Judge Marianne O. Battani of Wayne County (Ohio) Circuit Court ruled in 1986 that an infant girl—conceived in a glass dish with a couple's sperm and egg, but carried to term by a surrogate mother— legally belonged to the biological parents. "We really have no definition of 'mother' in our law books," the judge commented.

The first case of surrogate motherhood, where the surrogate was the biological mother, was decided by a superior court judge in New Jersey on March 31, 1987. By awarding "Baby M" to the biological father, who had paid a surrogate mother to bear a child from his sperm, the judge affirmed the legality of a surrogate contract, but did not touch the morality or biomedical aspects of the problem. The Vatican decree a few weeks before had already prohibited surrogate motherhood for Catholics.[13]

3

The Catholic hierarchy has had particular trouble dealing with the "right to die" issue, arising from recent advances in medical technology which can keep a comatose or brain-damaged patient alive for years. The issue can no longer be defined as euthanasia in its traditional sense. Now the patient may be in a permanent vegetative state, literally dead already, with heartbeat and breathing maintained only through machines doing the work of the body.

Euthanasia has always been condemned by the Vatican. "No one is permitted to ask for this act of killing, either for himself or herself or for another person entrusted to his or her care, nor can he or she consent to it, either explicitly or implicitly," Pope John Paul II proclaimed in 1980. But when the pope dealt with the impact of life-prolonging medical technology, he made a significant exception. "When inevitable death is imminent in spite of the means used," he ruled, "it is permitted in conscience to take the decision to refuse forms of treatment that would only secure a precarious and burdensome prolongation of life, so long as the normal care due to the sick person in similar cases is not interrupted."

The pope's exception was undoubtedly drawn from two precedents where Catholic patients had been kept alive by advanced medical technology. Karen Ann Quinlan, a twenty-one-year-old New Jersey resident, remained in a permanent vegetative state after respiratory arrest in 1975. Her family eventually sought court permission to stop all extraordinary treatment that would sustain vital life processes. The New Jersey Supreme Court approved, and the state's Catholic Conference called it a "morally correct decision." In 1976 Quinlan was removed from the respirator, transferred to a nursing home and remained in a deep coma until her death in 1985.

Brother Joseph Fox, an eighty-three-year-old member of the Catholic Marianist order, lapsed into a coma during an operation in 1979. Attending neurologists agreed that he was in a "permanent vegetative state." But when the Reverend Philip K. Eichner, his superior, asked the court's permission to withdraw the respirator, the district attorney of Nassau County, New York, as well as Catholic right-to-life groups, refused to accept the Quinlan precedent, and argued that this amounted to an act of killing as defined by euthanasia. With "clear and convincing evidence" that the patient had previously told his fellow Marianists that he wanted no life-sustaining procedures, New York's Court of Appeals said the respirator could be discontinued. Brother Fox, however, died while the case was still in court.[14]

Both before and after the pope's 1980 ruling, the complexity of the issue led to sharp contradictions in the official Catholic position. When "Living Will" legislation—allowing individuals well beforehand to establish clear directions for their terminal care—was introduced into the Connecticut legislature in 1979, the state's Catholic Conference opposed it. Although the bill passed the state senate 27 to 9, it was defeated by a close vote in the house after what the *Hartford Courant* called the "offensive scare tactics and irresponsible distortions used by the Connecticut Right-to-Life Corporation." Much of the right-to-life movement was beginning to equate euthanasia, as they called the Living Will concept, with their definition of abortion as "murder." Defeated in three succeeding years, the Connecticut bill was finally passed in 1985.

Similar legislation in Ohio, Virginia, and other states has been stopped largely as a result of lobbying by Catholic Conferences and right-to-life groups. Although a Massachusetts bill passed the house, it has long been stalled in the senate by legislators allied with the archdiocese. Massachusetts Citizens for Life attacked the bill as the "first step towards the ultimate legalization of euthanasia, which is currently classified as homicide."

"An opening wedge for the euthanasia movement," Catholics for Life in Rhode Island called Living Will legislation. The Reverend Robert Barry, a moral theologian, branded the Living Will as "legal approval for suicide, assisted suicide and non-voluntary mercy killing in some cases." Bishop Walter Curtis of Bridgeport, Connecticut, considered it "not a far step to legalizing murder or suicide."

In Virginia, the diverging Catholic positions led one diocese to support the Living Will while Bishop Walter F. Sullivan of Richmond blamed it for inducing a "social climate in which laws to permit suicide or the direct killing of the terminally ill could be accepted." Similarly, the Denver Archdiocesan Respect Life Commission favored Living Will legislation while Colorado right-to-life groups attacked it.

By 1984, the U.S. bishops recognized that Catholic positions had become so tangled that they issued guidelines withdrawing outright opposition to Living Will legislation and concentrating instead on correcting problem areas. Acting on those guidelines, Maryland's Catholic Conference in 1985 stopped objecting to a Living Will statute as long as its amendments were adopted. One amendment allowed a patient to direct continuation of life-sustaining procedures despite a previous declaration to remove them. Similarly in Missouri in 1985, the Catholic Conference insisted, among other changes, that the legislation narrowly define what was meant by a terminal condition.

As organizations such as the American Medical Association and National Council of Senior Citizens campaigned for the Living Will, a Lou Harris poll in 1985 reflected a public ground swell. Eighty-five per cent of those questioned approved the right of the terminally ill to instruct their doctors to remove support systems when no cure could be expected. Thirteen new Living Will acts were passed in 1985, and three in 1986, bringing the total to thirty-eight states and the District of Columbia.[15]

When food and water were included as part of a patient's medical support system, the issue became even more complex. The theological problem was whether to accept tubal feeding as the equivalent of any other life-prolonging procedure. The New Jersey Supreme Court recognized the right to terminate such feeding in the *Conroy* case in 1985.

Similarly, the Massachusetts Supreme Judicial Court ruled in 1986 in the case of Paul E. Brophy, who had been comatose since 1983, that tubal feeding was a form of "medical treatment," and that such feeding could be stopped.

But the case of Kathleen Farrell would push judicial interpretation even further. Farrell, a victim of Lou Gehrig's disease, was being cared for at home and was adjudged clearly competent to make the request to remove her respirator. She also refused artificial feeding. After her husband pleaded in court she had decided "on her own free will" that she no longer wanted to live, a New Jersey superior court approved the removal of all life-sustaining equipment. Although Mrs. Farrell died while the decision was being appealed, her case—along with those of two comatose patients—will be decided by the state's supreme court in 1987.

The Catholic Conference had approved the Quinlan decision earlier, but feeding obviously added a new dimension to the theological quandary. Now the Catholic bishops of New Jersey filed a brief in the Supreme Court, opposing removal of feeding tubes in all three cases on the grounds that starvation of patients on the verge of death should not be sanctioned.[16]

The bishops must have seen a difference between feeding and other life-sustaining equipment, and were troubled how the imminence of death, particularly for a competent patient, could be defined. Mrs. Farrell, as it turned out, died before a higher court could approve a halt to her feeding. Why should the bishops place feeding in a special category and make the imminence of death a moral issue taking precedence over Mrs. Farrell's right to take the decision into her own hands? The question, as with most church intrusions into medicine, comes down to a conflict between a priori theology and the right of a patient's individual choice. A decision on tubal feeding, whether by a competent person or the family of a comatose person, would seem to depend far more on dealing mercifully with an insoluble tragedy, as some courts have ruled, than with a theological definition of whether it amounts to killing by starvation.

Given the 1984 withdrawal of the bishops from outright opposition to the Living Will, it would seem that the church might be moving towards an acceptance of standard medical practices. Yet in the most obvious areas demanding change, such as birth control and voluntary sterilization, the Vatican maintains its rigidity against the progressive attitudes of some Catholic hospitals.

When Dr. John M. O'Lane studied 340 Catholic hospitals responding out of 598 questioned, he found that 44 supplied all family planning services in 1979. Twenty per cent—a slightly higher figure— supplied sterilization services. The most important insight of his study was that 47 per cent of Catholic medical staffs not performing sterilization stated that they wanted to do them. "It is nonsense to assert that what is theologically permissible in Canada, in the Netherlands and in 20 per cent of U.S. Catholic hospitals is not theologically permissible in the remaining U.S. Catholic hospitals," Dr. O'Lane protested.

This liberalizing trend, however, has recently been blocked by the Vatican. Although the Sisters of Mercy hospital system, the largest nongovernmental supplier of medical services in the country, had been performing sterilizations for at least a decade, a Vatican directive in 1983 ordered them to stop, and the hospital system's administrative director complied with the order to "avoid serious consequences."

According to the Reverend Walter J. Burghardt, editor of *Theological Studies*, the "dilemma will be taken underground." This process has already made sterilization the "most popular form of Catholic contraception," as shown by the studies of Father Andrew Greeley, the sociologist. The process has also intensified the splits within Catholicism. Most Catholics seeking medical services that conflict with the Vatican position (not just birth control but any procedure from organ transplants to artificial insemination) now ignore Rome, and turn to non-Catholic hospitals and clinics. Those U.S. prelates who recognize the need to raise their medical facilities to national standards —Archbishop Raymond Hunthausen, for example, was condemned for allowing sterilization in his diocese—will simply overlook infractions until Rome catches up with them. Catholic medicine and its striving for scientific objectivity cannot remain a prisoner of the Vatican indefinitely.[17]

VII

The Vatican Grip on Marriage, Divorce, and the Family

SINCE the essence of Catholic power is to keep control of marriage and children, canon law rules that to be "valid" all marriages must be made in the presence of a pastor or priest, or a deacon delegated by either of them. The rights of the state in civil marriage are ignored. Despite slight exceptions by the church in 1964 and 1967, the rights of a Protestant or any non-Catholic partner are similarly ignored. When a Catholic and Protestant asked the Vatican in 1967 whether they could be married by a Catholic priest in a Protestant church, they were told that a Catholic rite could be performed only in a Catholic church.

"For what is shocking to the Protestant, and to the Orthodox, too," protested the Reverend W. A. Visser 't Hooft of the World Council of Churches, "is that the non-Catholic party is treated as though he or she had no Christian faith to be taken seriously."[1]

The extent to which the church will go to impose obedience was demonstrated in 1962 in the case of two students at St. John's University in New York City. Harold Glenn Carr was due to graduate that spring. Greta Schmidt had only a term before graduation. They were married on March 12 in a civil ceremony at the Brooklyn Municipal Building, and a month later were married again before a priest of the New York archdiocese. On April 18 they were notified by a letter from the university that they had been dismissed for an act that was "gravely sinful" and a "source of public scandal." "The matter is especially serious," the letter concluded, "in the light of the recent pronouncement of the Vatican condemning the light and frivolous attitude of modern society in regard to the sacred contract of holy matrimony."

It might be argued that the slightly delayed church marriage hardly seemed frivolous. Moreover, the role of the university, rather than the church, in meting out punishment involved the deeper constitutional issue of whether St. John's had the right to inflict a religious sanction.

With the New York Civil Liberties Union representing them, the couple asked for reinstatement before the state supreme court. Questioning the legal power of St. John's to enforce canon law, the NYCLU claimed that it was a "quasi-public institution, chartered by the state and subject to its control, and its doors are open to the education of the public." Justice George Eilperin agreed that the university's power to impose "conformity" with "Christian education and conduct" was "too vague . . . to authorize dismissal," and ordered the students reinstated.

When St. John's appealed to the appellate division, the Civil Liberties Union stressed again the constitutional impropriety of an ecclesiastical law contravening standards "not immoral according to the standards of society in general." But the appellate bench supported the university's position that the civil marriage of Catholics is "invalid" and "seriously sinful," and the court of appeals, the state's highest court, upheld the ruling. The couple's punishment has never been altered. In a letter of July 11, 1985, the St. John's alumni relations office stated that neither Carr nor Schmidt had ever been listed among its graduates.[2]

Although such Protestant dignitaries as Arthur Michael Ramsey, the archbishop of Canterbury, have long protested Rome's derogation of other faiths, *Matrimonii Sacramentum* in 1966 still ruled that a non-Catholic minister and a Catholic priest could not perform a marriage "simultaneously" in "their respective rites." Protestant sects for centuries, however, have recognized the validity for their own constituents of a Catholic marriage.

The rigidity of canon law began to soften with Vatican Council II. Since 1964 an Eastern Rite Catholic and since 1967 a Roman Rite Catholic can marry validly before a priest of the "separated Eastern Rite Church" provided that "other requirements of law are complied with." The marriage of a Catholic and non-Catholic had always been degraded to second-class status, performed only in a church rectory or parish residence. But *Matrimonia Mixta* allowed a mixed marriage to take place in the church itself, and recognized its validity as long as the Catholic partner got a dispensation from "competent authority" and promised orally or in writing "to do all in his or her power to have all the children baptized and brought up in the Catholic Church."

Although canon law still forbids a Catholic to be married only by a non-Catholic minister or by a civil official, and two services, separate or joint, are also banned, the Vatican has finally allowed a non-Catholic minister to be present, and "after the celebration of the marriage [to] express some congratulatory remarks to the parties and say some prayers for them." At the mixed marriage of Jodi Daynard and Mark Polizzotti in August 1984 in New York City, for example, a priest and rabbi performed both Catholic and Jewish prayers and blessings in English and Hebrew. The bridegroom ended the ceremony by smashing a glass underfoot in the Jewish tradition.[3]

The Vatican's opposition to mixed marriages has always been an essential policy in its control of the family. Branding a non-Catholic partner a "member of a schismatical or heretical sect," Pope Pius XI in his 1930 encyclical, *Casti Connubii*, proclaimed "it is unlikely that the Catholic party will not suffer some detriment from such a marriage." Pius XII in *Sertum Laetitiae* in 1939 insisted that mixed marriages were "rarely happy" and usually occasion "grave loss to the Catholic Church." Father John J. Kane, in a study in 1952 of Catholic-Protestant intermarriage, concluded: "There is no such thing as equality of religion from the Catholic standpoint."

Yet as Catholics increasingly attended nondenominational colleges and achieved business and social status, their contact with other faiths boosted the rate of mixed marriages. Fifty-nine per cent of college students married outside their faith, one study showed. In the New York archdiocese in 1984, 21 per cent of Catholics who registered weddings with the church married Protestants or Jews. A National Opinion Research Center study in 1985 showed that a third of all marriages in urban areas involved a Catholic and non-Catholic.

Determined to increase the Catholic constituency, canon law decrees that the Catholic party has the obligation to work prudently for the conversion of the non-Catholic. The penalties can be severe for those who disobey. Mary Grace Hanusch, a twenty-seven-year-old teacher who had worked at St. Paul's Catholic High School in Bristol, Connecticut, for five years, was dismissed from her job in 1985 when she married a Lutheran and refused to pledge she would raise their children as Catholics. The archdiocese of Hartford ruled that her marriage was invalid and, therefore, required her dismissal.

Despite such pressures on the Catholic partner, mixed marriages have proved reasonably stable. Father John L. Thomas found in his study of the Catholic family that "religion as a factor in the breakdown of marriage was surprisingly rare, although 17 per cent of the cases [he studied] involved intermarriage." An Indiana study in 1967 showed that the survival rate of Catholic-Protestant marriages was almost 77 per cent. "If you are strong enough, you can beat those who would like to break up marriages like ours—and we are strong," a Catholic wife married to a Jew told Rabbi Albert I. Gordon.[4]

Vatican pressure against mixed marriages obviously results from the threat that the Catholic partner may leave the church—20 to 30 per cent of them convert to another faith, one study showed. "Therefore, to have offspring reared in another faith is a catastrophe," Father Kane proclaimed, "since it denies to the persons for whom one has the greatest love the grace of the sacraments and the solace of Roman Catholicism in life and death."

The Vatican has targeted children of a mixed marriage, much to the distress of other denominations. The Episcopal Triennial Convention declared in 1949 that "in no circumstances should a member of this church give any understanding, as a condition of marriage, that the children should be brought up in the practice of another communion." The Disciples of Christ a year later urged its parishioners not to "enter a marriage contract that places them in a disadvantage in their family relationship and in the training of their children.[5]

Significantly, many Catholics criticize the Vatican rule that children of a mixed marriage must be raised as Catholics. Branding it "another cog in the vast machinery of Catholic imperialism," *Commonweal*, a Catholic journal, pointed out that it "all but ignored the conscience of the non-Catholic marriage partner." Hans Küng, a Catholic theologian at the University of Tübingen and frequent Vatican critic, called it a "very sad and tragic situation" that virtually made children illegitimate in the church's eyes when the non-Catholic partner refused to agree to a premarital contract binding children to Catholicism.

Influenced by mounting protests and studies that showed the ineffectiveness of such rigidity (Father Kane found 50 per cent of children from intermarriage were reared as Protestants, 45 per cent as Catholics), Pope Paul VI relented slightly in 1970. The Catholic partner had only to make a sincere promise, not a written contract, that a child would be raised as a Catholic. Father Greeley, the sociologist, observed a "sigh of relief" across the country as Protestants discovered they "were no longer heretics but separated brothers."[6]

No matter how vigorously the Vatican applied its strictures, however, Catholic marriage and sexuality increasingly ignored canon law and followed national patterns. Fifty-seven per cent of Catholics under thirty years old remained unmarried compared to 41 per cent of Protestants, and by 1982, Catholics produced only 0.04 more births than Protestants. With contraceptive use among unmarried Catholic women higher than among the non-Catholic general population, 55 per cent of white, single Catholics between ages twenty and twenty-nine were sexually active, according to 1980 studies. And Catholic couples were living openly together before marriage. Bishop George H. Speltz of St. Cloud, Minnesota, called it a scandal to the community and the Reverend Thomas E. Kramer of Bismarck, North Dakota, refused such couples a church marriage since the diocese would be "giving tacit approval to your present behavior."

The Vatican ban on divorce—no civil authority can void a sacramental union between two Catholics or between a Catholic and non-Catholic—remains its harshest measure of family control. Pope Pius XI in 1930 excoriated divorce reformers as the "advocates of the neo-paganism of today." Pius XII tried to make the church dominant over the judiciary, warning the Union of Catholic Italian Lawyers in 1949 not to issue decisions in divorce that "would oblige those affected by it to perform . . . any act which in itself is contrary to the law of God and of the Church." Paul VI bitterly opposed reform legislation in Italy. When a limited civil divorce law was passed in 1970, he openly backed a referendum to repeal the law, which lost by a 3 to 2 margin. Then he intervened in the politics of the Christian Democratic party, seeking to weed out candidates for office who had opposed him.[7]

The church, with Cardinal Spellman directing strategy, made its decisive stand against reform in New York State. The state's divorce law had remained unchanged for 179 years—adultery being the only grounds for divorce—when state Senator Jerome L. Wilson finally put together a reform coalition in 1966. Everyone, including the courts, had always been aware of the multimillion-dollar racket in which lawyers and consenting spouses joined in collusion to have an accomplice be caught in bed with the husband so that photographers and witnesses could present evidence of adultery to the judge. Obviously, such an expensive cast of characters limited divorce to the wealthy, or to those who could pay the travel bills to Nevada or Mexico, where the laws were more cooperative than in New York.

The Powerhouse quickly went into action against the Wilson bill, which added cruel and inhuman treatment, an established period of separation, sodomy, imprisonment for three consecutive years, and other grounds to the previous limit of adultery. Assembly Speaker Anthony J. Travia assigned the bill to a committee he controlled instead of Judiciary or Codes, which would have been logical. Earl Brydges, the senate majority leader, assigned the bill to a committee headed by his close ally, Senator John H. Hughes. All were Catholics.

Charles J. Tobin, Jr., who had succeeded his father as the chief Catholic lobbyist at the capital, sent a "no affirmative action" letter to all legislators, which was generally tantamount to a death sentence for the reform bill. Wilson called these moves "seemingly a declaration of war."

The Spellman strategy, however, developed flaws. A considerable group of Catholics had joined Wilson's coalition, and its spokesman, New York City Council President Frank D. O'Connor, insisted that "we cannot tolerate one divorce policy for New Yorkers who can afford to travel to Mexico or Nevada and an altogether different policy for the poor." The Reverend Joseph D. Hassett, a Jesuit who headed Fordham University's philosophy department, told legislators that "when it comes to legal enactments, we should not force the religious and moral beliefs of one group on another." Monsignor Victor Pospishil, a Catholic priest of the Byzantine Rite who taught theology at Manhattan College, pointed out that the Eastern church had never stood for the "indissolubility of marriage," and that the Vatican ban on divorce was "historically unfounded and theologically unjustified."

As soon as Spellman saw his head count in the legislature dwindling, he ordered his political operatives to stall the Wilson bill with a diluted substitute. Its main feature was that a couple had to live apart for five years before a court could even consider a separation decree. The New York State Council of Churches and other organizations backing reform complained that the substitute would only continue the system of "fraud and collusion." To expedite passage, Wilson's coalition eventually agreed that a couple would have to live apart for two years before being granted a routine separation or a court decree. On April 27, 1966, the bill was approved by the assembly 152 to 7, and by the senate 64 to 1, and Governor Rockefeller signed it into law.[8]

Legal reform, of course, has not changed the Vatican's ban on divorce, nor the church's political tactics: the Baltimore archdiocese blocked a new divorce law in Maryland in 1982. For Catholics whose marriage has fallen apart, the church still offers only one alternative: a "Declaration of Nullity" from the Vatican on the grounds that the marriage was defective from the start as a result of such impediments as coercion, impotence, or a permanent refusal to have children. Few marriages, of course, qualify for annulment. Even when they do, the process is intricate and expensive except for a rare diocese that helps petitioners circumvent the roadblocks. Brooklyn, New York, for example, was once known as the "Reno of the Catholic church."

Annulment, consequently, has always been the province of the rich and influential, who paid at least $24,000. Since the Vatican has tried to cooperate with reigning monarchs, Princess Caroline of Monaco managed to get her first marriage invalidated, and remarried even before approval came through. Prince Stanislaus Radziwill, descendent of a ruling family of the past, and twice previously married and once divorced, still secured an annulment from Lee Bouvier, sister of Jackie Kennedy Onassis.

The annulment machinery has been simplified recently at many diocesan and parish levels so that the ordinary petitioner may not have to spend more than $250. Annulment Tribunals have become far more sympathetic to the plight of husbands and wives who prove that their conflicts are insoluble. By 1983, annulments had increased to 70,418 in the United States and Canada. Still, Mary E. Theriault of Maryland, who separated in 1947, complained, "They didn't lift a finger to help, and instead every time I went to confession I was put through the Inquisition again." It took her twenty-eight years for an annulment. [9]

The position of those Catholics who resort to civil divorce remains fraught with anguish. If they marry again while their first marriage is still valid in the eyes of the church, they can have no "sacramental participation," according to the *Catholic Almanac*. But they can attend mass and have their children baptized. Without a second marriage, the separated or divorced can receive sacraments. The Vatican even approves sacraments for those who have remarried as long as they live in a "brother sister relationship."

The continued rigidity of the Vatican has led to a divorce rate among Catholics that almost equals the national average, and has often forced them out of the church. National Opinion Research Center studies show the actual rate of ever divorced to ever married is 31 per cent for Protestants and 26 per cent for Catholics. Father Greeley claims that as a result of this exodus, one-fourth of those under age thirty who were baptized Catholics no longer define themselves as Catholics. By 1979, only 18 per cent of those in their twenties who were weekly communicants thought that divorce was wrong. [10]

The adoption system has often been manipulated by the Catholic church—and by other religions as well—to keep infants and children bound to the faith. The church contends that baptism is immutable. Once baptized, the offspring of Catholic parents, or one Catholic parent, can never be separated from his spiritual roots since the salvation that comes from Rome must take precedence over any alternative fulfillment of immediate needs or happiness. The church has consistently supported civil laws that guarantee its ends: laws in New York and Massachusetts, for example, that require the religion of the adopting parents to match that of the child "when practicable," laws with almost similar wording in Illinois, Maryland, and other states.

The hierarchy has repeatedly gone to court to reclaim adopted children. When Rouben and Sylvia Goldman, a Jewish couple from Marblehead, Massachusetts, adopted the illegitimate twins of an unknown father and a divorced Catholic mother who had agreed in writing in 1950 that the children would be raised as Jews, the Boston archdiocese appealed to Judge John W. Phelan to negate the contract. Phelan, a Catholic, ordered the twins turned over to Catholic welfare services, and the Supreme Judicial Court of Massachusetts upheld him on the basis that the "judge when practicable must give custody only to persons of the same religious faith as that of the child." The Goldmans spent years in litigation. Dedicated to the twins and afraid that a higher court would forcibly separate them, the Goldmans abandoned home and business and moved anonymously to another state. Despite continued pressure from the archdiocese, the Massachusetts Department of Public Welfare never found them.

In a somewhat parallel Massachusetts case in 1955, Marjorie McCoy, an unmarried Catholic, agreed to the adoption of her daughter, Hildy, by the Melvin Ellises. They had proved excellent parents for four years when McCoy went to court with the aid of diocesan lawyers, claiming she had not known the Ellises were Jewish and asking that Hildy be placed in a Catholic institution. After the Supreme Judicial Court of Massachusetts ruled in her favor, the Ellises took Hildy to Florida. The state sought to extradite the child, and the case became a burning issue, with most Protestant and Jewish groups insisting that Hildy's welfare and the Ellises' love should supersede the courts. Florida's governor eventually turned down extradition, and the Florida courts confirmed the adoption.

The hierarchy's anger at the loss of any child from the faith surfaced in the Gally case in 1952, when a Catholic child was adopted by a Protestant couple. *The Pilot*, a Boston archdiocese journal, branded it a "victory for the current secularist philosophy, which considers religion, any religion, of secondary or minor importance and the material advantage of life as of prevailing consequence."

Any attempts to moderate punitive adoption laws have been opposed by the hierarchy. When Assemblyman Leonard Yoswein introduced a bill into the New York State legislature in 1966 that would change the requirement that the religion of adopting parents must match that of the child, the Catholic Social Welfare Committee organized the opposition through Assemblyman Lawrence Murphy. The bill passed the assembly but was defeated in the senate.[11]

In fact, religious influence over adoption laws—not just that of the Catholic lobby—had long made it virtually impossible for any couple not church-affiliated to secure a child through established agencies. The New Jersey statute, like most state laws, required parents to declare their religion until John Burke, an atheist, and his wife challenged it in 1966. The New Jersey Supreme Court eventually upheld their right to adopt without religious affiliation.

The adoption policy of New York City changed in 1967. No longer would natural parents have to state their religion when placing a child for adoption. The assignment of foundlings would be made on the basis of the best parents available, not on the old system of rotation between the three major faiths.

This policy was broadened further in 1972 in New York State when a social service agency refused to accept an adoption application from Robert and Ann Dickens because he was an atheist and she had no religious affiliation. After the couple challenged the ruling, state courts ordered that the placement of foundlings must be based on the suitability of the applicant, and not limited to a matching faith or any faith, and that the child's welfare should take preference over religion, even if it conflicted with the religion of the natural mother. The Dickenses wanted more—the elimination of all religious factors from the adoption process. But the U.S. Supreme Court rejected their appeal for lack of a substantial federal question.

The hierarchy's determination to keep control of Catholic children has resulted in the church's holding them indefinitely in institutions rather than placing them with non-Catholic couples offering advantageous homes. "Catholic agencies won't make the effort to get children adopted," insisted Ira Levin, a social worker in New York City's Department of Health and Human Services. The adoption system, consequently, has been dangerously stalled. New York City Council President Carol Bellamy charged in 1981 that less than 20 per cent of 6,424 children available for adoption had been placed that year despite twice that number of applications from would-be adoptive parents. A few years before, U.S. Senator Alan Cranston (D-California) announced that 170,000 children nationwide were awaiting adoption or foster care placement.[12]

Not just Catholic agencies, but Orthodox Jewish ones as well, have often refused to accept adoptable children at random. Such discrimination has hit hardest at blacks, a discrimination challenged by the American Civil Liberties Union in federal court. Admission to an agency on the basis of religion contravenes the Establishment Clause of the First Amendment, ACLU contended, since public funds that go to religious agencies are being used to enforce one religious doctrine. ACLU also claimed that children in foster care must have access to family planning and abortion in compliance with U.S. Supreme Court decisions. Although most religious agencies in New York City made an agreement with the court in 1985 to meet ACLU's standards, Cardinal O'Connor forbade Catholic agencies to accept children at random and threatened to discontinue Catholic foster care.

In other states, particularly with large numbers of adoptable black children, many Catholic dioceses are following local codes allowing a mother to waive her request that her child be given to parents of her own faith. The Adoption Assistance and Child Welfare Act, passed by Congress in 1980, has put further pressure on religious agencies to seek effective immediate solutions. If they keep religious and color barriers, federal money can be withheld, and they can be taken to court. "For the first time, Catholics realized there wasn't one answer," explained Elisabeth Schüssler Fiorenza, a professor at the Episcopal Divinity School in Cambridge, Massachusetts. "It was the first step towards an adult Catholicity, namely, taking responsibility for one's own life."[13]

VIII

Money, Power, and the Media

I

No one knew better than John Hughes, the first archbishop of New York City in 1850, in fact, the first archbishop in the country, that money could become the symbol of religious power. Only fifteen years before, anti-Catholic mobs had tried to burn down "old" St. Patrick's in lower Manhattan. Hughes's embattled constituents had grown from 200 in 1785 to 200,000, mainly as a result of Irish immigration after the potato famines. Determined to force some respect out of the dominant Protestant society, he announced shortly after taking office that he would build a resplendent cathedral at Fifth Avenue and Fiftieth Street, and produce a "sensation in this new country."

Hughes wanted the church's spiritual aims translated into architecture, of course. St. Patrick's would be modeled on the European masterpieces at Rheims and Cologne. But above all, he wanted magnificence—a cathedral stretching 332 feet from Fifth to Madison avenues, its spires 330 feet tall—that would mark the emergence of Catholicism in America as a spiritual and financial power.

Hughes, who called Catholicism the "only true church on earth," quickly outclassed even the Episcopalians, the epitome of Protestant

99

wealth and elitism, for the cornerstone of the Episcopal cathedral of St. John the Divine was not laid until 1892. Still unfinished in 1986, its spires would be only 267 feet tall. St. Patrick's would remain 137 years later the preeminent religious structure in the nation, proof that a once persecuted minority could encase its success in stone.

The risks involved were integral to Hughes's ambitions. Since most Catholics then were day laborers and house servants, earning a few dollars a week, the archbishop had only a small core of shop owners and tradesmen who could afford to stake his plans. Visiting a hundred families personally, he wrung from each a pledge of $1,000.

His next gamble would be to locate the cathedral at Fiftieth Street, a hinterland of shanty towns occupied mainly by workers starting on the recently mapped-out Central Park. The city, in fact, virtually stopped at Fourteenth Street, and carriages had to plough through pools of mud a few blocks north. Yet Hughes would insist that this distant plot of land—purchased by a priest in 1810, presumably for a Catholic college, and deeded to the hierarchy in 1829 for $5,550—would soon dominate the city.

To stamp a final authority on his plans, the archbishop hired James Renwick, Jr., the foremost architect of the time. Descended from the Dutch patroon family of Brevoorts, and married to an Aspinwall, of equal primacy in the Protestant aristocracy, Renwick had made his mark as the apostle of the Gothic style with Grace Church at Broadway and Tenth Street. At least in size, St. Patrick's would quickly dwarf this Episcopalian gem of architecture.

The cornerstone of St. Patrick's was laid in 1858, but the official opening was delayed, partly by the Civil War, until 1879. During that period enough Catholic families had risen in business and finance to support the cost of construction. The Bouviers, for one, donated a chapel in honor of Michel Bouvier, who had arrived from France as a penniless immigrant in 1792 and made a fortune in Philadelphia and New York. His great-great-great-great-niece, Jacqueline, would become the wife of John F. Kennedy, the first Catholic president.

By the time the spires were completed, Hughes's "folly"—as the papers called it at first—had become the center for the mansions of the Vanderbilts, Astors, and other Protestant millionaires.[1] St. Patrick's truly represented success.

As Irish immigrants poured into Boston and Chicago, Poles into

Detroit and Hamtramck, and Germans into Milwaukee, the Catholic church has aways signaled its ascendency in the bricks and mortar of its cathedrals and churches. Following the Vatican's lead, money and pomp have become the handmaidens of power. By 1926, at the International Eucharistic Congress, the church could celebrate its wealth by transporting ten cardinals to Chicago in a seven-car train specially built for them by the Pullman Company. Cardinal William Henry O'Connell of Boston landed on the shores of Lake Michigan on his private yacht. "The Catholic church must be the biggest corporation in the United States," the Reverend Richard Ginder exulted in 1960. "We have a branch in almost every neighborhood. Our assets and real estate holdings must exceed those of Standard Oil, AT&T and U.S. Steel combined. And our roster of dues-paying members must be second only to the tax rolls of the U.S. Government."[2]

Since few dioceses release financial reports, the total wealth of the church in the United States in real estate, securities, and other assets remains incalculable. Even those reports made have been branded "incomplete and misleading" and a "very small piece of the pie" by the National Association of Laity, a dissident Catholic group, in 1972. The Reverend James A. Nash, executive director of the Massachusetts Council of Churches, set Catholic wealth at $100 billion in 1979. A few years before, Martin A. Larson and C. Stanley Lowell made a detailed study of the religious tax records in fourteen cities. Extrapolating from them, they estimated nationwide Catholic assets at over $168 billion, Protestant assets at $71 billion, and Jewish at $9 billion. Allowing for inflation, Catholic figures may well have reached $200 billion by 1986, certainly a cut above the $63 billion held by Exxon, the country's largest industrial corporation.

The most accurate basis from which to examine Catholic wealth is the financial reports of the Chicago and New York archdioceses. Chicago listed its holdings in real estate, securities, and other assets at over $2.3 billion in 1984 (lowering this figure the next year as a result of a study of insurable values). New York listed similar holdings at $1.2 billion in 1984.

The real-estate figures, however, hardly reflect a total picture of Catholic assets. In New York, for example, colleges, hospitals, religious orders, and other institutions are outside the archdiocese's jurisdiction and thus excluded. A survey of New York City's tax books shows hundreds of such excluded properties, including Fordham University's campus near Lincoln Center, assessed at about $23 million; and Cabrini-Columbus Hospital, assessed at about $17 million. Their land and buildings are worth many times that amount. City assessments are set far below real worth: consider St. Patrick's Cathedral, whose square block on Fifth Avenue and buildings are pegged at only $90 million. With such property excluded from the archdiocese report, and low city assessments, it would be a reasonable assumption that the value of Catholic real estate in New York City could reach $4 billion.

Another index of New York archdiocesan wealth—its stock and bond investments—gained $56 million in two years. Chicago's investments gained $24 million in one year. In fact, New York assets as a whole increased in value by about $800 million since the 1982 report. Total revenues for New York were over $276 million in 1984; for Chicago over $372 million in 1985.[3]

The Church of Jesus Christ of Latter-day Saints (Mormons) may have only 5.8 million members worldwide, but its skill at amassing wealth is unrivaled. According to a recent study by John Heinerman and Anson Shupe, the Mormons are worth more than $8 billion, with about $7 billion in meeting houses and temples, and they have an estimated annual income of $2 billion. In addition, they hold huge tracts of land in California ($84 million in Los Angeles County alone), in Georgia, and 30,000 acres near Disneyland in Florida. Their real-estate holdings, symbolized by the massive Mormon Temple and headquarters building, the tallest building in Utah, dominate Salt Lake City. They own an important hotel and newspaper there, a chain of TV and radio stations across the country, four insurance companies, the ZCMI department store, and clothing mills and farm equipment plants. By 1976, Larson and Lowell estimated the Mormons controlled 85 percent of the tax-exempt real estate in Salt Lake County, and similar assets, where their membership is concentrated, in Arizona, Idaho, New Mexico, Nevada, and Florida. With its high fertility rate, Mormon membership is expected to reach at least 12 million by the year 2000.

Religious power translates easily into political power. When Earl W. Baker, a Salt Lake City assessor, found a decade ago that many Mormon canneries and manufacturing plants were taking tax exemption on business enterprises, limited by the Utah constitution to places of worship and philanthropies, he began a routine investigation. Immediately the Mormon-dominated legislature changed the wording of the state constitution so that exemption would depend on the *purpose* rather than the use of property. A complex of Mormon plants and office buildings was thus able to hold its immune status.[4]

Similarly, the Reverend Robert Schuller, whose *Hour of Power* draws one of the largest Fundamentalist television audiences, was investigated in 1983 by the California State Board of Equalization. Although his Crystal Cathedral in Los Angeles, a mammoth glass structure shaped like a four-pointed star, qualifies for tax exemption, the state attorney general claimed that the commercial concerts on the premises, and their high-priced tickets and star-studded casts, could hardly be considered a religious function. Schuller, consequently, was billed for $400,000 in back taxes until religious lobbyists descended on the legislators and convinced them to pass a statute that prohibited the attorney general from subpoenaing the financial records of any church.

The line between authentic religious functions and business operations has always been shaky at best. A Catholic organization, the Knights of Columbus, combined profit-making and tax exemption when it bought Yankee Stadium in New York City in 1953 as an investment for its insurance funds. In a complex sale and lease-back deal, it secured a large income as well as a potential $1 million profit if purchase options were exercised. Christian Brothers, a Catholic order that runs the profitable California winery, had paid no taxes during the 1950s until the government claimed it owed $3.25 million in back taxes. Christian Brothers insisted it was "subject to the control of the pope," but a U.S. District Court ruled that the wine business was "not a church."

Although Congress in 1950 attempted to eliminate tax exemption for religious businesses, along with that of educational institutions and philanthropies, the church lobby was strong enough to block the religious category. It was not until the Tax Reform Act of 1969 that the word "religion" was put back into the law. Even then, churches won a five-year grace period before unrelated businesses became taxable.

Still, a Baptist church in downtown Miami, Florida, owned almost a square block of tax-exempt land used by parishioners for free parking on Sunday, but operated at a profit as a commercial lot during the week. In 1972 taxpayers challenged this commercial exploitation, but before the Supreme Court heard the *Diffenderfer* case, the Florida legislature eliminated this loophole. Since then, however, *Diffenderfer* has set a precedent that most religions have followed.

Beyond this mix of business and religion, tax exemption involves deeper First Amendment questions. Tax exemption is obviously a munificent privilege, allowing religious groups to save hundreds of millions of dollars a year. It is the base from which Catholic wealth and power—and that of all religions—has stemmed. Without it, neither Catholics, Mormons, nor any religion could have amassed their holdings.

In recognition of police, fire, and other governmental services, the Reverend Eugene Carson Blake of the United Presbyterian Church, later secretary general of the World Council of Churches, suggested in 1959 that religious groups should pay their "fair share" of taxes. The Unitarians, Presbyterians, and eventually the National Council of Churches supported this policy. The move, however, was purely voluntary, and no study has ever shown more than a trickle of money making up for the huge taxes surrendered by government.

The First Amendment's Free Exercise Clause originates from the belief that religion benefits the public at large and deserves to be fostered by tax exemption. Most Americans would undoubtedly support this concept, although the Reverend Nash calls "that assumption . . . dubious at best."[5]

Granted that religious tax exemption must be kept, we still have the troublesome question of whether the Free Exercise Clause should cover every religious activity that a church decides to promote. American travelers often run into teams of well-scrubbed Mormon youth seeking to win converts in fifty-eight countries around the world. These 27,000 missionaries undergo years of expensive training; their upkeep overseas is sizable, perhaps $100 million a year. Yet most of this is paid for by tax-exempt dollars that result in higher taxes for every U.S. citizen. It remains debatable whether a missionary policy overseas that may bring a handful of converts in Italy, for example, really benefits the advancement of religion in America.

Similarly, Catholic missions raise controversial issues. While the church's famine relief in Africa, as well as that of other religions, has met the highest standards of charity, should Catholic missionary policy in Africa deserve unchecked tax exemption? While Congress has constantly supported family planning for Africa, the Catholic church still inveighs against birth control despite population growth that threatens minor economic gains. The Society for the Propagation of the Faith in America is the largest contributor towards Catholic foreign missions. Why, then, should U.S. citizens pay higher taxes to support religious tax exemption for missionary work that goes against their aims?

The core of the problem is whether tax exemption should be granted indiscriminately. By granting it to the U.S. Conference of Bishops, must we automatically support every cause the bishops undertake? Must we also support every outrageous cult? The Reverend Nash pinpoints "tax-exempt charlatans who fleece the pious on public broadcasting and a number of so called cults and churches [which] are just plain harmful to humanity."

Insisting that tax exemption is an unassailable right under the Free Exercise Clause, essential to religious liberty, the National Council of Churches and most mainstream religions object to any governmental selection process in deciding what faith deserves this privilege. As the NCC's Reverend Kelley claimed: "It is precisely because government will not be able or willing to recognize those churches that are most effectively performing the function of religion where it is most needed that government must not be responsible for picking and choosing among churches [and would-be churches] on the basis of its own [political] preferences and predilections."

Once we accept this principle, the dilemma is that every cult and charlatan must be allowed to solicit funds on radio and television and build their money and power through tax exemption. Otherwise, we would be limiting tax exemption to Episcopalians, Catholics, and other traditional faiths; and recent religions, such as the Mormons, who were outcasts not long ago, would remain outcasts. To protect tax exemption for the majority, we must concede that what seems like a fraudulent cult today can become a mainstream faith tomorrow.

The ultimate dilemma, of course, is whether tax exemption in itself ranks as a constitutional right. Few have questioned it since President Grant and Speaker Blaine wanted it confined to religious edifices and graveyards in their post–Civil War amendment. The U.S. Court of Appeals for the Tenth Circuit, in the *Christian Echoes* case in 1972, called it a "subsidy" and a "privilege, a matter of grace rather than right." Yet this privilege has become so built into the system that once a religious body has been granted tax exemption under Sec. 501 (c) (3) of the Internal Revenue Service tax code, it automatically retains it. By contrast, philanthropies and other nonreligious groups in the same category must have their applications examined and renewed periodically.

In effect, tax exemption implies a conflict between the Free Exercise and Establishment clauses that has been largely ignored. While the mainstream religions have succeeded in building it into a right, tax exemption obviously involves aid to religion that could be questioned under the Establishment Clause. James Madison, the principal author of the First Amendment, considered it unconstitutional for churches to be exempt from taxes levied on the lay public. Paul G. Kauper, professor of law at the University of Michigan, characterizes tax exemption as a "substantial aid to religion" and concludes that "its constitutionality is, therefore, subject to doubt."[6]

The conflict has never been completely resolved by the U.S. Supreme Court. The one approach to it was the *Walz* case in 1970, and the Court avoided the central issue. Frederick Walz, who owned real estate in New York City, sued the tax collector under a New York State law providing religious tax exemption, and asked for the return of that portion of his property taxes he would not have paid if churches had also been taxed. His brief contended that tax exemption constituted an establishment of religion prohibited by the First Amendment.

With only Justice William Douglas dissenting, the Supreme Court upheld tax exemption. But it never took up one of the traditional tests it long employed in First Amendment cases: whether tax exemption significantly aided religion. Instead, its reasoning was based almost solely on the entanglement test. If tax exemption were nullified, the government would become excessively involved in the whole process of valuations of church property, tax liens, and tax foreclosures. It was almost as if the Court was emphasizing governmental bookwork in order to dodge the conflict between the Free Exercise and Establishment clauses.[7]

The conflict, however, has become critical. Tax exemption is the base on which the Catholic church and Fundamentalist preachers, such as Jerry Falwell and Pat Robertson, have built their political power. Tax exemption, in effect, has been exploited far beyond its original purpose of sustaining the free exercise of religion. Instead of leading to religious liberty, it has led to property and religious empires.

2

Under the peculiar legal concepts of "corporation sole," most Catholic bishops in the United States take total control of all real estate, stocks, and assets in their dioceses, and no internal or external check can limit their power. The individual bishop and his aides reign as a one-man corporation, and few underlings have dared to challenge the abuses of this rule. Bishop Leo T. Maher of San Diego, California, was accused in 1985 of deeding a four-bedroom, diocesan-owned house to his female secretary and helping her obtain a $160,000 condominium for $50,000. Monsignor Benjamin Hawkes, vicar general of the Los Angeles archdiocese, reportedly transferred $1.5 million in church funds as a loan to a friend to buy a home.

Still, these seeming transgressions are paltry compared to the regal trappings which Cardinal John Patrick Cody of Chicago lavished on himself and close friends with the church's tax-exempt dollars. Cody lived like a monarch in a three-story gingerbread mansion with nineteen chimneys on the edge of Lincoln Park. He collected art and rare books. He traveled in a limousine with crimson-strutted wheels, brandishing the license plate "Illinois 1." When he was accused in 1981 of misappropriating church funds, his lawyer retorted that Cody was answerable only "to Rome and to God."

Cody's flagrant reign damaged morale among his clergy to the point that 34 per cent of his priests resigned in the twelve years after 1968, and his seminaries had only seven students. He cut subsidies to black and inner-city parishes. He threatened one priest with suspension unless he left the peace movement. Another priest, who had taken part in a strike at a Catholic institution, was banned from speaking in Chicago. "Priests Accuse Cody of One-Man Rule," the *Chicago Sun-Times* described this confrontation in 1975, when other bishops had secretly begun to deplore his instability.

The favorite recipient of Cody's financial excesses was Helen Dolan Wilson, whose father had married Cody's aunt in 1913. They described themselves as "cousins," although she purportedly acted as the cardinal's housekeeper from 1969 to 1975. Most of this time she traveled with him on trips to Rome or lived in Florida in a $100,000 home that Cody had helped her build. She also leased a luxury apartment on Chicago's Gold Coast and held a $100,000 insurance policy supplied by Cody. Her housekeeper's salary in this period amounted to only $11,500 a year; but her lawyer admitted she had a net worth of at least $350,000. The *Sun-Times* claimed she had amassed $1 million.

Cardinal Cody also bestowed his largesse on Helen Wilson's son, David, an insurance agent. The cardinal saw to it that he handled the archdiocese's pension plans, group auto plans, and other insurance programs which produced generous commissions. The cardinal loaned David $30,000 to buy his St. Louis home. The archdiocese's lawyer gave this explanation of these surprising transactions: "Many people give money to the church under ambiguous circumstances, and the church leader decides if the money is his own gift or one intended for the church itself."[8]

Since tax-exempt religious funds cannot be applied to personal use, Cody's finances were investigated by a federal grand jury. The jury repeatedly subpoenaed archdiocesan records, but Cody placed himself above the law. Until the day he died in 1982, Cody ignored all subpoenas.

Cardinal John Krol of Philadelphia, however, has outdone contemporary prelates as the master of money and power. In his corner suite on the twelfth floor of the Philadelphia archdiocesan offices, he sits behind an ornate desk, a tall, stern, aloof, domineering wheeler-dealer of politics. His windows have a dazzling view of the city's art museum. His efficiency is reflected in the desktop computer terminal behind him; his elegance in his fleet of cars and sprawling estate, with sand trap and putting green; in the gourmet restaurants he patronizes; in the gold-button cuff links shown off by crisp French cuffs.

As president of the National Conference of Catholic Bishops in 1972, he became a crony of Richard Nixon's, often traveling with him on the White House yacht, *Sequoia*. His close friendship with President Reagan sealed the White House–Catholic alliance. Krol stood at Reagan's side at Doylestown, Pennsylvania, and other campaign rallies in 1984, dressed in his cardinal's robes and often praising him so fulsomely that it seemed tantamount to a political endorsement, which would breach the federal law controlling tax-exempt religious organizations.

Krol's manipulation of the appointment of John J. O'Connor, then an unknown Pennsylvania bishop, to be archbishop of New York City in 1984, confirmed his achievements as a power player. Pope John Paul II wanted a ruthless hard-liner to force some orthodoxy on the American hierarchy. President Reagan needed a conservative ally in the country's richest diocese. Krol wanted a successor in his right-wing image. It was a perfect blend of interests.

Krol has never failed to capitalize on the coincidence that his ancestors came from the same Tatra mountain region of Poland as John Paul II, the first Polish pope, and Krol is probably his closest friend in the United States. When Wojtyła was a Polish cardinal, Krol used his White House connections to support him in his clashes with the Communist government. He reportedly lobbied American cardinals in the election of Wojtyła to the papacy.

Krol has built intimate links to the most reactionary clique at the Vatican, mainly through Archbishop Paul Marcinkus of Cicero, Illinois, who acted as papal bodyguard and advance man until he was promoted to head the Vatican bank. There Marcinkus entrusted many Vatican investments to Michele Sindona, a shoddy Italian financier whose banking network extended to New York. When it collapsed, Sindona was given a twenty-five-year sentence for fraud in a U.S. penitentiary, and sentenced in Italy as well, but Krol insisted in 1983 that "Sindona was a broker, nothing more."

Born in Cleveland in 1910, Krol was a doctoral student at Catholic University in Washington, D.C., when he shrewdly offered his services to the apostolic delegate, Archbishop (later Cardinal) Amleto Cicognani, and often drove him around the capital and on vacations. Once he heard Cicognani and another cleric discussing a complex point of canon law in the back of the car. Krol said he knew the solution and offered to write it up. His legal skill so impressed the archbishop that he got him an appointment as chamberlain to Pope Pius XII, launching Krol's career which advanced to auxiliary bishop of Cleveland and archbishop of Philadelphia in 1961.

Krol has always ruled Philadelphia like a fiefdom. For years he manipulated the local press through friends on the news desks who tailored or killed stories to fit his interests. During the anti-Vietnam riots of the 1960s, he was accused of reporting participants to the Federal Bureau of Investigation. Fifty priests in his archdiocese were fired recently for celebrating experimental masses. Krol "could not conceive of religious freedom," according to William Leahy, an ex-priest who accompanied the cardinal during Vatican II.

"Krol is conservative beyond belief," asserted Babette Joseph, a member of the Pennsylvania House of Representatives. He backed the Vatican's rigid stand in *Humanae Vitae* against changing the birth control ban. At Vatican II, he opposed liberalization of marriage laws and other reforms. "The Vatican Council was aborted here in Philadelphia," said an ex-diocesan priest who served in Rome. At the 1976 "Call to Action" in Detroit, attended by a thousand lay delegates as well as the hierarchy, he fought off seemingly temperate revisions— public declaration of church finances and parish participation in the choice of bishops, among others—and denounced proponents as a "naïve group of little old ladies." He told a reporter in 1986 that the spread of AIDS was an "act of vengeance" against the "sin" of homosexuality.

Krol's application of money and power at the state capital and the Philadelphia City Council has made him one of the most awesome lobbyists among Catholic bishops. Although many legislators wanted Congresswoman Geraldine Ferraro, the Democratic vice-presidential candidate, to march in Philadelphia's Columbus Day parade in 1984, Krol's office told its city council allies that there would be organized demonstrations against her. Ferraro, consequently, stayed away from the parade.[9]

Krol's influence throughout the state set off a boycott of Planned Parenthood clinics by the Allentown diocese. Planned Parenthood had long been a member of the United Way, a prestigious agency which runs a centralized fund drive among businesses and corporations and divides the money among community charities. But in 1981 the Allentown diocese urged donors not to give to the United Way unless Planned Parenthood was ousted, charging that Planned Parenthood was "showering these young people with contraceptives and provocative literature" and "amoral and anti-Christian sex education programs."

One newspaper in the diocese, the Reading *Times*, lamented that "in a nation built on religious tolerance, we are witnessing a growth of intolerant religions." The Reading *Eagle* called it a "move that will not only jeopardize the agency, but the community as a whole." Still, Krol persisted, and Planned Parenthood was forced out of the United Way in 1983, joining 42 out of 190 Planned Parenthood clinics similarly ousted by Catholic and Fundamentalist boycotts.[10]

3

The boycott has become an effective tool of Catholics and Fundamentalists, controlling what people read and what they see on the stage and screen. One recent target has been Jean-Luc Godard's film *Hail Mary*, which was banned in Brazil in 1986 after pressure from Pope John Paul II and the local hierarchy less than a year after the new civilian government announced the end of all censorship. The film tells the story of a teenager named Marie and her boyfriend, Joseph, both incredulous when she finds herself pregnant although still a virgin. The pope and Cardinal O'Connor denounced it after its opening in New York the year before. Neither reported having seen it, but in his charge that it "distorts and insults the spiritual significance" of Christian faith, the pope must have assumed that it paralleled the birth of Jesus.

When *Hail Mary* opened at the New York Film Festival at Lincoln Center, picket lines and phone calls, mainly organized by the Catholic League for Religious and Civil Rights, forced the distributor to cancel a public run. In Boston, the Sacks theater chain dropped the film after similar pressure. It opened in nearby Cambridge only when the city manager worked out an agreement with the theater owner that would guarantee public safety against threats of violence. "I'm glad I'm not living in the Middle Ages because I would be dead," Godard noted.

The Catholic League also made a target of *Sister Mary Ignatius*

Explains It All for You, an Obie Award–winning play by Christopher Durang. Its theme—which the league deemed so dangerous to the public that it tried but failed to have the play banned in Chicago, St. Louis, and Detroit—pits parochial school graduates against religious dogma and the nun who tried to inculcate them.

Branding the play an "unrelenting assault on Catholic education," the league turned out its picket lines again in 1985 at Nassau County Community College near New York City. This time it had a peculiar ally in Dennis Dillon, the county district attorney. Although Dillon had been elected by voters of every faith, he announced that "you can't do this to the Catholic community without the Catholic community showing its rage." The college's president, however, Dr. Sean Fanelli, who happened to be a former Catholic brother, stood by the First Amendment and allowed the play to open. It played to sold-out houses.

The Fundamentalists have concentrated on book censorship. In New Mexico, a dictionary was banned from schools because it contained the "most obscene words imaginable," and four hundred words were cut from William Shakespeare's *Romeo and Juliet* because of "sexually explicit material." Insisting that every word of the Bible must be accepted as scientific truth, Fundamentalist lobbies have tried to purge any treatment of evolution from textbooks, and publishers have often yielded to these pressures to save their markets. Arkansas and Louisiana, among other states, have passed laws requiring that "scientific creationism," as the Fundamentalists call the biblical story, must be given equal emphasis in class with the theory of evolution, but these laws rarely hold up in court. When a Baptist pastor condemned The Living Bible, an easy-to-read version of King James, students at the Temple Christian School in Gastonia, North Carolina, tossed copies into a bonfire.[11]

In the belief that "God and Satan are eternally at war for the souls of humankind," as the Colorado Education Association described the campaign, books that don't fit Fundamentalist morality have been purged from school libraries. Some lower courts have tolerated these purges. But after the Island Trees, New York, school board removed eleven books, including a Pulitzer Prize–winning novel by Bernard Malamud, the U.S. Supreme Court in a 1982 decision ruled that books could not be banned by local officials "simply because they dislike the ideas contained in those books." Fundamentalists still boasted in 1984 that they had eliminated ten of twenty-one targeted books from Texas schools and pressured the Wal-Mart department store chain in 1986 to remove virtually all teen and rock-oriented publications from more than eight hundred outlets.

This boycott of movies, plays, and books, of course, is only part of a broader Catholic-Fundamentalist drive to stamp their morality on the country through the political process. The Reverend Jerry Falwell, founder of the Moral Majority, bluntly proclaims that "God has led me to wage a Holy War against the moral sins that threaten America." The religious conservatives saw that the media was essential to control, and much of their money and power has concentrated on shaping public opinion through radio and television.[12]

The most secretive power player among Catholic extremists has been Harry John of Milwaukee, heir to a Miller brewing company fortune and head of the DeRance Foundation. On its 1983 tax return, DeRance listed assets of over $185 million, revenues of almost $26 million, and a capital gain over the previous year of almost $19 million. A gaunt, monkish man who allows no pictures of himself to be taken, John combines ruthlessness with eccentricity. He once preferred going to jail rather than paying the mortgage on the house of his ex-wife, and was released only after handing over $10,000.

In 1983 he gave $350,000 to radio and TV programming; $100,000 to Morality in Media, a conservative pressure group; and $50,000 to the Christian Broadcasting Network, run by the Reverend Pat Robertson, the Fundamentalist preacher. Vehemently opposed to birth control, he gave $400,000 that year to Catholic organizations promoting the "rhythm method." Equally opposed to Liberation Theology in Latin America (he has been called "more Catholic than the pope"), he gave over $1 million in 1983 to the International Institute of the Heart of Jesus in order to combat liberalizing trends in the church.

Already the owner of stations in California and Texas, John made his most ambitious grab for media power in 1983 by announcing—with a message of congratulations from President Reagan—that he was establishing a Catholic television network. His base was Santa

Fe Communications in Los Angeles, which set out to buy a string of TV stations. In the process, John spent $83 million of DeRance funds, and his ex-wife and his longtime associate, Donald Gallagher, went to court to oust John from the foundation's board of directors. In a pretrial deposition, Erica John claimed that the papal pro-nuncio, Archbishop Pio Laghi, met with her in 1984 and threatened that "if we didn't do something right away, that he would remove . . . the name of our organization" from approved church lists. "Without the church approval, we cannot remain classified as a charitable organization." In 1986 the Wisconsin Circuit Court barred John as a director, an unprecedented legal step against a foundation's founder, but he has appealed the decision.[13]

Another Catholic television and cable complex, featuring the *Gulf Coast Catholic Hour*, was built by Bishop Mariano Garriga of Corpus Christi, Texas, trustee of the Sara K. East Foundation, whose assets of $300 to $500 million come from oil drilling and 400,000 acres of ranch land.

Even more effective—although smaller—than Harry John in building a media base for Catholic conservatives is Mother Angelica, the feisty abbess of Our Lady of the Angels Monastery not far from Birmingham, Alabama. Since 1981 she has run the Eternal Word Television Network, which reaches 1.6 million subscribers through 105 cable systems, and started broadcasting twenty-four hours a day in 1987. Her programs, "up-linked" to Sat Com III R, are picked up from the satellite by each cable company.

Mother Angelica appeals to Fundamentalists as well as Catholics. "The guy in the living room and the man in the pew don't have to be knocked on the head with social justice all the time," she declared in defining her conservative programming. Her funding comes from broadcast appeals, as well as from the DeRance, Grace, Raskob, and other right-wing foundations. Her ability to combine fervor and ebullience before the camera has made her the only Catholic star to approach Monsignor Fulton J. Sheen, who reached as much as a third of the television audience in the 1950s. Her TV talks, cassettes, and videotapes have quickly established her as the "one-woman network for Jesus."

The real base of religious power, of course, is commercial stations. The Catholic church owns television stations in Brownsville, Texas;

Memphis, Tennessee; and Tucson, Arizona; but its strongest cluster is in New Orleans, where the Jesuit-run Loyola University owns WWL TV as well as WWL AM and FM radio. These stations obviously give the Jesuits a considerable influence over the programming that reaches New Orleans. And since the stations are CBS affiliates and sell commercial time, they also provide income to the church.

It is difficult to find how much income. Before the Tax Reform Act of 1969, the profits from religious-owned businesses usually escaped any taxation. With a five-year grace period, this loophole was ostensibly plugged by 1974. But even then, Sec. 502 (b) (17) and Sec. 7605 (c) provide some far-reaching immunity. For example, services licensed by a federal regulatory agency (such as the Federal Communications Commission licensing of radio and TV stations) can often exclude gross income from trade or business, and only an IRS regional director has the authority to investigate potential violations. Since the FCC stopped requiring financial reports of stations it licenses in 1981 (and kept them secret before then), there is no way of knowing how the Loyola stations separate their commercial income from their tax-exempt income, or what the income of any religious broadcaster amounts to.[14]

One of the few cases investigated by the FCC came about as a result of an exposé by the Charlotte (North Carolina) *Observer* of WJAN-TV in Ohio, which was owned by the Reverend Jim Bakker, a Fundamentalist preacher, and his Praise The Lord (PTL) Network. Bakker had raised hundreds of thousands of dollars on the air, supposedly for his overseas ministries, but it was credited to his own domestic projects and payment of his personal bills. Bakker and his wife were paid a salary of $100,000. They lived in a $449,000 home in Palm Springs, California, and in a church-owned home in South Carolina near the $150 million resort complex built by PTL. Bakker's brother, sister, and parents were also on the PTL payroll. But when the FCC subpoenaed Bakker's financial records, he immediately sold WJAN. The FCC claimed it could only act against someone who still owned a station, and thereupon dropped the investigation by a hotly disputed 4 to 3 vote.

The FCC was more persistent in its charges against the Reverend Eugene Scott and his Faith Center Inc., a 10,000-member congregation in Glendale, California. After studying evidence that Scott had engaged in fraudulent fund-raising on the air by soliciting funds that were diverted for uses other than those advertised, the FCC took away his license for a San Francisco TV station and a Los Angeles radio station. In December 1985 the U.S. Supreme Court refused to review a lower court decision against Scott.

Avoiding the controversy that surrounds such propagandists, the Catholic Telecommunications Network still influences at least 1.5 million Catholic homes. Established in 1981 by the U.S. Conference of Catholic Bishops, it broadcasts fifteen hours a week on television and fifteen hours on radio through cable systems in seventy-seven dioceses. Its programming emphasizes values—*Video Edition*, for example, examines the spiritual implications of the news. It continued to ban commercials through 1986, but allowed financial appeals not exceeding thirty seconds per half hour.

The dominant money and power in religious broadcasting remains with the Fundamentalists. They began buying stations in the 1920s, recognizing that their flamboyant style of preaching was particularly attuned to the airwaves, and that an audience that could be moved by sin and healing could be equally moved to dig into its pockets. Television lent itself even more to the thunder and oversimplified message of Fundamentalism. The final mix—the fusion with politics—came recently, particularly after the Fundamentalists made abortion and other sexual issues into political campaigns.

By 1986, Fundamentalist broadcasting had become an empire, at times rivaling the popular programs on CBS and other commercial networks. The Fundamentalists own 192 TV stations (not including ten of low power) and 1,134 radio stations.

The Mormons own three television stations and seven FM and five AM radio stations, all in important population centers. They also hold a major bloc of Times-Mirror Corporation stock, making them a power in another media empire. Although the Mormon purchase of California stations in 1968 was opposed by three of seven Federal Communications Commission members, two Mormon members on the commission were able to push through approval. When Mormon-owned radio station KSL came up for renewal in 1968, some Salt Lake City residents opposed the church's media control, and a U.S. Department of Justice petition argued that it would "perpetuate the high degree of concentration in the dissemination of local news and advertising that now exists in Salt Lake City." But Mormon influence on the FCC succeeded in keeping the church's monopoly position.

Fundamentalist media growth has been rapid. In 1972 the Christian Broadcasting Network (CBN) had the only religious TV station in the country. Eventually, CBN owned four in key centers such as Dallas, as well as five radio stations, but sold many of them in order to concentrate on its cable network, which claims to reach 30.5 million household subscribers. Recently the Southern Baptist Convention launched the American Christian TV system, and the Reverend Jerry Falwell, the Moral Majority leader, purchased a cable television network called Liberty Broadcasting to provide twenty-four-hour programming.[15]

Fundamentalist coverage goes far beyond their owned stations. Their networks buy time on other commercial stations: Falwell's *Old-Time Gospel Hour*, for example, carried on 350 TV and 450 radio stations; and PTL expanding to 180 stations and 1,300 cable systems. By contrast, the Methodists, Presbyterians, and other mainline Protestant groups do not own a single TV or radio station, and their time on NBC and other commercial network programs has been severely diminished.

The superstar preachers command huge audiences. The Reverend Robert Schuller reaches 1,277,000 television households, according to Nielsen ratings; *The Jimmy Swaggart Show* claims an audience of 8 million viewers. A recent Nielsen survey showed that 33 million homes watch one of the top ten at least a few minutes each month.

The Reverend Pat Robertson's religious appeals purportedly bring in $230 million annually, which is tax-exempt. He supported the Freedom Council, also tax-exempt, which became instrumental in his political campaigning. In Michigan, using Fundamentalist churches as recruiting centers, the Freedom Council organized delegates in precinct elections for state delegates, spending almost $300,000. In Indiana, state Senator James Butcher also used Fundamentalist churches as his base in winning the Republican primary for Congress. Robertson raised $30,000 for that campaign.

Although Robertson as a minister can run for office, the U.S. Tax Code precludes him from using tax-exempt facilities in political races. The now-defunct Freedom Council has been questioned by the IRS in connection with possible abuse of its tax-exempt status by helping

Robertson's campaigns. The IRS has refused to comment on the affair, but the Freedom Council has reportedly tried to convince former employees to sign an agreement, with a $100 payment to each, not to disclose any records, data, or other information about the organization.

Fundamentalist broadcasting was somewhat tarnished in March 1987 when the Reverend Jim Bakker, head of the PTL television ministry (along with his wife, Tammy Faye), admitted to a sexual encounter with a woman seven years before and to a blackmail payment to hush up the incident. After resigning from PTL, Bakker was reported to have received $4,800,000 in salary and payments in the previous twenty-seven months.

The impact of religious broadcasting, however, must be examined beyond superstar ratings. A study by the University of Pennsylvania's Annenberg School of Communications in 1984 found that 13.6 million people regularly watch religious programs in general. But since this figure is based on 2.4 people per family, and the religious audience is predominantly widows and widowers, the estimate should probably be reduced to 9.2 million viewers or less.

Religious broadcasting has been analyzed by Dr. William Fore of the National Council of Churches as a "kind of totalitarianism," selling a "superficial magical God." In a typical program on CBN, the Reverend Pat Robertson will be down on his knees, his arms raised to heaven. A telephone call comes in from a woman in a wheelchair, suffering from curvature of the spine. "The Lord is straightening that out right now, and you can stand up and walk," he cries. The woman may claim to rise from her chair, at least for that moment on television. Robertson plunges on, wheedling the audience for donations, hammering repeatedly that the more cash the audience sends, the more Jesus will love them. The main stock in trade of the Fundamentalist preacher is selling miracles to the sick and desperate. The Annenberg study revealed that 5 per cent of the viewing audience who participated claimed to have been healed.

Robertson, in fact, has developed a more sophisticated style than other preachers, a homespun style not unlike Jimmy Stewart's. The son of a former U.S. senator from Virginia, he graduated Phi Beta Kappa from Washington and Lee University, took his law degree at Yale, and served as a Marine captain during the Korean War. Founding CBN in 1960, he expanded its headquarters at Virginia Beach, Virginia, into a $35 million complex. In addition to broadcasting, it holds a law school and other educational facilities. Robertson's television showcase, *The 700 Club*, claims 300,000 members, each paying $15 a month dues.[16]

The struggle against sin—the concept of human experience pitting Christ against anti-Christ—underlies the incessant Fundamentalist appeal for money. Each day is a crisis for those seeking to be "born again." "For, if our program goes off the air," The Reverend Rex Humbard warned in a supposedly last-ditch fund drive, "there are men, women, boys and girls who will spend eternity in hell." When Humbard made another appeal to pay his debts, he received $4 million immediately, although he and his sons had just bought a $650,000 home in Florida.

The Fundamentalist struggle against sin—a republic ruled by Christ, a "theocracy," James Dunn of the Southern Baptists calls it—has moved to a new dimension. The Fundamentalists had previously reached lower-middle-class white Americans whose problems had been ignored. They were born again; they considered themselves healed; they were given a new sense of esteem. But as the Fundamentalists transferred their moral aims into political aims in the last decade, they reached a wider audience. By concentrating their attack on specific issues, such as ERA, abortion, and sex education, they became the spearhead of a larger crusade that placed the individual viewer in the mainstream of action. The viewer was involved not just with individual, but with national salvation.

Using skilled technocracy, Oral Roberts handles 20,000 pieces of mail a day on his computers. PTL processes 478,000 phone calls a year. Falwell claimed that he registered 3 million new voters in 1980. Half of all religious programs were targeted at politics, the Annenberg study showed. As the Moral Majority became a pillar of the Reagan administration, the Fundamentalists produced a new phenomenon in America: the complete fusion of religion and politics.

At first their support of political candidates was more subtle than that of the Catholic church. But by 1980, the Bishops of the Episcopal Church complained that the "use of religious radio and TV and local pulpits in support of particular candidates in the name of God distorts Christian truth and threatens American religious freedom." As Fundamentalist ambitions soared, Pat Robertson was soon boasting, "We have enough votes to run this country." By 1987, he was considering a race for the presidency, entering party caucuses in Michigan and other states to test his strength. Whether he becomes a serious contender or not, money and media control have proved to be the foundation of the Fundamentalist-Catholic alliance and have brought it to a peak of power.[17]

IX

Catholics and Fundamentalists Against the ERA

W HEN thousands of women delegates met in Houston, Texas, in November 1977, as the climax of the International Women's Year, Phyllis Schlafly staged a counterdemonstration nearby. Her balloons and banners mocked the IWY as the "International Witches Year." This was standard convention hoopla, of course. But beneath the speeches and cheering Schlafly had engineered a dangerous shift of power. Her Eagle Forum, the most diligent foe of the Equal Rights Amendment, had penetrated the IWY delegations from Missouri, Ohio, Washington, and other states—in Hawaii, for example, the Mormons took over 63 per cent of the state but made up only 3.2 per cent of the state's population. While the Mormons had previously stayed aloof from the abortion controversy and the anti-ERA alliance, they now became a fundamental part of Schlafly's campaign.

"Emancipation, independence, sexual liberation" and other feminist issues were branded by N. Eldon Tanner, a member of the Mormons' First Presidency, as "Satan's way of destroying woman, the home and the family—the basic unity of society."

Spencer W. Kimball, the Mormons' octogenarian president, would shortly send out 8,000 letters to the national leadership, coordinating the anti-ERA campaign in a special committee of the ruling Council of Twelve Apostles. With orders carried out by a phone call from Salt Lake City to the heads of each regional "stake," the chain of command was authoritative and efficient. Each stake had five to ten ward bishops, comparable to a Catholic parish priest. Each bishop controlled at least 2,000 members. "The structure exists where I can make 16 calls," boasted a Florida leader," and by the end of the day, 2,700 people will know something."[1]

The Mormons and Fundamentalists added a new discipline to the Catholic campaign against the ERA, for the Catholics were split. Most of the hierarchy violently opposed it, in contrast to increasing support from lay Catholics. Only twenty-four archbishops and bishops out of 385 eventually came out for ERA. One bitter opponent, Cardinal Cody of Chicago, brought other Illinois bishops and the political machine of Mayor Richard Daley into his camp. Although Bishop Norman F. McFarland of Reno, Nevada, attacked ERA constantly, Sister Maureen Fiedler, national coordinator of Catholics for ERA, tried to organize the state. Almost daily she passed out leaflets in front of the cathedral. Finally a priest threatened to have her arrested. The combination of Catholics and Mormons, the two largest religious blocs, eventually stopped ERA in Nevada.

Seventy-three per cent of the American public supported ERA by 1982, according to a Lou Harris poll. Twenty-four per cent of white Catholics were "strong" for it, 36 per cent "somewhat" for it. Still, even though the U.S. Senate and House of Representatives had passed the ERA amendment by the overwhelming margins of 84 to 8 and 354 to 23, respectively, and though 30 state legislatures out of the required 38 had ratified the amendment, the Catholics, Fundamentalists, and Mormons concentrated such political pressure on the remaining legislatures that ERA was defeated.

The incessant theme of the opposition was that ERA would destroy the American family. Schlafly, a Catholic, stressed that "God intended the husband to be the head of the family." She hammered at the "differences between the sexes—innate differences—which we ignore only at the peril to the family and civilization as we know it." When she led a picket line around the White House, she appealed to

President Jimmy Carter's wife, Rosalynn: "Let us stay home and be mothers, too." She claimed that on any application form she put down "Mother" as her occupation.

Homosexuality became an obsession with the opposition. "NOW [The National Organization for Women] is for pro-lesbian legislation so that perverts will be given the same legal rights as husbands and wives," Schlafly declared. She warned that ERA would lead to marriage certificates for male and female couples and to unisex toilets. The anti-ERA campaign in Iowa, organized by Donna Le Porte, a Catholic, featured TV spots showing two men caressing on the grass, implying they would be able to marry under ERA.[2]

Many nuns, working for ERA, attributed the hierarchy's vehemence to the church's long-standing dehumanization, and even hatred, of women. "The church is totally sexist," charged Sister Marjorie Tuite, coordinator of the National Assembly of Religious Women. "Not only is the church anti-woman, but if the bishops had come out for ERA, they would have had to come out for equality everywhere," insists Sister Fiedler.

Dr. Mary Daly, a rebel theologian who taught at Boston College, a Catholic institution, accuses the church of perpetuating a "myth of feminine evil." The church's hatred has not only "excluded women from the priesthood, but even a man who is contaminated by marriage to a woman is forbidden to function as a priest," points out Daniel Maguire, professor of moral theology at Marquette University.

Fundamentalist politicians reiterated the need for male dominance. State Senator John Young of Oklahoma asserted that "God created woman to be a helpmate to man." U.S. Senator Roger Jepsen (R-Iowa) demanded that we keep the "status role between men and woman . . . as it has been historically understood."

The threat to male supremacy coupled with a moral breakdown—teenage pregnancy, abortion, venereal disease, and homosexuality were among the targets—fused the Catholic-Fundamentalist alliance against ERA. But subconsciously there were deeper fears. The alliance dreaded the emergence of what might be called the "New Woman," who would topple the balance of society on which the right wing is based. Through education and responsible jobs, she was challenging her husband and often outreaching him. She was reshaping the old concept of homemaker, rearing children while on the job through day-care centers or employed help, even creating a home without a male and having children outside marriage. All this ambition and independence not only threatened the religious values of the alliance but the ideal of society it promoted. An American Christian Cause letter warned that "Satan has taken over the reins of the 'women's liberation' movement . . ." Bishop Thomas J. Welsh of Arlington, Virginia, predicted tha ERA would give women "equal rights to be tank commanders in the Army."

Another threat was that ERA could divide the opposition churches. Sonia Johnson, a Virginia Mormon, was excommunicated because of her work for ERA. One Mormon woman became committed to women's rights while her husband was an official at Harvard University. But when the couple returned to Salt Lake City, and Elizabeth Dunn, a NOW organizer, telephoned her about the upcoming ERA vote, her husband would not allow her to come to the phone.

"Wherever I went, I met Catholic women who told me how sexism had alienated them from the church," said Sister Fiedler. In Iowa, she spent four days with Bishop Maurice J. Dingman of Des Moines and convinced him to become one of the few bishops who came out for ERA. He even gave his cathedral for an ecumenical service of support. When anti-ERA pickets surrounded it, he went out on the step and explained at length why he had changed his stand.[3]

Despite national support for ERA that reached 73 per cent, the Catholic-Fundamentalist alliance was able to block it in essential state legislatures by concentrating their money and political and business clout on swing votes. Trade-offs and vote switches were crucial in Nevada, Oklahoma, Florida, and Illinois. Eight Nevada legislators, previously committed to ERA and in most cases supported for election by the women's movement, turned against ERA overnight. Last-minute deals by senate majority leader Jim Gibson, one of two Nevada representatives to the highest councils of the Mormon church, may well have been responsible. Furthermore, an estimated 95 per cent of the Mormon vote came to the polls in one of the church's most concentrated election campaigns. The Oklahoma Farm Bureau, owner of insurance companies whose discriminatory rates against women would have suffered from ERA's passage, lobbied legislators close to the insurance business and claimed credit for the defeat of ERA in that state.

Although the ERA coalition in Indiana was able to elect a Democratic and pro-ERA house and senate for the first time in the state's history, ERA passed the senate by only one vote. "On the day of the Indiana vote, little boys wearing seersucker suits with white shirts and blue ties, and little girls in frilly dresses were lobbying," recalled Eleanor Smeal, NOW's president. "They were almost caricatures." One senator decided to switch and vote anti-ERA at the last minute, and was only dissuaded by a phone call from Rosalynn Carter.

Shlafly and Neal Maxwell, a high Mormon official, reached large audiences together in Florida, Nevada, and other states. "We saw that it was a pattern. . . . They were the professionals. We were the amateurs," concluded Smeal.

In Florida, state Senator Dempsey Barron, whose law firm represented sixteen insurance companies, was instrumental in legislative lobbying against ERA. An analysis by NOW showed that women are charged approximately twice as much as men for medical insurance and disability coverage. Instead of the 10 to 20 per cent advantage women were given on life insurance premiums, the advantage should be closer to 40 per cent. Combining auto, medical, disability, and life insurance premiums and pension plans, NOW estimated that a woman's total costs during adult years exceeded a man's by $15,732.

When the house passed a new state insurance code that eliminated discrimination against women, Barron put over a compromise bill that kept most of the previous unfair rates. In 1982, after the house passed the ERA again and the women's movement prepared a last-ditch campaign in the senate, Barron worked behind the scenes through his insurance and business interests to line up a 22 to 16 vote against the amendment. One legislator who had previously been for ERA switched his vote and protested that "God had told me to do it." Women organizers later found that he had gone bankrupt with a half-million dollars in loans, and that business pressure had convinced him to defect.[4]

While the National Council of Catholic Women campaigned hard in Florida, backed by all the state's bishops, Mormon money and canvassing made the critical difference. "You saw their boys everywhere in their typical white shirts and black ties, bicycling from door to door, distributing leaflets," recalled Jennifer Jackman, a NOW organizer. In 1978 the Mormons raised $60,000 in the last seventeen days before elections, $13,000 from California alone. The money was funneled through a Florida organization called Families Are Concerned Today (FACT), and put into 425,000 leaflets and a statewide advertising blitz. The *Sacramento* (California) *Bee* revealed that "FACT had funded the successful campaigns of three anti-ERA state senators."

Similarly, Mormon money and workers were thrown into the anti-ERA campaigns in Missouri and Virginia. "We're just seeing the tip of the iceberg of the church's power," Sonia Johnson insisted. "It's the most powerful new right-wing group we have."

State Senator Pat Frank, whose opponent was funded by the Mormons, charged that Mormon money had been used in Florida in violation of the U.S. Tax Code prohibiting religious support of political candidates. A local IRS official admitted, "We do have a duty to see that organizations that are tax exempt follow the rules." But no investigation apparently was made. When the *Miami Herald* suggested that the Mormons could lose their tax exemption, a Mormon spokesman agreed "things were undoubtedly done that on review shouldn't have been done."[5]

Although the Illinois legislature had imposed a mammoth obstacle by requiring a three-fifths vote for ratification in contrast to a simple majority in most states, ERA failed by only five votes in the house in 1980. The Republican party, which had dropped a pro-ERA plank from its platform for the first time in 1980, was strongly influenced by John Birch Society extremists. "The Republican party has not only deserted women's rights, it has actually led the attack against them," declared Eleanor Smeal.

Sister Maureen Fiedler and other women spent thirty-seven days fasting in the capitol rotunda at Springfield, Illinois, in an attempt to influence legislators. She admitted the risks were "frightening," especially when a low potassium level sent her to the hospital. The ERA, however, had to deal with Phyllis Schlafly on her home turf, and she not only had well-organized branches of the Catholic Daughters of America and the National Council of Catholic Women, but her Eagle Forum was strong among down-state Fundamentalists. Right-to-life committees constantly leafleted Catholic churches, and many priests criticized pro-ERA legislators by name. The women's movement managed to gain the support of Jane Byrne, the new Chicago mayor, but it could never swing the last few votes in the house. In 1982, ERA failed again by four votes.[6]

Schlafly, a Catholic, usually worked outside Catholic channels and showed particular skill in building her Eagle Forum to a membership of 50,000. Although reared in gentility despite her father's financial reverses, she was adored by that fringe class of Fundamentalists who had few of the economic benefits enjoyed by Schlafly and most upwardly mobile Americans.

Born Phyllis MacAlpin Stewart in St. Louis in 1924, she was educated by the Sacred Heart nuns during three years of elementary school, four years of high school, and her freshman year at Maryville College. She was a striking, if not beautiful, young woman, tall and willowy with a china-white complexion, blue eyes, and almost golden hair. Like other socialites, she attended Junior League dancing classes. When her father became unemployed during the Depression, she worked at grinding jobs during three years at George Washington University, but still graduated Phi Beta Kappa. She would always criticize the "Eastern establishment," blaming it, for example, for the "sellout" of Taiwan to the Chinese Communists. Nevertheless, she chose Radcliffe for her M.A., again working to support herself and getting her degree in only seven months.

Her Catholic credentials were impeccable. She attended mass regularly and was married in the St. Louis Cathedral to Fred Schlafly, a Catholic and wealthy lawyer from Alton, Illinois. A friend traveling with her on a political tour was amazed that she knelt at her bedside each night and said her prayers. The Vatican made her and her husband members of the Knights and Ladies of the Holy Sepulchre. After a visit to the Vatican in 1980, the *Phyllis Schafly Report* announced: "Phyllis had the great privilege on November 26 of speaking with Pope John Paul II and presenting him with a copy of 'The Power of the Positive Woman' and copies of the *Phyllis Schlafly Report*. The Holy Father said, 'I give you my cordial blessings on your movement.' "

Her husband's politics were probably decisive in pushing her towards conservatism. Fred Schlafly had always been linked to right-wing extremists. He lectured for Dr. Fred Schwarz's Christian Anti-Communist Crusade Schools. He worked closely with Clarence Manion, former dean of the Notre Dame University Law School and a founding member of the John Birch Society. Robert Welch, the society's founder, called her a "very loyal member" in 1960. Phyllis always denied membership, although she spoke at Birch meetings. Her base in Republican politics was on the right. Her organization, STOP ERA, was allied with the Defenders of American Liberty, which supported Major General Edwin A. Walker after he was dismissed from his Army command for distributing right-wing literature to his troops.

Schlafly's political rhetoric followed the turgid generalizations of these groups, the linking of unconnected events to achieve an illogical conclusion. Attacking President Harry Truman for not unleashing General Douglas MacArthur on the Chinese mainland, she declared: "If the Truman administration had fought the Chinese Communists as hard as it is fighting the steel industry, the war in Korea would have been over long ago." Her sexual rhetoric usually followed the same logic. In 1981 she told a U.S. Senate committee on sexual harassment: "Virtuous women are seldom accosted."

Her sources of funding came from these same extremists. Her associate, Kathleen Teague, admitted that Jay Van Andel, the ultra-conservative founder of the Amway Corporation, was "one of Phyllis's biggest donors." She added, "Oh, yes, we are talking about big, big money." Van Andel gave $25,000 to the Eagle Forum Legal Defense Fund in 1982 and $30,000 in 1983. Schlafly said she got $33,492 from the right-wing insurance magnate W. Clement Stone in 1970. She also received contributions from the American Conservative Union and the Conservative Caucus. Howard Phillips of the caucus listed $50,000 for Schlafly in her North Carolina and Florida anti-ERA campaigns. She may have been financed by the Cardinal Mindszenty Fund in St. Louis, which is headed by her sister-in-law, Eleanor Schlafly. One of its biggest contributors is Patrick Frawley of the Schick-Eversharp Corporation, another angel of the Right.

Even at age thirty-six, with an expanding family, she was eager for political power, and ran for the presidency of the Illinois Federation of Republican Women in 1960 and 1962, winning both times. As the next presidential election approached, she forecast the emergence of conservative Republicanism with U.S. Senator Barry Goldwater (R-Arizona) as its candidate. A slim volume she wrote, *A Choice Not An Echo*, sold astonishingly well and made her something of a minor powerbroker in Goldwater's nomination at the Republican convention. Goldwater remained one of her principal heroes: she called him "Defender of the American Way of Life." Yet the senator has consistently voted for abortion rights and severely criticized the divisive impact of right-wing one-issue politics on American society.

There is a further irony of apostasy in her immediate family. Her younger sister, Odile, postponed marriage until age thirty-four, married a divorced man, left the Catholic church, and became a Presbyterian like their Scottish grandfather.

In 1952 and 1970, Schlafly ran for Congress and lost. In 1967 she tried unsuccessfully for the presidency of the National Federation of Republican Women. In all cases, she represented the extremist wing of the party. She was considered not just exotic but troublesome by moderates attempting to steer a centrist course after Goldwater's crushing defeat in 1964. Her political career, in fact, seemed to be at a dead end.

It was then that she made the portentous decision to strike out on her own and build her own political base. Her first step was the *Phyllis Schlafly Report* in 1967, a monthly newsletter with a feisty, biting tone, aimed at conservative middle-class women. Schlafly recognized a constituency which had been voiceless before: women concerned with moral corruption, a growing drug culture, and rampant sex among teenagers. Her *Report* soon had a circulation of 20,000.

Schlafly had also become an articulate, witty speaker, quick at thrust and parry, confident in the most heated debate, skilled at putting her opponents on the defensive. Her organizing ability had been honed in years of Republican infighting. When she and her supporters later lobbied the Illinois legislature, they passed out boxes of freshly cooked apple pies, and Schlafly announced, "I'm for Mom and apple pie." She made her impact on the North Carolina legislature by assemblying 2,000 women, praying and singing, around the capitol. When she was organizing Illinois against ERA, she claimed 20,000 women workers in the state, with a coordinator in each legislative district.[7]

Her next important steps were to launch an attack against ERA in her *Report* in 1972 and establish the Eagle Forum as her organizing instrument in 1975. She played on the fears and anger of her constituency, branding ERA proponents a "bunch of anti-family radicals and lesbians and elitists." Her questions went to the core of her audience's insecurities. Would laws requiring a husband to support his wife become unconstitutional under ERA? Would child support and alimony be restricted or abolished? Would women be subject to the draft? Would labor laws, protective of women, be abolished? Would the Catholic church be forced to ordain women and give up single-sex schools?

Her plunge into ERA politics with STOP ERA was certainly motivated by her own ambitions, the realization that she had grasped an issue that could propel her to national leadership. But there was a deeper impetus, coming from her Catholicism, that would soon bring important consequences.

The Catholic church had been seriously isolated in its early struggle against abortion and ERA. State after state, starting in 1967— Colorado, Oregon, Hawaii, and others—passed abortion reform laws, climaxed by the sweeping New York law of 1970. When the U.S. Supreme Court legalized abortion everywhere in 1973, the church's opposition was hesitant.

Hoping to build a coalition in every parish, the Catholic bishops issued a "Pastoral Plan" in 1975 that blueprinted a political strategy against abortion. The bishops wanted to enlist mainstream Protestants and Orthodox Jews, but only a token few joined. What the hierarchy needed to break out of its isolation was a huge bloc of new support. Ironically, this would come from the Fundamentalists, who had always been in the vanguard of anti-Catholicism, particularly in the South. It was Schlafly's skill at building a platform through her Eagle Forum—as appealing to Fundamentalists as to Catholic conservatives—that made the Fundamentalists give up their past animosities for a new alliance aimed primarily at ERA and abortion.

Schlafly supplied the theoretical glue and glamour. Three other Catholics supplied the political machinery and technocratic wizardry. Paul Weyrich, whose father was a German immigrant and who converted to Eastern Rite Catholicism, headed the Committee for the Survival of a Free Congress. Terry Dolan, a lawyer, ran the National Conservative Political Action Committee and was largely responsible for deciding how much money would be thrown behind right-wing candidates. Richard Viguerie, publisher of the *Conservative Digest*, was an early master of electronic mailing lists, pinpointed at prime right-wing activists in every district in the country. At his luxurious office in Falls Church, Virginia, he developed a bank of 250,000 rich donors and claimed he raised $30 million a year.

Before 1979 the Fundamentalists had been largely inactive as a national political force. They had a moment of notoriety with the Scopes trial in 1925 over the issue of "creationism," but the country brushed it aside as histrionics. They had been partially responsible for blocking Al Smith for the presidency in 1928. But the Depression had exhausted the Fundamentalist base—the small farmers and tradesmen of the South and Midwest—and swept them into the Roosevelt-Truman majorities. Only with the nomination of Jimmy Carter for the presidency in 1976 would the Fundamentalists glimpse a national outlet for their aims. But Carter's veneer of born-again Christianity turned out to be liberal at its core. The Fundamentalist preachers on radio and TV still represented religious revivalism rather than an aggressive politics.

It was not until 1979 that the Fundamentalist Crusade Against Abortion took off on a twenty-city tour, and Schlafly, Viguerie, and Weyrich addressed a Religious Roundtable luncheon that September to formalize the Fundamentalist-Catholic alliance. It was not until 1979 that "born-again" Christianity achieved respectability, and the Reverend Jerry Falwell propelled himself and other warriors against sin onto the political stage under the banner of the Moral Majority. His organization, in fact, was not even mentioned in *The New York Times Index* until 1980.

Schlafly's skill in building the Catholic-Fundamentalist alliance became even more critical after dissension in the church following the Vatican's continued ban on birth control in 1968. ERA intensified the split. Although a majority of Catholics supported ERA, the National Conference of Catholic bishops, in contrast to almost every Protestant and Jewish organization, took no official stand. Most bishops, in fact, worked openly against ERA.

To cover the church's abdication of women's rights, Catholic strategy was to insist that ERA would bring a rash of court cases expanding the legalization of Medicaid abortion. Consequently, U.S. Congressman James Sensenbrenner (R-Wisconsin) tacked on an amendment to ERA guaranteeing that its passage would not "grant or secure any right relating to abortion or the funding thereof." The thesis was that ERA and abortion were inextricably linked, and U.S. Congressman

Henry Hyde (R-Illinois), the main Catholic spokesman in the House, proclaimed that everyone from "the Catholic bishops to the National Right to Life Committee" believed that a "vote for ERA without the Sensenbrenner abortion-neutral amendment is a pro-abortion vote."[8]

Once the old congressional bill approving ERA expired without the necessary number of state ratifications (and with Bishop Thomas J. Welsh of Virginia leading the prayer service at Schlafly's celebration), the Catholic hierarchy flooded the House with telephone calls against a new bill. As a result, ERA was defeated in 1985, with only 278 House votes for it and 147 opposed, six short of the necessary two-thirds majority.

The Catholic hierarchy's strategy of linking ERA to abortion depended on a highly twisted version of constitutional reality. Any state's control over abortion stemmed from the constitutional right of privacy and "would not be affected one way or another by the passage of ERA," according to Thomas Emerson, a Yale Law School professor.

But the church hammered at this linkage as early as 1978 when the National Right to Life Committee, its close ally, set out to defeat U.S. Senator Richard Clark (D-Iowa). Priests across the state attacked Clark by name, a potential violation of the U.S. Tax Code. On the Sunday before election day, hundreds of thousands of leaflets, stigmatizing Clark for both ERA and abortion, were distributed in church parking lots. Although polls had shown Clark 10 per cent ahead, this last-minute deluge helped his opponent, Lieutenant Governor Roger Jepsen, win by 26,000 votes. A *Des Moines Register* study showed that the Catholic attack had swung 20 per cent of the normally Democratic vote to Jepsen that would have gone to Clark.[9]

The church kept pushing the linkage between ERA and abortion through 1984, when a state ERA bill came before the voters of Maine. Schlafly crisscrossed the state, raising the abortion specter. With money pouring in through her Eagle Forum and the National Right to Life Committee, the ERA coalition was outspent seven to one. Although the bill had already been backed by the governor and state legislature, the vote went 63 to 37 per cent against it.

A similar ERA bill was introduced into the New York State legislature in 1984, strongly backed by Governor Mario Cuomo. It passed the Democratic-controlled assembly, but the Catholic hierarchy concentrated on the Republican-controlled senate. Hammering at its persistent thesis, the state Catholic Conference insisted that ERA was "not an economic equity measure but a pro-abortion funding tool."

Constantly busing parishioners to the capital, upstate bishops were able to turn ten Democrats from the Buffalo area, who had been generally supportive, against ERA. Although a Marist College Institute of Public Opinion poll showed 74 per cent of voters for ERA, and Warren Anderson, the Republican majority leader of the senate, spoke for it, the bill never got out of senate committee. Governor Cuomo, a Catholic, complained: "Look what happened in my last legislative session—the Catholic Church killed the ERA."

Everything about Schlafly's strategy in building the Catholic-Fundamentalist Alliance had an apocalyptic ring, as though ERA had brought Christianity to the edge of disaster. The New Woman would destroy the home. Homosexuality would destroy the sacrament of marriage. Degeneracy would destroy America as surely as it had ancient Rome. "The 'liberated' Roman matron, who is most similar to the present-day feminists," she wrote in *The Power of the Positive Woman*, "helped bring about the fall of Rome through her unnatural emulation of masculine qualities, which resulted in a large-scale breakdown of the family and ultimately of the empire." Such visions of doom may have helped defeat ERA for the moment. But in the long run, Schlafly was intensifying the ever-growing split in the Catholic constituency. She was producing a polarity in American society as a whole that hardened the fanaticism on both sides.[10]

X

Politics and Money at the Vatican

T<small>HE VATICAN</small>, always claiming to be the spiritual ruler of Christendom, has, in fact, sought political supremacy as well for over a thousand years. Its ambitions to control emperors and kings were never checked convincingly until Henry VIII of England established his own church in 1534, followed by the onrush of Protestantism. The Inquisition was Rome's political tool against dissent, and the trial of Galileo in 1633 became pivotal to the Vatican's counterattack against rebellion.

When Galileo's astronomical studies confirmed that the sun, rather than the earth, was the center of the universe, he was not only challenging Catholic teachings but the infallibility of the pope. A "prisoner of the Inquisition," as John Milton called him, broken and ill under the threats of torture, Galileo was forced to recant and was punished with house arrest until his death a few years later.

It took more than three hundred years for the Vatican to admit that Galileo had been "wrongfully" condemned. Presiding over a meeting of the Political Academy of Sciences at the Vatican in 1979, Pope

John Paul II declared that he had "suffered greatly at the hands of churchmen and church bodies."

If the exoneration of Galileo represents one aspect of Vatican policy, John Paul quickly proved himself a master of the power game. Pius XII after 1945 had sought to make the Christian Democratic party in Italy virtually his personal vehicle. John XXIII abandoned this policy. But by 1985, John Paul was back in politics, ordering his priests to campaign from the pulpits for Christian Democratic candidates in an effort to oust mayors and city councils that had run the most populous cities for at least a decade. Taking a "major role in the elections," as Senator Carla Ravaioli of the Sinistra Independente (Independent Left) party described it, the pope helped the Christian Democrats gain 34 per cent of the votes against 29 per cent for the Communists. Although the Vatican had previously considered the Socialists anathema, the pope gave his pragmatic blessing to a Christian-Socialist alliance which ousted the Communists in Rome, Venice, Milan, Turin, and other cities.[1]

Despite its spiritual claims, the pragmatic factor has always dominated Vatican politics. Its aim is the survival and supremacy of the church even at the expense of moral considerations. And while recent popes have taken a constructive part in the quest for peace and nuclear control, the overall record reflects essentially selfish ends, and Pius XII's relations with Nazi Germany remain the most disastrous example of that twisted morality.

Pius virtually ignored the most monstrous single crime in history: the annihilation of 6 million Jews in Nazi death camps. He not only made just rare attempts to intervene against Nazi genocide, but he failed to use the spiritual prestige of the papacy to attack this mounting horror. He expressed no moral outrage against the gas chambers and remained almost completely silent during the war.

It was not that the facts didn't reach him from the start. His own nuncios reported the deportation of Jews to death camps from Bucovina and Bessarabia in 1941, and the killing of Jews in Slovakia. The Reverend Pirro Scavizzi, a hospital train chaplain, wrote him twice of the "systematic slaughter of Jews" in 1942. The situation in Poland was transmitted to the Vatican officially in 1942—the bishop of Lwów recording 200,000 Jewish deaths just in his diocese. A memorandum in the files of the Vatican's Secretariat of State describes the death camps near Lublin and Brest Litovsk by early 1943. Yet, when Harold Tittmann, assistant to President Roosevelt's personal representative at the Vatican, asked the pope to associate himself with the Allied resolution of December 1942 condemning the "bestial policy of cold-blooded extermination," Pius declined. There was "some exaggeration for the purposes of propaganda," he insisted.

The pope made one slight reference to the Holocaust. In his Christmas message of 1942, he spoke of "hundreds of thousands of persons who, without any guilt of their own, and only for reasons of nationality or origin, were destined for death or progressive destruction." Without mentioning Nazi Germany or extermination camps, the reference was so veiled that it fails to qualify as a moral protest.

Pius's statement of June 1943 on the suffering of Polish Catholics was hardly more explicit. The evidence that many Catholic priests throughout Europe had been murdered by the Nazis brought no Vatican outburst. When a bomb, hurled in Rome, killed thirty-three German soldiers, the pope branded it a senseless provocation. But he never condemned the Nazis for rounding up 335 Romans and murdering them in retaliation. And when the Nazis began to hunt down the Jews of Rome in the fall of 1943—over 1,000 were shipped to Auschwitz on October 18 alone—there was no further protest from the pope.

After the Allied liberation of Rome in June 1944, Pius no longer had the excuse of a possible Nazi invasion of the Vatican and danger to its personnel. Still, he refused to take any moral stand on the massacres at Auschwitz, which reached their highest daily quota at this point.

A few affirmative acts by the pope must be balanced against his negative record. In Slovakia, Hungary, and Rumania, Vatican intervention slowed down the exterminations temporarily and undoubtedly saved many lives. With the knowledge and approval of the pope, more than 4,000 Jews, according to some sources, found refuge in monasteries and religious orders in and near Rome, and Pius offered 50 kilograms of gold as ransom for two hundred Jewish leaders.

Pius's calamitous silence in most cases must also be set against the framework of the church as an institution. The Catholic Center party was instrumental in bringing Hitler to power, and the Catholic church in Austria supported Chancellor Engelbert Dollfuss's clerical fascists. Both before and during the war, the German Catholic press rarely wavered in its enthusiasm for the Nazis. During his early service as a nuncio in Berlin, Pius himself became ardently pro-German and welcomed the supernationalism from which the Nazi movement sprung. The Concordat with Hitler that he signed as pope in 1933 was a natural development of his prejudices, and it effectively squelched most potential opposition in the hierarchy. With rare exceptions, the German bishops lined up willingly behind the regime.

In a prophetic letter of June 11, 1940, Cardinal Eugene Tisserant of Paris warned that "history may be obliged in time to come to blame the Holy See for a policy accommodated to its own advantage and little more." Vatican historians have tried to palliate the Vatican record, but it can never escape the selfish motivations that Pius considered advantageous to the church with little regard for morality. Obsessed with the destruction of Soviet communism, he saw the success of German arms as the only means to that end. Even as the evidence of Nazi atrocities piled up, he shunned the accuracy of the evidence and could never rate the spiritual responsibility of the church above its temporal interests.[2]

Enamored of all things German, he feared to do anything that would bring the German people to blame him for their defeat, and to force Catholics to choose between their church and their state. His long-range policy was to maintain Vatican neutrality throughout the war so that the Vatican would emerge as an uncommitted power that could negotiate between combatants and block the spread of communism. His pragmatism failed in the end. While some Jewish groups praised his isolated efforts against genocide, the general verdict would tally with that of the *Christian Century*, a Protestant journal: "Pius XII was at best mediocre."

The ultimate test, of course, was that the Vatican had abandoned its own standards. It had abdicated its mission. It not only failed the Jews and many others, but as Father John Morley wrote: "it also failed itself because in neglecting the needs of the Jews and pursuing a goal of reserve rather than humanitarian concern, it betrayed the ideals it had set for itself."

Nor did the Vatican recoup itself after 1945. It had long been implicated in the escape of high-ranking Nazi war criminals from

Europe, but the evidence remained debatable until the recent discovery of a May 15, 1947, report, labeled "Top Secret," that was prepared by Vincent La Vista, a lawyer listed as a U.S. State Department officer and military attaché to the American Embassy in Rome. "The role of the Vatican [in these escapes] is now confirmed," concluded Charles R. Allen, Jr., an expert on war criminals who uncovered the La Vista report and many ancillary documents. The La Vista report, according to Allen, established the Vatican's culpability "in aiding and abetting the escape of scores, if not hundreds of SS and other Nazi genocidists—and it did nothing to bar their flight from justice."

One of the more notorious war criminals, aided by the Vatican's "monastery route" in escaping from Europe through the 1950s, was Klaus Barbie, a Gestapo officer branded the "butcher of Lyons." The Reverend Stefano Dragonovic, a Croatian priest in Rome, engineered his escape in collaboration with the U.S. Army's Counter Intelligence Corps. He also had access to documents of the International Red Cross, which may or may not have known whether its documents were being used.

The La Vista report suggested in its evidence that Walter Rauff, an SS colonel charged with massed gassing of Jews, escaped through routes "operating under protection of the Vatican." Dragonovic, head of the Croation section of a Vatican agency, Pontifical Assistance, was responsible for the escape to Argentina of many Yugoslav fascists, known as Ustachi. Two other key figures in planning the escape routes were a little-known Hungarian priest named Gallov and Monsignor Alois Hudal, an Austrian who was Bishop of Elia and a resident of the Collegio Teutonica de Santa Maria dell'Anima in Vatican City.[3]

Neither La Vista, himself a Catholic, nor any of the experts on these documents has ever claimed that Pope Pius XII himself had immediate knowledge of this connivance with war criminals. Yet it has been proved that the planning went up to the highest levels of the Vatican Secretariat. The Reverend Robert Graham, a noted Catholic historian, insists that Dragonovic and others operated on their own, but admits that the pope "could have easily suspected" what they were doing. The justification for this unholy alliance between church officials and war criminals remains puzzling. La Vista's explanation is that those involved believed it was crucial to keep vehement anti-Communists and dedicated Catholics working in Latin

America and other areas to serve the church's struggle against Russia. He calls their motivation "simply the propagation of the Faith." Whatever the confused reasoning of American intelligence, the Vatican, or at least part of it, conspired in a perversion of justice that further darkens its wartime record.[4]

The Vatican's treatment of the state of Israel reflects this same type of politics. When Pope Pius X was sounded out on the possibility of a Jewish state in 1904, he reiterated an almost 2,000-year policy of persecution, declaring that "Jews have not recognized our Lord; we cannot recognize the Jewish people."

It was not until the Second Vatican Council in 1965 that *Nostra Aetate*, Declarations on the Relations of the Church to Non-Christian Religions, reversed the church's insistence that Jews were collectively responsible for Christ's death, the basis of its condemnation from the start. This step would begin the healing process.

Still, as a political power, the Vatican remained adamant in its refusal to grant formal recognition to Israel. It demanded that Jerusalem, the Israeli capital, should be made an international city, but then backed off subtly by demanding the internationalization of Christian shrines. In December 1986 the Vatican blocked Cardinal O'Connor's agreement to meet with top Israeli officials in their offices because it did not recognize Jerusalem as the capital. Determined to increase its influence over Christians in Lebanon and other Arab countries, who represented a larger power base than the few Christians in Israel, it continued to play off terrorist factions against the Jewish state by dealing with the Palestine Liberation Organization and even welcoming Yasir Arafat at the Vatican.

Pope John Paul II, however, knew how to balance his political aims. In a brilliant conciliatory move, he visited Rome's central synagogue in April 1986, the first recorded papal appearance at a synagogue anywhere. No mention of Israel was made in his address, and so the nonrecognition policy continued. But greeting Jews as "our elder brothers," his words were tender. He reaffirmed the Vatican's recent stand against anti-Semitism "at any time and by anyone." Most important of all, in an obvious reference to Pope Pius XII's disastrous silence on Nazi Germany, he expressed his "abhorrence for the genocide decreed against the Jewish people during the last war, which led to the holocaust of millions of innocent victims."

At the end, he embraced a handful of Jewish survivors of the Nazi roundup of October 16, 1943, that had sent thousands of Roman Jews to their deaths in gas chambers—an act that Pius had refused to condemn. "The Jewish community of Rome, too, paid a high price in blood," John Paul lamented.[5]

The Vietnam War continued a policy that attempted to combine anti-communism and Catholic hegemony. When France pulled out of Vietnam after the 1954 Geneva agreements, some Catholic officials saw the chance to make South Vietnam a Catholic base and a symbol of resistance to the encroachment of communism from North Vietnam. With China lost to the Communists, Vietnam became a strategic theater that ostensibly would block Chinese troops pouring over the border to the aid of Ho Chi Minh's government.

For part of the hierarchy, in the United States particularly, South Vietnam represented the possibility of another state, like Franco's dictatorship in Spain, where religion could be fused with politics. There was one special problem, however. South Vietnam, at most, had a population that was 10 per cent Catholic, while Buddhists made up at least 80, perhaps 90, per cent of the country. Cardinal Spellman, working with a Washington lobby put together by Joseph Kennedy, President Kennedy's father, had to sell the illusion that South Vietnam was a Christian territory, the only significant Christian stronghold on the Asian mainland. Once U.S. troops entered South Vietnam, Spellman glorified them as "holy crusaders engaged in Christ's war against the Vietcong and the people of North Vietnam."

Pius XII's support of Spellman's lobby remains uncertain, but Malachi Martin, a former Jesuit priest then working at the Vatican, claims that the pope "turned to Spellman to encourage American commitment to Vietnam." On his frequent trips to Vietnam, where he was treated with the pomp of a state dignitary, Spellman billed himself as the "Vicar of the Armed Forces," although he was only vicar of Catholics among the troops. But Cardinal Alfredo Ottaviani, the second most influential figure at the Vatican, reinforced the illusion by insisting that Spellman "was speaking as the religious head of the American Army."[6]

Cardinal Spellman had virtually created the Catholic cabal that would rule South Vietnam. He met Ngo Dinh Diem, an almost unknown politician, when he was at Maryknoll Seminary, not far from New York City, in 1950. By August 1954, in an address to the national convention of the American Legion, Spellman was preaching the importance of Vietnam as the hinge in America's containment strategy that would ensure Catholic security.

Diem's family was Spellman's device to bring about American intervention. They were not only rabid anti-Communists but completely dedicated to the church. Although President Dwight D. Eisenhower had tempered the brinksmanship of John Foster Dulles, his secretary of state, the Spellman lobby convinced the administration to force Ngo Dinh Diem on Emperor Bao Dai, a Buddhist, and make Diem the South Vietnam prime minister. Another Diem brother was archbishop of Vietnam. A third brother would become head of the government's secret police.

By 1955, in a coup engineered by the Central Intelligence Agency, Diem overthrew the monarchy and Bao Dai fled the country. Diem established a dictatorship with his power stemming from a network of 1,000 Catholic parishes. Since the French had already developed the educated Catholic elite into an administrative class, it was easy for Diem to promote Catholics into almost every key government post. They made up the highest ranks of the Army. Nearly every governor of every province was a Catholic. It was commonly accepted that advancement in the government depended on religion. In 1962 alone, the diocese of Saigon reported 70,000 baptisms to the Catholic faith.

Once John F. Kennedy became president and his administration bought the concept that Vietnam was crucial to resisting worldwide communism, American food and aid built Diem's Catholic base. Most of it was funnelled through Catholic Relief Services, the primary recipients often being the 150,000 troops of the South Vietnamese militia who, with their families, made up a bloc of 600,000 Diem partisans. Whether the White House was aware of it or not, American food and aid reached few Buddhists. The *National Catholic Reporter* and other newspapers eventually revealed this scandal, which shook the Diem government as well as Cardinal Spellman's manipulations to maintain Catholic dominance.

Despite the propaganda campaign of Tom Dooley, a Catholic doctor and U.S. Navy lieutenant operating out of Haiphong, whose best-selling books hammered at the agony of Catholics in North Vietnam, Diem's secret police destroyed the facade of religious tranquillity in the south. It raided Buddhist temples, the centers of protest against the Diem dictatorship, and closed them. It jailed and killed thousands of monks. Many monks set themselves on fire in a suicidal demonstration against oppression.

By November 2, 1963, the political turbulence, food scandals, and disintegrating military resistance to North Vietnam convinced the White House that Diem had outlived his usefulness. Although Cardinal Spellman defended them until the end, a military coup, abetted by the CIA, assassinated Diem and his brother, Ngo Dinh Nhu, the secret police chief.

But nothing really had changed. The new president, Nguyen Van Thieu, was also a Catholic, and the church still dominated the government. Obsessed with Vietnam as the bulwark of the U.S. containment policy, President Lyndon B. Johnson poured increasing troops into the country. The White House certainly had no involvement in Spellman's plans, but the cardinal continued to push his holy crusade. Pope Paul VI, however, now saw the futility of a military solution and no longer wanted the Vatican linked to a corrupt government that had eliminated the Buddhists as a centrist force. As part of his new policy of negotiations, the pope declared in his New York speech at Yankee Stadium in October 1965 that "Politics do not suffice to sustain a durable peace." Spellman still insisted that "Total victory means peace," but he had lost the gamble to build a Catholic state as a bastion against communism in Asia.[7]

No recent pope more determinedly represents the Vatican duality of religion and politics than John Paul II. He handles politics with consummate showmanship. Not just the first Slavic pope and the first non-Italian pope since 1522, he is the first Vatican superstar. A master manipulator of the press, seemingly created for the media age, he radiates cheer and confidence. His instincts are for the spectacular. Arriving at a foreign airport, he will often fling himself to the ground and kiss the earth. After his investiture he fielded questions from the press in what was probably the first journalistic thrust and parry in Vatican history, speaking in Polish, Italian, English, French, and Russian. He has turned his appearances into theater, greeting by 1985 at least 200 million people on twenty-four worldwide and Italian trips.

Dignified and massive at ceremonials, his broad, hunched shoulders conveying athletic prowess, the pope likes to ignore protocol. He plunges into crowds to kiss babies. He became the first pope to hear confessions at St. Peter's, and baptizes babies and presides over marriages. On a trip to Poland in 1979, he stayed up late at night with a young chorus of Polish folksingers at a "Sacrasong" festival. As a cardinal visiting Rome, he was noted for constantly wearing a threadbare cassock and battered hat, and even hitchhiking to the beach.

With two doctoral degrees in ethics and moral theology, he was invited on a trip in 1976 not only to speak at Catholic colleges, but at Harvard, Princeton, and Stanford as well. In his Harvard speech, "Participation and Alienation," he insisted that the spiritual vacuum left by socialism could only be filled by Christianity. He published a book of poetry in 1963. Another book, *Love and Responsibility*, stresses the primacy of marriage and the danger of birth control and abortion, a theme that dominates his teaching.

Trained in discipline by his father, a retired professional soldier, the pope maintains an inflexible schedule of push-ups after breakfast each morning, jogs and bikes around the Vatican gardens, and plays tennis with his secretary. At his summer residence at Castel Gondolfo, he swims daily. Before assuming the papacy, he was a dedicated skier, canoeist, and mountain climber. As a student at Poland's Jagellonian University, he joined a theater group emphasizing poetic declamation and still sings at gatherings. This early training as an actor contributed to the showmanship that has characterized every appearance.

The pope rules a bureaucracy as supreme monarch, the largest in the world: 4,000 archbishops and bishops, 400,000 priests, and almost one million nuns and brothers, controlling a worldwide constituency of 855.6 million people. At the top of this absolutist structure sits the Roman Curia, the Vatican's ruling body, and its Secretariat of State. A bevy of congregations and tribunals radiate from the pinnacle. The Congregation for the Doctrine of the Faith, once known as the Inquisition, maintains theological discipline. The Roman Rota decides legal questions. The Congregation for the Evangelization of the Peoples supervises foreign missions and collects contributions from around the world.

Papal domination of the appointment of bishops is actually a nineteenth-century concept. As late as 1917, when the new Code of Canon Law was drawn up, about seven hundred, or roughly half, the existing bishops were appointed by the Holy See. The remainder were usually elected by cathedral chapters.

The perpetuation of this absolutist system, reinforced by the iron hand of papal infallibility, has stirred a wave of protest among those seeking to bring more communal decision-making into the church. Hans Küng, a Catholic theologian, asserts that Pope Pius IX in 1870 bullied the bishops into approving infallibility, and that the doctrine itself should be declared invalid. Küng was immediately muzzled along with a long string of dissenters from Father Leonardo Boff in Brazil to Father Edward Schillebeeckx in Holland, and most recently, Father Charles Curran at Catholic University in Washington, D.C. Pope John Paul II, after a prior move towards enlightenment in the Second Vatican Council, has reinstated total autocracy. When Cardinal Justin Darmoujuwono of Indonesia begged the pope to ease the clerical shortage by ordaining older married men, the Vatican announced the cardinal "had resigned for health reasons," which was double-talk for his demotion to parish priest.

The strongest rebellion has centered in the Netherlands, Latin America, and to some extent, the United States. In 1985, when the pope visited Holland, already in rebellion against Rome, and a poll of Catholics showed only 3 per cent approving the trip, rioters clashed with the police and threw rocks and bottles at the pope's car, injuring more than eight people. "Others are at least willing to acknowledge that they're sinners," a Vatican official complained. "The Dutch are not."

When Archbishop Raymond Hunthausen was accused of deviance from Vatican orthodoxy, the pope sent investigators to his Seattle diocese. Hunthausen had allowed Dignity, a homosexual group, to meet at his cathedral, ignored sterilizations being performed at a local Catholic hospital, and withheld part of his federal taxes as a stand against nuclear buildup. The archbishop was warned to use "greater vigilance" against birth control, divorce, and homosexuality and eventually had his authority in five areas, including moral issues, turned over to his auxiliary bishop. "One of the more sordid tales of U.S. church history," the *National Catholic Reporter* called the investigation.

Cardinal Joseph Ratzinger, a powerful member of the Roman Curia and the pope's main bludgeon against dissent, contends that American

Catholics have been taken over by hedonism, and that nuns, in particular, have succumbed to a "feminist mentality." Dissension "seems to have passed over from self-criticism to self-destruction," he proclaims. Küng retorts that Ratzinger's rigid orthodoxy stems from fear, and that "just like Dostoyevsky's Grand Inquisitor, he fears nothing more than freedom."

In strengthening his autocratic system, Pope John Paul II has increasingly depended on three reactionary organizations. Communione e Liberazione, with a membership of 60,000 Italian youths, became the Vatican's shock troops in recent campaigns against liberalized divorce and abortion legislation. The elite Sovereign Military Order of Malta—whose recent members include Cardinal Law of Boston and drugstore tycoon Lewis E. Lehrman, a former candidate for governor of New York and Jewish convert to Catholicism—ships food and medical supplies to its El Salvador warehouses for anti-Communist operations, and aids "contra" units in Nicaragua.[8]

But the vanguard of Vatican absolutism is Opus Dei, often known as the "Holy Mafia" and totally committed to anti-communism and right-wing politics. Founded in Spain in 1928, its 74,000 lay members (and 1,200 priests) around the world are drawn mainly from doctors, lawyers, journalists, and other influential professions. Opus held important positions in Franco's cabinet in the last decades of his regime, has considerable sway over General Augusto Pinochet's dictatorship in Chile today, and has penetrated the inner circles of the Christian Democratic party in Italy. Opus, in fact, has become so crucial to the pope's rule that in 1982 he made it a personal prelature, the only movement in the church to have the autonomy of a prelate and priesthood of its own. In addition, the Vatican approved the first step towards securing canonization for its founder.

The top rank of members, called numeraries, live in special Opus communities while holding jobs in business or professions. They are pledged to celibacy, intensifying their dedication with periods of self-flagellation. Women numeraries usually sleep on planks until the age of forty. As the fanatical arm of Vatican policy, Opus represents virtually a church within a church. "A malignant growth in the body of the church," John Roche, an Oxford University professor and former member, calls it. Father Andrew Greeley, a U.S. sociologist, labels it "authoritarian and power-mad . . . a semi-fascist institution, desperately hungry for absolute power in the Church and quite possibly very close now to having that power."[9]

In the Vatican duality of spiritual and political aims, the essential ingredient is money. Two branches of the Roman Curia administer Vatican finances: the Administration of the Patrimony of St. Peter (APSA) and the Institute of Religious Works (IOR). APSA handles stocks, bonds, real estate, and other liquid assets. IOR is the Vatican bank, the secret agency of a sovereign state, removed from Italian banking regulations. Since it takes many wealthy Italians as private clients, and their deposits are not subject to exchange controls, the Vatican bank could become on occasion the conduit for funneling funds to Switzerland and hidden accounts elsewhere.

The Vatican is rich, one of the richest entities on earth. But since it keeps its holdings in fanatical secrecy, no accurate assessment can be made. While Malachi Martin has traced $20 billion in investments, an indefinable amount of real estate—and, of course, its paintings, manuscripts, and other treasures—could bring its total wealth far higher.

What is known is that the Vatican controls a number of convention centers around Rome, exempt from Italian taxes, and other commercial properties. It provided much of the backing for recent construction in lower Manhattan and Montreal, and once controlled the Watergate complex in Washington, D.C., through a company it owned. But beyond that, palazzos have been willed to the Vatican for centuries, and thousands of acres have been owned by monasteries around key cities. Among income-producing properties, the Vatican owns an estimated 5,000 apartments and one-fifth to one-fourth of all the land and buildings in Rome.

Vatican investments reach into almost every facet of Italian industry, even an interest in the Istituto Farmacologico Serono, headed by Prince Giulio Pacelli, the nephew of Pope Pius XII. But it hastily sold its shares after the press reported that the company made birth control pills.

The church's alliance with the Christian Democratic party further enhances its business interests. When the City of Rome built an enlarged airport at Ciampino, the land was bought from Prince Torlonia, a member of the Vatican inner circle, and contracts for the main terminal, runways, and hangars were placed with church-controlled companies. An Italian law of 1962 established a dividend tax on all shares on the country's stock exchanges, but although the Vatican owed at least $37 million, and the government announced in 1968 it would be paid, the treasury failed for years to calculate this running debt.

With all its assets, the Vatican has plunged in recent years into manipulations that could only be described as illegal and into scandals that have soiled its name. These revelations, many in court records, indicate that some top officials and advisers of the church have turned out to be thieves, and thieves on an enormous scale.

A series of disasters started in 1969 when Pope Paul VI decided that revenues could be increased only by moving large church assets into foreign investments and enlisting the sharpest moneymen to advise the Vatican. His first move was to name Archbishop Paul Casimir Marcinkus, whose talents had impressed him years before in the Secretariat of State, as chairman of the Vatican bank.

Marcinkus was an odd choice. A second-generation Lithuanian from Cicero, Illinois ("I'm from the place Al Capone came from," he often announced), Marcinkus became known as the "gorilla." He was six feet three inches tall and weighed 230 pounds—a bulk that made him efficient as the pope's security guard and "advance man" on the New York trip of 1965 and the Philippines trip of 1970. Marcinkus was also dedicated to golf and expensive restaurants, and in both locales he entertained financial contacts and gleaned nuggets of information that the Vatican found valuable.

Marcinkus would shortly appoint one of the most flamboyant stars of Italian finance, Michele Sindona, his chief collaborator at the Vatican bank. "I consider him a friend," Marcinkus declared. Born in Sicily and trained in law by the Jesuits at the University of Messina, Sindona demonstrated his shrewdness early in dubious grain trading with the U.S. Army, investing the proceeds in private banks and corporations after he moved to the big time in Milan. There, he ingratiated himself with Paul VI, then Giovanni Montini, archbishop of Milan. He claimed to have raised $2.4 million for Montini's charities, and contributed loyally to the Christian Democratic party. Sindona was also accused of being the largest Mafia conduit for washing drug profits between Sicily and the United States.[10]

While he was making himself a multimillionaire as a private operator, Sindona impressed the Vatican with his manipulations. His position was confirmed at a later court trial in New York, at which his lawyer, former federal judge Marvin E. Frankel, described him as "an advisor and aide to the Vatican in the management of its properties. . . ." Sindona handled the sale of Vatican interests in Società Generale Immobiliare, which not only controlled the Watergate but such hotels as the Grand in Rome and the Gritti and Danieli in Venice. He managed all foreign currency speculations for the Vatican and transferred $40 million in Vatican funds to a Luxembourg bank.

When Sindona gained control of the Franklin National Bank in New York in 1972, he moved to New York, living sumptuously at the Pierre Hotel. But his seizure of Franklin National would trigger his downfall and eventually his death. Sindona was shuffling funds desperately between his banks to cover shortages when the Swiss government caught up with this sleight of hand in 1975 and closed his Finabank. Italy placed his Banca Privata Italiana in compulsory liquidation. The U.S. District Court in New York ruled that he had misappropriated $45 million from Franklin National and sent him to jail.

Franklin's collapse seriously damaged the Vatican bank, its loss estimated at anywhere from $160 to $330 million. Luigi Mennini, the highest lay official of the Vatican bank, was convicted of fraud in Italy. A U.S. court, in addition, fined the Vatican bank for an improperly documented purchase of Vetco Industries stock.

This was only the beginning of the financial disaster into which Sindona had led the Vatican. Carlo Bordoni, Sindona's chief associate, testified in a memo to the Italian government's investigating magistrate that the Vatican bank's "gigantic speculative operations" had resulted in "colossal losses."

The Vatican, moreover, owned minority shares and had board representation in at least three Sindona-controlled banks: Banca Unione and Banca Privata Finanziaria in Milan, and Finabank in Geneva. John J. Kenney, the U.S. attorney trying the Sindona case, charged the Vatican bank with "engaging in transactions which would not comply with the religious tenets of the Vatican or the Roman Catholic Church." When Bordoni described in court how lire were allegedly passed through the Vatican bank's account at Banca Privata, converted there into dollars, and then siphoned into Swiss accounts under "fantasy" names, Sindona's lawyer, Frankel, asked whether the Vatican's role was partly illegal. "For tens of millions of dollars, for hundreds and hundreds of billion lires," Bordoni replied.

In an even blunter summary of Bordoni's testimony, Frankel spoke of the "furtherance of alliances in dirty Vatican operations between certain prominent Christian Democrats in Italy." The Christian Democratic party reputedly got two billion lire from Sindona in 1973 alone, and its frequently elected prime minister, Giulio Andreotti, became a Sindona consultant after leaving office.

Yet, with all these revelations of illegal dealings between the Vatican bank and Sindona, the Vatican still agreed to supply three videotaped character witnesses for Sindona's trial: Cardinal Giuseppe Caprio, supervisor of Vatican economic affairs; Archbishop Marcinkus; and Cardinal Sergio Guerri, a former Vatican executive. Their testimony was only canceled at the last minute by the pope.[11]

All this time, Marcinkus remained hidden away in Vatican City, protected from Italian authorities, so that his links to Sindona could not be uncovered by the investigating magistrate. It was assumed that Pope John Paul II would fire him. Instead, he was promoted to be "mayor" of Vatican City.

Sindona, who had already been convicted in Milan for embezzlement, was extradited from his U.S. jail to stand trial again in Italy. The charges were not just bank fraud; now they included the murder of Giorgio Ambrosoli, the lawyer liquidating Sindona's banks, and drug trafficking. On March 22, 1986, four days after the court had sentenced him to life imprisonment, Sindona died in jail from drinking coffee laced with cyanide. The official inquiry ruled it a suicide.

Archbishop Marcinkus collaborated even more closely with Roberto Calvi of the Banco Ambrosiano. The Vatican bank was a stockholder in Ambrosiano, probably its principal stockholder, and its Panama and Luxembourg "shell" companies, and was a founding shareholder of its Bahamas affiliate, on whose board Marcinkus sat as a director.

Calvi worked his way to the presidency of Ambrosiano, aided in large part by Sindona, who needed links to the Vatican establishment. Ambrosiano had been a depository for rich Catholics since 1896, so close to the church it was known as the "bank of the priests" and, until recently, depositors had to produce a baptismal certificate. Sindona, manipulating Calvi, may have introduced him to Marcinkus, but the archbishop claimed he met him through the Milanese curia.

Expanding Ambrosiano rapidly once the Vatican had become a stockholder, Calvi was soon making shaky loans, transferring capital overseas in violation of Italian currency laws and using the depositors' money to buy Ambrosiano stock himself. By 1975, the Vatican bank was enmeshed in Ambrosiano's stock speculations. Calvi may also have been financing right-wing governments in Latin America.

When Italian investigators found many accounts drained to cover Ambrosiano's speculations, Calvi was arrested in 1981. He thought he was protected by his allies in the "P-2 lodge," a secret reactionary society that included high officials in the military, government, and business, possibly aimed at the overthrow of the state. In addition, he tried to use "letters of comfort" from the Vatican, which admitted ownership of some Ambrosiano shell companies, to stall off his creditors. But Marcinkus insisted the letters had been repudiated.

Calvi was sentenced to four years in jail. In April 1982 an official of Ambrosiano was shot by a gunman, who accused Calvi of setting up the attempted assassination. In early June, Calvi's secretary jumped to her death from Ambrosiano's headquarters building. On June 18, Calvi was found hanging from Blackfriars Bridge in London, with ten pounds of rocks and concrete attached to his body and $16,000 of assorted currencies in his pockets.

Although the Italian government handed down a verdict of suicide, Calvi's widow claimed her husband had been killed because of a "risky political and economic operation" he was trying to work out between the Vatican bank and Opus Dei. The Vatican denied it, and Mrs. Calvi could offer no proof.

But when Dr. Francesco Pazienza, a Calvi adviser under indictment for embezzling $200,000 from Ambrosiano, was extradited from New York to Italy in 1986, he claimed to be an Italian intelligence agent. The White House denied any knowledge of this role. Still, a former U.S. ambassador to Italy affirmed that Pazienza had worked as a "channel" between the Reagan administration and the Italian government. Pazienza had also been Calvi's agent in trying to find a buyer for his Ambrosiano stock. Pazienza was still in jail in Italy awaiting trial in early 1987.

Whether or not the Calvi scandal involved international intelligence operations as well, the only certainty was that Ambrosiano's collapse had cost the bank's creditors $1.3 billion and deeply implicated the Vatican. In 1984, still claiming it had been duped by Calvi, the Vatican announced that it would accept its moral obligations and pay $250 million to the bank's creditors. Since claims ran far beyond this amount, the Vatican had made an advantageous settlement.

The ultimate question, of course, was why Archbishop Marcinkus and the Roman Curia had allowed the Vatican to be taken over by swindlers like Sindona and Calvi. Its insistence that it was an unknowing victim remains a dubious defense. The Vatican bank was technical owner of at least 10 per cent of Ambrosiano, and in reality controlled it. The Vatican Bank owned shell companies that owed Ambrosiano over $1 billion. Yet Marcinkus stayed as a director of Ambrosiano's affiliate in the Bahamas until a few days before the collapse. Beniamino Andreatta, the Italian treasury minister, had even warned the Vatican to get out of the Ambrosiano debacle shortly after the official investigation started.[12]

On February 25, 1987, Italian magistrates investigating the Ambrosiano debacle issued arrest warrants for Marcinkus, Mennini, and other officials of the Vatican bank, charging them as "accessories to fraudulent bankruptcy." Significantly, the Vatican indicated that all those charged would be safe from arrest as long as they stayed within Vatican territory under the 1929 Lateran Treaties establishing the Vatican as a separate state. In this case, it was convenient for the pope to assume the role of a head of state rather than the head of a world religion, which had been the argument for sending a U.S. ambassador to the Holy See.

The Vatican's plight stemmed, to begin with, from its fanatical demand for secrecy. Italian financial circles were always suspect: their political ties could lead to a leak of Vatican affairs. The Vatican also refrained from calling on advisers from Wall Street, even the most devout Catholic, for U.S. law requires a constant disclosure of profit and loss and other financial transactions, which the Vatican abhors.

The Vatican's plight was compounded by its failure to train a core of clergy in banking and finance. Archbishop Marcinkus was totally inexperienced. Calvi, at least, came from the Catholic banking world, and with a long tradition of animosity between church banks and civil banks, it was logical that the Vatican should depend on him without any check on his operations.

Sindona's Sicilian background fit Vatican specifications even more. Sindona thrived on the Sicilian penchant for intrigue, a Vatican trait as well, and like most Sicilians, he leaned towards a conservative church and conservative politics. Furthermore, Sindona's years of wheeling and dealing in Milan added qualities of daring and innovative international finance that the Vatican thought it needed. Sindona, in fact, had always wrapped himself in such secrecy that until 1972 the press could obtain only two photographs of him, both taken by reckless photographers, known as paparazzi, who wormed their way into the most private functions to come up with a picture.

The Vatican's willingness to risk its finances with Sindona and Calvi was based as well on a changing international and domestic climate. Catholicism was becoming a Third World religion. New population bases in Latin America and Africa, riddled by poverty, could hardly fill its coffers. And with the once abundant flow of money from the United States and Western Europe drying up, particularly after continuation of the birth control ban disillusioned many of the faithful, the Vatican was forced to take chances it would have shunned before.

The Italian political situation intensified the Vatican's needs to gamble in international securities. The continuing strength of the Communist and Socialist parties convinced the Vatican that domestic business and industry would suffer, and consequently depress its shares on the stock market. If the Christian Democrats lost control, a leftist government could pass taxes and regulations that would damage church investments. The Vatican's decision to move large assets overseas obviously required the services of supposed experts like Sindona.[13]

All these factors contributed to a psychological hunger for the "big kill." The Vatican may not have succumbed to outright greed, but it certainly became a plunger.

Even after the Sindona and Calvi debacles, the Vatican has taken few steps to train a financial staff among the clergy or bring in outside experts. Its political ambitions continue to outrun its resources. Determined to expand its influence in Africa, for example, which demographers predict will hold 350 million Catholics by the year 2000,

John Paul II's trip in 1985 tried to align the continent's political leadership with the church. In Cameroon, the pope gave a long private audience to Paul Biya, its president—"an unusually long meeting," a Vatican spokesman acknowledged—for, despite Biya's shoddy record on human rights, Cameroon's population is 35 per cent Catholic and a fertile ground for continued conversion.

Yet, at the same time that it assiduously cultivates black governments, a Vatican-controlled bank, the Banca di Roma per la Svizzera, took part in floating a new issue of South African bonds in 1986. Seemingly, the hunger for profits can still produce a partnership with a racist state, and the Vatican's religious-political aims are in conflict with its investments.[14]

XI

Radical Nuns and
Troublesome Priests

I

THE STRONGEST CHALLENGE to the "monarchical model" of the Vatican, as Sister Jeannine Gramick called it, would come from inside the church, from the long-docile nuns. "What is this part of the church that responds as in the days of the Inquisition?" demanded Sister Joselma Gartner. "Who are these men who behave as if they have power over women, over our consciences, over our very lives?"

At the First Women's Ordination Conference in Detroit in November 1975, the challenge became a political movement. Many nuns were asking the unthinkable: equality in the hierarchy, the right to be ordained as priests, a step so drastic that Bishop James S. Rausch of Phoenix predicted it could cause the "biggest schism in the history of the Church."

Determined to reassert his authority, Pope John Paul II tried to "round up the strayed American sisters and return them to total institution-like corrals of the pre-Vatican II design," Sister Lillanna Kopp pointed out. Most nuns ignored the pope.

By January 1985, the pope became sterner with religious dissidents and insisted: "To be faithful to the Church . . . is to accept with docility its teachings." As if to underscore the warning, *L'Osservatore Romano*, the Vatican's semi-official voice, stressed that "There can be no true, visible membership in the Church, without assent to all and every one of the dogmas it professes." The confrontation reached its peak with a full-page ad in *The New York Times*, challenging the Vatican's total prohibition of abortion. Signed by twenty-four nuns, the "Catholic Statement on Pluralism and Abortion" claimed that a "diversity of opinions regarding abortion exists among committed Catholics."

David Riesman, the Harvard sociologist, concluded: "This disturbance is being described as a little squabble among nuns. It reminds me of the fact that the problems raised by Luther were dismissed at the time as a little squabble among monks."[1]

The rebellion had its roots in the women's movement and the civil rights movement of the 1960s as well as in Vatican II. *Gaudium et Spes*, the Pastoral Constitution on the Church in the Modern World, ruled in 1965 that "all the faithful, clerical and lay" possess "freedom to express their minds humbly and courageously about those matters in which they enjoy competence." Many nuns, particularly from the Maryknoll Sisters and the Sisters of Loretto, took this papal encouragement seriously and were in the front lines at Selma, Alabama, when the police clubbed down black marchers. Nuns were jailed in Washington, D.C., during anti-Vietnam demonstrations at the capital. They led anti-nuclear demonstrations and invaded MX missile bases. In a Lithuanian Catholic neighborhood of Cicero, Illinois, during a march with Dr. Martin Luther King, Jr., a brick was thrown at a nun by a Catholic boy, shouting, "And that's for you, *nun*!" They organized Network, a "Catholic social injustice lobby" with 7,000 members, to pressure Congress against the Vietnam War and for the ERA. "The death of King called me to *act* for justice," said Sister Maureen Fiedler, "to put my body where my words had been."[2]

One of the first groups of rebel nuns joined the United Farm Workers Union in organizing the fruitpickers of California, mainly of Mexican-Catholic background, struggling to improve their subsistence wages. The local hierarchy opposed religious activism at first; Monsignor A. J. Willinger of the Monterey-Fresno diocese castigated a priest for his "unadulterated disobedience, insubordination and breach of office." Cesar Chavez, a devout Catholic who organized the union on the principles of nonviolence, admitted "there have been a few good priests. But most of them have opposed me." After Chavez went on a month-long fast in 1968 to force attention on the strike, a large contingent of nuns and priests marched with him behind the Thunderbird flag of the union and the banner of Our Lady of Guadalupe.[3]

In their struggle to reverse 2,000 years of male domination that had reduced them virtually to infantilism, the dissident nuns had to combat the church's doctrine on the status of women. Its base is Paul's decree that women "are not permitted to speak, but should be subordinate even as the law says." Paul announced that "I permit no woman to teach or to have authority over men; she is to keep silent" (I Cor. 14:34–35). The First Epistle to Timothy, probably written by a disciple of Paul's, demeans women further through its judgment that Eve was "deceived and became a transgressor" (2:9–15).

The chief rationale behind the inferiority doctrine, of course, is the fact that Jesus included no woman among the Twelve Apostles. This did not seem to block the Marcionites, Montanists, and Gnostics in the early centuries from appointing women as priests, but their credibility was tarnished when these sects were eventually declaimed as heretics. Some biblical scholars, on the other hand, have pointed out that even if Jesus did not call women to the Twelve, he called no Gentiles either, only Jews, making it difficult to be certain of Christ's intentions.

"But in the Bible there is nothing formal or explicit, nothing for or against," declares Father Yves Congar, the French theologian. "One cannot adduce any New Testament text in support of the ordination of women," concludes John L. McKenzie, a biblical scholar at De Paul University. "One cannot adduce any New Testament text in support of the ordination of men."

Moving into this vacuum, Elisabeth Schüssler Fiorenza, a Catholic teacher at the Episcopal Divinity School in Cambridge, Massachusetts, insists that the "church can entrust the apostolic ministry and power to whomever it chooses without maintaining any historical-lineal connection to the Twelve."[4]

Under the influence of the women's movement, nuns asserted their independence by leaving convents and other institutions and forming small home groups of six or ten. By "forging new experiences of community," as Sister Rea McDonnell called it, they were building democratic sisterhoods and a web of feminine power. They elected their governing councils. Decisions were reached by consensus. And these nuclei were soon translated into nationwide organizations.

The National Assembly of Religious Women, concentrating on issues of peace and justice from a feminist perspective, has grown to 2,500 members. The National Coalition of American Nuns, dealing with women's issues in the church, has 2,000 members. The Leadership Conference of Women Religious speaks for 650 officers of the Catholic sisterhoods. The Black Sisters Conference and Las Hermanas, representing Hispanic women, often align themselves with these groups. All told, the rebels represent approximately a third of the country's 114,000 nuns.

One factor above all—educational achievement—provided a springboard for independence. Sixty-five per cent of women religious have master's degrees and 25 per cent have doctorates, far outclassing their bishops (priests not even in the running), with 24 and 10 per cent, respectively. Of the 1,537 members of the Adrian Dominican congregation by 1983, 1,144 had M.A.'s and 94 had Ph.D.'s.[5]

None of these advances, however, have markedly improved the long-range aspirations of American nuns, who often refer to themselves as the "battered women of the church." Still objects of what Sister Francis B. Rothluebber of Wisconsin's Columbiere Meditation Center calls "conformity, manipulation and victim-like surrender," many nuns have resigned. Recruitment of new sisters has dwindled. In two decades after 1966, their total membership fell from 181,421 to 115,386.

After leaving her order, Diane Christian recognized "how repressive it is to women," and branded the "apolitization of Catholic women . . . the most powerful manipulative tool after infantilization." Angela Fina, also a former nun, blamed "terror, fear . . . the whole Catholic guilt thing that really worked." Barbara A. Cullom of the Women's Ordination Conference accuses the system of making "a woman in today's Catholic Church . . . like being invisible, and that is in the *good* times."

In its efforts to discipline women religious who have not only marched and picketed but entered politics as well, the Vatican decreed that no priest or nun could hold a political or governmental office. The ban was aimed primarily at Father Robert Drinan, a U.S. Representative from Massachusetts, an abrasive liberal who became particularly distasteful to his cardinal and the pope with his consistent votes for abortion rights. But the effect of the ban has fallen mainly on nuns.

Sister Agnes Mary Mansour, director of Michigan's Department of Social Service, was ordered by the Vatican in 1983 either to denounce and refuse to handle government-funded abortions, which were part of her responsibilities, or resign from the Sisters of Mercy. She decided she could do more good by staying in office.

Two other members were forced out of the Sisters of Mercy when they were elected to office in Rhode Island. In both cases, they weighed their constricted effectiveness as nuns against their contributions as officeholders. "It's a whole movement on the part of church women to identify where are the places we should be today in service with and for the people," decided Sister Elizabeth Morancy, a nun for twenty-four years who had already been given special recognition by her bishop for legislative achievement as a state representative.

Sister Arlene Violet, a nun for twenty-three years and a supporter of ERA and abortion rights, also kept her post as the first woman elected state attorney general. "What the decision came down to," she announced, "was being a Sister of Mercy in name only or being a Sister of Mercy in reality."

As part of the church's opposition to homosexual rights, Sister Jeannine Gramick, co-director of New Ways Ministry in Washington, D.C., an advocacy and education center for gay and lesbian Catholics, was ordered to leave her post.[6]

The National Coalition of American Nuns has become particularly jarring to the church with its stand on sexual issues. In 1982 it had lobbied against the Hatch Act in the U.S. Senate, which would have allowed individual states to restrict or abolish the right of abortion. A few years later, it came out for a program of contraceptive services in junior and senior high schools in order to cut the soaring rate of teenage pregnancies. The rebel nuns are obviously aware they are reaching a sensitive nerve. "The church is afraid of losing control of sexuality," explains Sister Fiedler.

The abortion ad, which appeared on October 7, 1984, was the

most drastic challenge to Vatican authority that had yet been made. It was a carefully considered step, planned and debated for well over a year. Although issued under the aegis of Catholics for a Free Choice, a Washington, D.C., organization supporting abortion rights, nuns took an important part in shaping it. The signers included such leaders as Sister Fiedler, Sister Marjorie Tuite of Church Women United, and Sisters Margaret Ellen Traxler and Ann Patrick Ware of the National Coalition of American Nuns.

Everyone recognized that this was the ultimate confrontation. Since the U.S. Supreme Court decision of 1973, the American hierarchy had worked furiously to overthrow it, and some bishops had even labeled it the number-one issue in the 1984 presidential campaign. While a few signers claimed that their purpose was to rouse debate, they must have known that the Vatican stand was unshakable. The ad claimed it was based on an "adherence to principles of moral theology, such as probabilism, religious liberty and the centrality of informed conscience." But these theological twists and turns could hardly be expected to make any impression on the Vatican. The only words in the ad that really counted were that abortion "can sometimes be a moral choice." This was the gauntlet that had been flung down. There was no way of evading the fact that nuns and theologians, among other signers, intended to challenge the Holy Office.

The church's reaction, as might be expected, minced no words. Abortion had been branded an "unspeakable crime" by the Vatican, and Archbishop John May of St. Louis represented the fury of the hierarchy in his statement: "For a sister or priest to deny the teachings of the church is a scandal . . . a flagrant, flashy and deliberate affront."

Moving quickly to enforce its authority, the Vatican charged that the signers of the ad were "seriously lacking in 'religious submission of will and mind' to the Magisterium." The Sacred Congregation for Religious and Secular Institutes (CRIS), the pope's enforcement arm, thereupon ordered all signers to make a "public retraction" or face the "explicit threat of dismissal" from their orders.

Dismissal, of course, meant that signers could lose their jobs and future assignments as well as their church-owned living quarters. Since many nuns were of advanced age, the punishment was ominous. But while the four priests and brothers retracted at once, not one of the nuns or theologians budged. "What's to retract? What did we say that isn't the truth?" asked Sister Donna Quinn, executive director of Chicago Catholic Women.

"I can't go against my conscience," insisted Sister Traxler, a member of the School Sisters of Notre Dame for forty-four years. Sister Fiedler saw abortion as the crux of the church's debasement of women. "Women must have determination over their lives and bodies, including the procreative process," she declared. "The bishops refuse to admit women can make decisions. They ignore women on abortion, even to save the life of the mother. They rarely speak out on battered women or rape."[7]

The position of these nuns was largely supported by the change in American theological thinking. A study of the membership of the Catholic Theological Society, the College Theology Society, and the Catholic Biblical Association was made shortly after publication of the abortion ad. Of almost five hundred answering the questionnaire, 62 per cent said abortion should not be called murder. Sixty per cent opposed the canon law ordering excommunication for those involved in abortion. Forty-nine per cent believed abortion sometimes could be a moral choice.

Even before the Vatican moved forward on its threats of punishment to the signers of the ad, the local dioceses brought other forms of pressure. Sister Gramick had a workshop on homosexuality canceled by diocesan officials in Florida, and the New York and Brooklyn archdioceses withdrew sponsorship of a retreat she gave for campus ministers. Anne Carr, a professor of theology at the University of Chicago, resigned as one of five women consultants to the bishops' committee drawing up a pastoral letter on women; the obvious assumption was she was forced out. Boston College and two other Catholic colleges, in Minnesota and Washington State, canceled their speaking invitations to Daniel Maguire, the Marquette University theologian, another signer.

Monsignor John P. Languille, director of Catholic Social Services in Los Angeles, ordered that no more clients be sent to the House of Ruth, a shelter for homeless women run by Sister Judy Vaughan, also a signer. Languille tried to stop payment on a $500 check owed the shelter. "Whether or not the Vatican demands we leave religious life, whatever, there is nothing that can separate us," announced

Vaughan, who holds a doctorate from the Chicago Divinity School. "We have the energy to stay in the struggle."

The enormous emphasis that the Vatican gave the abortion ad had a peculiar logic. Catholic women had been in the forefront of the referendum drive which legalized abortion in Italy. In fact, two Catholic countries, Italy and Poland, showed the highest rate of abortion in Europe. Yet neither the Vatican nor local bishops ever threatened to punish these women leaders, or even harassed them. The assumption must be that the radical wing of the American church, particularly its nuns, was considered such a threat to Vatican control that their disciplining ranked as the first priority.[8]

A second ad, a "Declaration of Solidarity," which was pitched at the free speech issue, appeared in *The New York Times* on March 2, 1986. This time it was signed by more than 1,000 Catholics, including forty nuns and five priests. Its argument was that "Catholics who, in good conscience, take positions on the difficult questions of legal abortion and other controversial issues that differ from the official hierarchical positions act within their rights and responsibilities as Catholics and citizens."

The abortion issue had seemingly been pushed aside by the larger issue of papal authority. In fact, Sister Patricia Hussey, a signer of both ads, now placed the stress on "control and authority and attempts by the hierarchy to impose themselves in our lives." They were more than nuns: "We must also be who we are as women of integrity," she said.

For a while it looked as though the Vatican threat of punishment for the nun-signers had been diluted by a diplomatic solution. Although none of the nuns had retracted, six members of the Sisters of Loretto agreed to a four-sentence explanation that began, "We had no intention of making a pro-abortion statement." Others also had supposedly cleared themselves, for a press release from the Vatican on July 21, 1986, asserted that eleven sisters had retracted their positions in the first ad.

This provoked heated denials. The eleven claimed that the Vatican had twisted their statements, and that they had not budged from their original stand. It was a ploy to isolate them from Sister Hussey and Sister Barbara Ferraro, who had now been singled out specifically by the Vatican with a threat of disciplinary action. They had been in religious orders for nineteen and twenty-four years, respectively, and now were co-directors of Covenant House, a day shelter for the homeless in Charleston, West Virginia. "We no longer have burnings at the stake," Hussey declared, "but we have burnings of careers and psyches."

By late 1986, the confrontation between the Vatican and the radical nuns was still at an impasse. "It's been simply terrible," concluded Sister Traxler, "and it's not over yet . . . the Vatican has a sexist obsession which it can't see beyond."9

The problem is to delineate a clear pattern in the rebellion. Certainly, the ordination of women is a prime objective, but the struggle, at least for the radicals, goes far beyond that. They are concerned with all aspects of domination—in the church, of bishops over Catholics as a whole and over women in particular; in society, of the rich over the poor, of whites over blacks. They are concerned with radicalizing the church, with Liberation Theology, with shoring up the Sandinista government against the autocratic church in Nicaragua. They are concerned with nuclear war and its elimination. The pastoral letter of the bishops on nuclear arms is just a hesitant first step for them.

If this pattern seems amorphous, their ultimate aim is well defined. "We want a revolution in the church," states Sister Fiedler. A summary of a 1985 meeting, published in *Probe*, the organ of the National Assembly of Religious Women, concludes: "We would like to render the Vatican powerless. . . ."

In the end, the Vatican is always the target. The concept would seem to call for a totally new church, with most of Rome's power eliminated. But for many, it is the old church, the original church. Sister Kaye Ashe defines a "community of equals." Sister Tuite wanted a return to the communal church of the first centuries after Christ. "It would be a return to the original plan of 'The People of God,' a church in the original meaning of the Gospel, a church with shared responsibilities and dignity for women, blacks, gays, for everyone. We are revolutionaries because we are Christian."

Sister Lora Ann Quinonez, executive director of the Leadership Conference of Women Religious, foresees a church "where the clergy would marry if they want, where nuns could choose to be celibate or married, where the sense of community would be all important." Sister Ferraro argues, "We must resist by naming the oppressor, by resisting the evil of the hierarchy. The issue is power and control over our lives." Sister Marilyn Thie, associate professor of theology and religion at Colgate University, insists that the radicals "must learn to live resistance."[10]

This concept may be visionary, and no one expects the Vatican to yield the power it has accumulated over two millennia. Yet there is some precedent in the "base communities" in Latin America— thousands of Catholic groups that have developed independently of the bureaucratic church. The confrontation produced by the abortion ads also illuminates a long-range strategy that may be aimed at an increasing attack on Vatican authority. Abortion, in this perspective, is hardly the issue. The right of dissent, of pluralism in the church, comes closer to the real purpose. The radical nuns may be seen by history as hardheaded tacticians, building a consensus of power against the Vatican that may eventually produce as explosive results as Martin Luther's little band of monks unleashed four centuries earlier.

2

The rebellion also came from the Catholic clergy, who sided with the nuns in their demand for ordination. Priests for Equality, an organization with 2,100 members in thirty-four countries, issued a "Pastoral on Equality" in 1984. "Jesus acknowledged the dignity of women and their equality with men in the sight of God, in whose image he knew they were created," the pastoral declared. "God is as much Mother as God is Father." This fusion of interests between priests and nuns has undoubtedly influenced lay Catholics, for recent studies show 47 to 52 per cent backing the ordination of women in 1985.

A large part of the clergy, moreover, was in conflict with the Vatican in its demand for the option of marriage if a priest decides to choose it. The National Federation of Priests' Councils in the United States came out for clerical marriage in 1971, and religious and lay delegates from 152 dioceses, meeting in 1976 as a "Call to Action," also approved it. From a 1970 study, Father Andrew Greeley reported that "four-fifths of the priests in the country believed that married men should be ordained priests and that priests who had left the active ministry to marry should be permitted to return (though only two-fifths of the inactive priests actually wanted to return to the ministry and only about one-fifth to the kinds of work that they had been doing before they left the ministry)."

This movement for a married clergy has produced strong reactions in Rome. The tenet that a priest belongs to God alone, that his total being must be dedicated to his mission, that a wife could somehow defile the purity of a male elite class—all these strictures are at the core of papal thinking. Perfection has become equated with complete separation from the taint of a woman's body. "I had been brainwashed into believing that celibacy was the something extra, the distinguishing mark for those who were 'perfect,' " explained Robert Eder, a former priest.

On a more practical level, celibacy gave added control to Rome, making a priest less expensive to maintain and easier to transfer to another post. Above all, it was the final technique of subservience. "I began to see," Eder concluded, "that celibacy helped to induce docility and submission to authority, in so far as it made the priest dependent, really dependent, on the structure itself."

Nothing in the New Testament, however, provides any basis for the Vatican's rigidity on celibacy. Some apostles and their disciples married, and in the early centuries marriage was optional for priests as well as deacons. It was not until 390 that Rome began to push for celibacy. The First and Second Lateran Councils in the twelfth century finally made marriage invalid and illicit, although infringements of the rule persisted. And Roman Catholic clergy of the Eastern Rites have always kept the tradition that priests can marry before their ordination.

Despite the fact that the celibacy issue is partially responsible for the decline in seminarians from 47,500 to 12,000 in the last two decades, the hierarchy maintains an attitude of abhorrence towards the resignation of a priest and his subsequent marriage. "I am excommunicated, anathemized, damned because I had committed matrimony . . . consigned to hell's fire," explained Edward F. Henriques, a Catholic priest for sixteen years before he married and entered the Episcopal clergy.

There are troubling undercurrents to the celibacy issue that the

Vatican has chosen to ignore. In Latin America and the Philippines particularly, priests often establish "unofficial" marriages: one priest reported that eleven of thirteen clergy in his area maintained this arrangement. Bishop Peter Koop of Brazil found the situation so critical that he wrote the Vatican, "We have to make a choice right away: either to multiply the number of priests, both celibate and married, or look forward to the collapse of the church in South America."[11]

In Africa, the Vatican confronts a similar dilemma. It considers the continent, as it considers Latin America, the most fertile source of expansion for the Catholic church. Yet it is blocked by a traditional opposition to celibacy, which holds that celibacy amounts to self-indulgence rather than self-sacrifice, and that a young man shirks his responsibility to his family and community by refusing to have children. Many in the African hierarchy insist that celibacy cannot work. "African culture does not find in permanent celibacy an authentic human value that deserves to be lived," asserts Father Matungulu Otene, a Jesuit from Zaire. Father Aylward Shorter, a British scholar of the African church, estimates that each year Africa has two hundred fewer priests to serve two million more Catholics.

But if the Vatican can brush aside conflicts caused by the celibacy rule, it has been severely embarrassed by the homosexual issue and the notoriety given it in 1984 with the publication of *The American Pope*, a biography of the late Cardinal Francis Spellman of New York. In the advance galleys, its author, John Cooney, cited evidence of the cardinal's homosexuality. But after protests by the diocese and examination of the evidence by the publisher, the passages in question were cut before publication.

A year later, the *National Catholic Reporter* charged that there was "blatant homosexuality" among priests in training at Catholic seminaries. Father Robert Nugent, former co-director of New Ways Ministry, referring to bishops, rectors, and other church leaders, admitted that "none of them wants others to know they are even dealing with homosexuality in their institutions."

In the case of a Louisiana priest convicted of pedophilia, J. Minos Simon, a lawyer representing parents suing for damages, asserted that the Lafayette diocese was a "safe haven" for homosexuals and that "someone in authority knowingly condones homosexual behavior." Simon's views were hardly objective, but he pinpointed the central problem when he observed that "what happened here is rooted in celibacy."

A more documented portrayal of the problem came in 1985 with a book, *Lesbian Nuns: Breaking Silence,* in which present and former nuns described their own sexual lives and the impact of lesbianism on their sisterhoods. The book caused such consternation that when a Boston television station scheduled some of the authors for interviews, an aide to Cardinal Bernard Law branded the show an "affront to the sensitivity of Roman Catholics" and forced its cancellation. One result of this censorship was that sales rose to 125,000 copies, and softcover rights went for considerable money.

Despite the persistence of the church in attempting to blot out references to its homosexual problem, some priests refused to be silenced. In a letter to *The New York Times,* the Reverend William Hart McNichols, a Jesuit, insisted: "Cardinal Spellman's sex life does not matter, but Cardinal Spellman's homosexuality does indeed matter. It matters to thousands of people whose jobs, relationships and whose very lives are threatened because of their sexuality, all the while being forced to view and eat the hypocrisy of their church."

Referring to the incidence of homosexuality in the hierarchy, Kevin Gordon, a former Christian Brother, who directs a homosexual think tank in New York City, stated, "Although there obviously isn't any hard data, priests and nuns tell me that 40 per cent to 60 per cent is more like it." A Detroit seminary faculty member set the figure at "one-third, and maybe more."[12]

The hierarchy may have felt justified in ignoring the evidence on homosexuality, but it could not suppress the revelations in 1985 about pedophilia, which involved the critical legal charge that a few clergy had long been victimizing students, altar boys, and Boy Scouts in their care. Evidence had been accumulating for some time, fueling "old suspicions against the Catholic church and a celibate clergy," the *National Catholic Reporter* charged. "All too often, complaints against the priest involved are disregarded by the bishops, or the priest is given the benefit of the doubt."

But a string of recent convictions shocked the hierarchy out of its complaisance. A priest in Thousand Oaks, California, pleaded no contest in court to three charges of child molestation. A priest in

Portland, Oregon, was convicted of three sexual abuse misdemeanor counts and sentenced to five months in jail, admitting he had been sexually involved with boys for fifteen to twenty years. A priest in Boise, Idaho, was sentenced to seven years for lewd behavior with a minor male, and investigation showed he had a twenty-year record of illegal sexual contact with boys. The charges—more than forty cases in two years—have spread to Rhode Island, Pittsburgh, Newark, New Jersey, and San Diego.

One case in the Cajun country of southern Louisiana proved particularly damaging to the church, since it had ignored or squelched a mound of evidence for ten years. In 1986, Father Gilbert Gauthe, a forty-one-year-old priest in Lafayette, was sentenced to twenty years in prison after confessing that he had raped or sodomized at least thirty-seven—perhaps as many as seventy—children. Boys were sodomized before mass, and oral sex took place in the confessional.

The church's spiritual standing has suffered. The father of one victim in Portland, noting that his son was no longer a churchgoing Catholic, concluded that the "last thing we discuss in our family now is religion." But the damage has been financial as well. The Lafayette diocese alone and its insurance companies may end up paying at least $10 million as a result of lawsuits to the families of the victims, and most insurance companies are excluding sexual abuse coverage from future policies.

No psychological studies have proved that pedophilia results from the imposition of celibacy. Still, the homosexual problem haunts the church, and its furious denunciations of it contrast oddly with the Vatican's refusal to consider the demands of the dissident priests for a married clergy. Even marriage for deacons, an order below that of priest, was defeated in the last Vatican Council by a vote of 1,364 to 839.[13]

Relying on its usual interpretation of natural law, the church brands homosexual acts a "grave transgression of the goals of human sexuality and of human personality and are consequently contrary to the will of God." But the *New Catholic Encyclopedia* emphasizes the church's more immediate concern: "The homosexual act by its essence excludes all possibility of transmission of life. . . ." Like birth control, abortion, and voluntary sterilization, homosexuality cuts off the possibility of birth, limiting the pool of adherents on which the church's survival depends. By offering an alternative to marriage, it threatens the Vatican's control over sex, children, and the family.

Ironically, the Old Testament has only one undisputed injunction against homosexuality, Leviticus teaching that "Thou shall not lie with mankind as with womankind: it is abomination" (18:22). Although the word "sodomy" derives from the city of Sodom in Genesis, and the word "know" in this passage has often been interpreted to mean knowing carnally, many biblical scholars consider this a dubious interpretation (19:4–11).

Four passages from Paul in the New Testament are generally considered condemnations of homosexuality. Again, biblical scholars differ, and Father John J. McNeill, a Jesuit priest critical of traditional interpretation, insists that "Nowhere is there a specific text which explicitly rejects all homosexual activities as such independent of the circumstances."

The very sensitivity of dealing with homosexuality and pedophilia among its clergy is undoubtedly responsible for much of the fury with which the church responds to any threat to its authority. As a church-affiliated institution, Georgetown University thought it had a religious sanction to stamp out any hint of homosexuality by refusing to give Gay People, a campus organization, office space and equal recognition with other student and faculty groups. Gay People challenged the university in court in 1984 on the basis of the District of Columbia's anti-discrimination ordinance, joined by the local government and fourteen members of the university's Law Faculty.

In a confrontation setting a precedent for other Catholic campuses, the university argued that its religious freedom under the First Amendment superseded homosexual rights. Lawyers for Gay People insisted that by accepting federal funds for building construction, Georgetown was a secular institution and no longer shielded by its claim to impose religious dogma at will. After a lower court ruled for the university, Joe Izzo, a former campus minister, charged that the administration, afraid of losing alumni contributions, was "running scared shitless." The court of appeals reversed the lower court in 1985. Gay rights groups, it said, must be given the same status as any other group in the elimination of racial and sexual discrimination.

In October 1986, Cardinal Joseph Ratzinger, head of the Vatican's

Sacred Congregation for the Doctrine of the Faith, issued a directive forbidding Father McNeill, who is also a practicing psychotherapist, from ministering to homosexuals and talking publicly about his work. McNeill, author of the book *The Church and the Homosexual*, and a critic of the Vatican's recent homosexual guidelines, refused to obey the ban, and the Jesuits began procedures to expel him. "Part of the issue has always been their own fear of being unwilling to deal honestly and openly with the fears of their own sexuality," McNeill stated. "You have to understand, too, that the issue comes back to authority. They feel that their authority is very much at stake, that they are losing control."[14]

Forbidden by Cardinal O'Connor of New York to hold masses as a group, Dignity, a homosexual organization, conducted its last service at St. Francis Xavier in Manhattan on March 7, 1987. Then a thousand homosexuals marched into the streets, chanting "We are the church."

Refusing to accept the First Amendment line between church and state, Catholic officials continue to insist that its stand on homosexuality must have priority over governmental policy. Cardinal O'Connor of New York has long been the unrelenting bullyboy of this approach. When Mayor Edward Koch issued Executive Order 50 to ban discrimination in city agencies against homosexuals as well as other minorities, O'Connor brusquely refused to obey the order and took the case to the state's highest court. The court of appeals ruled against the city, saying the mayor was establishing his own social policy.

The introduction of a gay rights bill in the New York City Council in 1986, prohibiting discrimination against sexual orientation in housing, employment, and public accommodations, angered O'Connor even more. Ordering his pastors to denounce the bill from their pulpits and urge their constituents to lobby the council against it, O'Connor proclaimed that "Divine law cannot be changed by federal law, state law, county law or city law, even by passage of legislation by the city council."

Again, as with abortion and other issues, the church was insisting that its interpretation of divine law was the only valid one despite the fact that most Protestant and Jewish groups, and Catholic groups such as the National Assembly of Religious Women and National Coalition of American Nuns, supported the bill. Again, the church refused to accept the line between church and state. Legislation reflecting the will of society, it insisted, must never conflict with Catholic teaching. When the bill passed by a large margin, O'Connor promised to challenge it in court, but eventually allowed Catholic agencies to sign the required city contracts.

The emotions stirred by homosexuality in the Catholic hierarchy obviously reflect deep strains of fear and guilt. The possibility of a married clergy would unravel a thousand years of sexual suppression. "I am a Catholic, I am a feminist, I am a lesbian," announced Mary Hunt, a coordinator of the Women's Alliance for Theology, Ethics and Ritual. "Many in our church, married, single, and religious women, are lesbians. We need to unlock this dimension."[15]

XII

Liberation Theology:
Challenge to the Vatican

FATHER CAMILO TORRES could be considered an aberration. Few priests have taken up arms and joined the guerrillas in the jungles of Colombia, where he was killed by government troops in 1966.

Yet Torres represents far more than a clerical alliance with revolutionary peasants. He came out of a long ground swell of protest within the Latin church, a movement known as Liberation Theology that has torn the church from its elitist past and insisted that religion must deal above all with the needs of the poor. Liberation Theology has created a new kind of church, a "People's Church" rooted in decision-making by the masses in direct opposition to the autocratic rule of the Vatican.

If the Vatican could ignore, as it did, a rebellious cleric who turned to violence, it was deeply concerned about the movement that produced him. Liberation Theology, in fact, has been the most direct internal challenge to Roman power in this century. It has not only spawned well over 100,000 lay groups, known as "base communities" and often operating independently of the hierarchy, but it has become a symbol of dissent for radical nuns and priests in the United States and elsewhere, particularly for many Catholic Hispanics and blacks.

Although both the Vatican and disciples of Liberation Theology are apt to tone down the movement's consequences, it has certainly produced an increasing split in the church. "Avoid everything that would make one think that a double hierarchy . . . exists in the church," Pope John Paul II warned in recognition of this threat in a 1985 speech in Peru.

Born in Bogotá in 1929, Torres was ordained a priest in 1954 and took graduate studies at the University of Louvain, in Belgium, where he came under the wing of Gustavo Gutiérrez, the Peruvian theologian credited with coining the name Liberation Theology. Back in Bogotá, Torres was appointed student chaplain at the National University. A dashing and impulsive figure, he knew how to rouse student audiences. Accused of fomenting disorder, he was dismissed from his post in 1962.

He worked with peasants in a Rural Action Unit. When peasants formed the Yopal project to defend themselves against the encroachment of large landowners, Torres attacked the government for allowing more than two hundred peasant deaths and imprisonments. He urged the nationalization of banks and industries. He drew huge crowds at his meetings and was constantly watched by government spies. Determined to remain the spokesman for peasants, workers, and students, he requested a return to lay status in 1965 at the age of thirty-six, but remained a Catholic.

All during 1965 he addressed meeting after meeting. When the police tried to stop him from speaking in Medellín, students rioted and pelted the police with bricks. Torres and a hundred others were arrested. He was putting out a radical paper for the United Front, the first issue of which sold 30,000 copies in a few hours. "They know," he said of the poor, "that the only road left open to them is that of armed struggle. . . . Not one step back! Liberation or death!"

Even his closest friends did not realize he had been in contact with the Army of National Liberation guerrillas. After a speech in mid-October, he slipped away and joined a unit in the San Vicente jungle. He was armed with a Colt revolver when his unit clashed with government troops on February 15, 1966. Torres was hit by rifle fire and killed instantly along with at least six guerrillas. His death, announced two days later, was followed by riots throughout the country. "They say they killed him with a gun," students and workers would sing, "but Camilo Torres died to live."[1]

Torres represents only a handful of guerrilla priests, among them Father Domingo Lain in Colombia, Father Gaspar García Lavina with the Sandinistas in Nicaragua, and Father Conrado Balweg in the Philippines. Their militancy may be a rare step, but the concept of Liberation Theology motivating them has spread so widely in Latin America that the continent could be classified as having a divided church. This presents a special threat to the Vatican since Latin America, already the base of Catholicism, holds 42 per cent of the world's 810 million Catholics. (France, Italy, and Spain, with the largest Catholic populations in the West, have 140 million.) At the present rate of population growth, at least half of all Catholics will live in Latin America by the year 2000.

It seems ironical that in lands where the church has always been allied with the aristocracy and military, the growth of Liberation Theology should come out of a fusion of poverty and the priesthood. As the overwhelming burden of poverty brought the clergy closer to the mass protests of the early 1960s, theologians such as Gutiérrez and Jean Luis Segundo of Argentina saw that the aims of the church must be inextricably linked to the political struggles of the destitute. Segundo called it a "revolution in the classic conception of Christianity."

Eighty per cent of the capital wealth was controlled by 5 per cent of the population of Latin America in 1984. In Brazil, a fourth of the people live in absolute poverty, and almost 43 per cent of the land is owned by one per cent of the aristocracy. In Peru, two-thirds of the work force are often unemployed or earn less than $38 a month. In El Salvador, a few families control property equal to that of 80 per cent of the people.

Liberation Theology called for the eradication of poverty to the exclusion of any other issue. "I am helping this poor man here. I don't care if he were a guerrilla, a religious or a non-Catholic," insisted Father Pedro Arrupe, retired head of the Jesuits.

Liberation Theology further demanded that the poor had to be "protagonists of their own liberation," as Gutiérrez expressed it. No longer would the church simply hand out charity or advise "patience and resignation," the traditional formula that many priests now opposed. The poor had to become their own vehicle of liberation: a revolutionary force, an "engine" of social revolt.

Leonardo Boff, the Brazilian theologian soon to be silenced by the Vatican, envisioned a "concrete theology related to daily life." No longer appeasing the poor in return for the promise of eternal salvation, the church would stress the "primacy of action." Gutiérrez concluded: "Universal love comes down from the level of abstractions and becomes concrete and effective by becoming incarnate in the struggle for the liberation of the oppressed."[2]

A major obstacle for Liberation Theology was creating a synthesis between the traditional spiritual quest of the church and the new emphasis on concrete action. Gutiérrez saw the solution in a constant reinterpretation of the Bible—"illuminating history with the word of the Lord of history," he described it. We must immerse the "gospel message in the concrete, in the here and now, if the transcendent is to be revitalized," he taught. "The universality of Christian love is an abstraction until it becomes a political reality."

Above all, Liberation Theology had to overcome constant accusations by the Vatican and many Latin American bishops that it was rooted in Marxism. It often makes use of Marxist dialectics. Raúl Vidales, a Mexican theologian, sees Liberation Theology as the "dialectical interplay between ongoing concrete history and incarnation of the divine message." Boff admits that "Marx and his comrades interest us to the extent that they help us better understand the reality of exploitation and point to possible ways of overcoming the capitalist system." Drawing on the most basic Marxist tenet, Gutiérrez insists that "class struggle is a fact, and neutrality in this matter is impossible."

Although all these liberation theologians claim they use Marx only as an analytic tool, there is a constant tension between insistence on class struggle and opposition to capitalism and the Vatican's traditional teachings. Father Avery Dulles, a Catholic University theologian in Washington, D.C., considers praxis—Marxist terminology for analyzing structures of injustice in order to achieve specific Marxist aims— "important for better understanding of the Gospel." But he warns it must not be made the "supreme norm of truth and morality." The Vatican charges that Liberation Theology depends primarily on praxis.

Jon Sobrino, a theologian from El Salvador, sums up this clash when he asks "whether the main interest of Liberation Theology is Christ or liberation."

Certainly, in its vehemence against U.S. intrusion in Latin America, whether Chile or Nicaragua, and against U.S. exploitation of the continent's economy, Liberation Theology draws heavily on Marxism. "The greatest danger in Latin America is not Marxism but capitalism," Boff insists.

Only a minority of Latin American bishops have supported Liberation Theology, and even fewer have dealt with the political forces that could implement it. Dom Helder Cámara, a Brazilian archbishop, calls for a "line of socialization adapted to Latin American needs." Sergio Méndez Arceo, bishop of Cuernavaca, Mexico, claims that "our underdeveloped world has no resource open to it but socialism." But neither defines a form that socialism would take or how it would be carried out. The problem, of course, is that except for a brief period in Chile, the continent has had little pragmatic experience to draw on. But a broader problem is that Liberation Theology is essentially inspirational. It wants to organize the poor, but it fails to describe the long-range ends of organizing.

Liberation Theology, in effect, speaks more of what it is against than where it is going. One of its prime targets is the backing of dictatorships and military governments by the partnership of the Vatican and the United States, using the cloak of anti-communism. "I don't understand why it is necessary to combat communism with fascism," Helder Cámara argues.[3]

The Vatican's stand against Marxism, by contrast, has been implacable for almost a century. It abhors the atheistic basis of Marxism. It rejects the concept of class warfare, Pope Leo XIII attacking the "notion that class is naturally hostile to class" in *Rerum Novarum* in 1891. Pius XI assailed Christian socialism as an enemy of capitalism and private property in *Quadragesimo Anno* in 1931. Six years later, he branded communism as "intrinsically wrong" in *Divini Redemptoris*.

Eventually, the Vatican softened its rigidity. Although *Gaudium et Spes* in 1965 reiterated the necessity of private property, it allowed for some public ownership when the ruthlessness of capitalism had to be tempered by critical human needs. In *Populorum Progressio* in 1967, Paul VI blamed rich nations for not doing enough to alleviate hunger and misery. In *Laborem Exercens* in 1981, John Paul II deplored the "disproportionate distribution of wealth and poverty" and called for a "levelling out and a search for ways to ensure just development for all."[4]

Liberation Theology became virtually the central issue at the Medellín conference in Colombia in 1968, attended by almost all Latin bishops and Paul VI, the first pope to visit the continent. Reflecting Sobrino's thesis that "institutionalized injustice" brought "institutionalized violence," much of the debate focused on popular uprisings. In *Populorum* the year before, Pope Paul had ruled that "any insurrection is legitimate in the very exceptional case of evident and prolonged tyranny that seriously attacks the rights of the person and dangerously harms the common good of the country. . . ." Could the church condone insurrection only against a Communist government as Pius XII had done in Hungary in 1956? Or were revolts against Latin dictatorships equally legitimate? The pope evaded specifics, but a critical test would come in Chile not long afterwards.

Eduardo Frei, a Christian Democrat, had been elected president in 1964 with the backing of the Central Intelligence Agency and the church. But when his pledge of land distribution and other reforms remained unfulfilled, the Catholic Left joined a six-party Popular Unity coalition behind Salvador Allende, the Socialist leader. Priests and nuns in the "Group of 80" would organize Christians for Socialism (CS), the first plunge by Liberation Theology into campaign politics.

After Allende's election to the presidency in 1970, he took certain socialist initiatives, such as land distribution and the nationalization of copper and a few other industries. Cardinal Raul Silva Henriquez of Santiago worked with the government at first. But by 1972, he charged that Christians for Socialism was committing the "Church and Christians to the struggle on behalf of Marxism and the Marxist revolution" and "turning Christianity into a ridiculous caricature by reducing it to a socio-economic and political system."

Fearing a Marxist base on the continent, the Nixon administration, through the CIA and Chilean land and business interests, had cut off financial aid, staged street demonstrations, and brought the country to the point of economic collapse. In September 1973, General Augusto Pinochet Ugarte toppled Allende in a military coup. Allende was murdered. As many as 20,000 of Allende's followers were killed and 80,000 were jailed.

Cardinal Silva now legitimized the Pinochet dictatorship in his speeches, and in a pastoral letter, the bishops of Chile thanked the general for saving the country from Marxism. But as murder and torture continued, part of the hierarchy tried to rescue the remaining Christian Socialists through safe havens and underground emigration. Silva himself seemed ambiguous. Father Gonzalo Arroyo, who had belonged to the Group of 80, condemned the "silence of the cardinal and most of the churches in general. . . ."

The next conclave of Latin American bishops at Puebla, Mexico, in 1979 reflected the Pinochet coup and the swing towards conservatism. The nonvoting delegates were largely handpicked by Cardinal Alfonso López Trujillo of Colombia and Father Roger Vekemans, a Belgian priest who succeeded in rigging the attendance and makeup of the conclave with $25 million a year from the West German Catholic churches and contributions from the ultra-conservative DeRance Foundation of Wisconsin. "So worried were the conservatives that the bishops at Puebla would be influenced by liberation theologians," reported Robert McAfee Brown, a U.S. Protestant theologian, "that the latter were unceremoniously excluded from entering the seminary walls within which the enclave was held." Friendly bishops had to pass them papers and notes each evening.[5]

In a critique of "socio-political radicalism" obviously aimed at Liberation Theology, Pope John Paul II warned the clergy at Mexico City that "you are not social directors, political leaders, or functionaries of a temporal power." Ignoring the military uprising against Allende, he would repeat constantly that social justice "cannot be obtained through violence." He insisted that the "Church does not propose a concrete political or economic model in its social doctrine. But it shows the way, presents principles."

Even if the Vatican ignored Allende, it had to recognize the increasing alignment of priests and nuns with worker and peasant movements and its consequent toll. In Argentina by December 1977, at least thirty priests were murdered by security forces. In El Salvador, at least seven priests were murdered between 1978 and 1981, and four North American women missionaries were murdered by the National

Guard in 1980. All told, almost a thousand clergy in Latin America were assassinated, imprisoned, or simply missing, accentuating the split between the militant clergy and Vatican support of dictatorships and military governments.

Archbishop Oscar Arnulfo Romero of San Salvador, who preached constantly against injustice and refused to cut his ties to the radicals, pointed out that "we do not overlook the sins of the left also. But they are proportionately fewer than the violence of oppression." Four of the country's bishops complained to the Vatican that Romero had been taken over by Marxism. On March 24, 1980, he was celebrating evening mass when a shot rang out and he fell near the altar. Rushed to the hospital, he died a few minutes later.[6]

Despite all attempts by the conservative hierarchy to suppress radical elements generally grouped under the banner of Liberation Theology, its principal offshoot—the Communidad Eclesial de Base, or "base communities"—has expanded volcanically. Each base consists of ten to a hundred people organized and led by the members themselves. While they often serve as an adjunct to the parish church and the local priest may be invited to meetings, they represent a sharp break from an ecclesiastical structure that has always been run from the top. They are a training ground in democracy. Decisions are made by a consensus of peasants and workers. Boff calls them a "new church" which has cut itself off completely from the "monopoly of social and religious power."

At least 90,000 base communities have sprung up in Brazil, a thousand in Chile, large clusters in El Salvador, Guatemala, Mexico, Nicaragua, and Peru—an estimated 150,000 in Latin America as a whole. "If you abolished them all, I don't know what would be left of the church," says Harvey Cox, a Protestant theologian at Harvard University.

At weekly meetings, the bases analyze their poverty and oppression through the Gospels, and often translate their conclusions into cooperative projects. At Campos Elyseos near Rio de Janeiro, they organized a health center. At Itabira, Brazil, they built a housing project; at Santa Fe, they built a day-care center and organized against rising utility rates. When a ranch owner sent forty men to take away a peasant's farm at São Benedito at a time such expropriations were often ignored by the government, the prayers of the base community "gave us the courage to back Manuel more in his cause, which is now in the courts," a member related. Moving into politics, legally, to be sure, but often suppressed by the conservative hierarchy and right-wing governments, base communities led demonstrations in Brazil after 1978 and were instrumental in organizing the Workers party. Similar political action has expanded to Peru and Venezuela.

But Nicaragua represents the most serious confrontation between a politicized church and the Vatican. Its base communities, known as the "People's Church," draw support from an estimated 75 per cent of all priests and nuns. Pope John Paul II may frame the issue in anti-Communist terms, but his real fear presumably stems from the reality of a divided church.[7]

Although Archbishop Miguel Obando y Bravo welcomed the Sandinista troops to Managua when they overthrew the Somoza dictatorship in 1979, the first provocation by the new government was the appointment of four priests to high posts. The pope ordered them to resign. All refused, including Miguel D'Escoto Brockman, the foreign minister, trained in the Maryknoll order outside New York City, and Ernesto Cardenal, minister of culture. "I cannot conceive of a God that would ask me to give up my commitment to the people," argued Cardenal.

The archbishop soon became the symbol of the anti-Sandinista opposition, condemning the Sandinistas as an "alien ideology." His attempt to purge the People's Church centered on Father Uriel Molina, head of the Antonio Valdivieso Ecumenical Center in Managua, which James Goff, a Presbyterian minister there, calls a "critical supporter of revolutionary social change." When Obando tried to force Molina to leave the country, he ignored him. Molina blames the pope for targeting him as the "head of the so-called 'popular church.' "

The archbishop's campaign meshes well with President Reagan's strategy. At Santa Fe, New Mexico, as a candidate in 1980, Reagan was already demanding that "United States foreign policy must begin to counter—not react against—liberation theology." Reagan's spokesman Patrick J. Buchanan inveighed against "liberated nuns and Marxist Maryknolls." The Maryknoll order has long trained clergy and lay volunteers to work with radical groups in Latin America, and published the most important texts of Liberation Theology.

U.S. Senator Jeremiah Denton (R-Alabama), a Reagan ally, held hearings before the Senate Security and Terrorism Subcommittee, which investigated the "influence Marxists have had on churches" but mainly tried to tar Catholic and Protestant clergy who had aided Liberation Theology in Latin America. Radical priests and nuns in the United States, in fact, are increasingly aligned with Liberation Theology, and the Quixote Center in Washington, D.C., dedicated to worker and peasant movements, has shipped $27 million in medical supplies to Nicaragua.[8]

In a quest for money that reflects the Vatican–White House coalition, Archbishop Obando went to New York in May 1984 to meet with officials of W. R. Grace, a corporation with extensive chemical holdings in Latin America. Its president, J. Peter Grace, is a conservative Catholic and close associate of Reagan's. Although there was no proof that Grace donated money, the archbishop explained he needed funds to train cadres for evangelical, not military, objectives, but he didn't rule out organizing to oust the Sandinistas.

For the Sandinistas, consequently, the pope is the "pope of the West, the pope of imperialism," and they claim that his objective is not only the destruction of the government but of the People's Church which supports it. The Sandinistas charge Obando with aiding the anti-government, "contra" guerrillas based in Honduras. After accusing a priest of supplying explosives to the contras, they deported ten non-Nicaraguan priests. They expelled one of Obando's bishops on similar charges and closed down the Catholic radio station.

While the church and Reagan administration see these acts as human rights violations, the Sandinistas consider them solely defensive measures. Father Robert Drinan, the former congressman, claims there is "no persecution of the church in Nicaragua." Father William Callahan, a Jesuit with Sandinista leanings, contends that the "number of priests and religious kicked out by the government totals about 30 while the bishops and Obando have forced upwards of 200 out [of the country] for being sympathetic with the revolution."

The Vatican assault on Liberation Theology intensified with the May 1984 issue of *30 Giorni*, a conservative Catholic magazine. It carried a cover with a satiric cartoon of a guerrilla priest, pistol on belt and bandana cloaking his face, saying mass in a jungle clearing. The lead article by Cardinal Joseph Ratzinger, prefect of the Sacred Congregation for the Doctrine of the Faith, hammered at clerical and lay Catholics who "identified with class." The pope continued this theme on his Latin American tour with another condemnation of those "considering the poor as a class in struggle."

Ratzinger got tougher in a thirty-six-page analysis of Liberation Theology in September 1984, branding it a "pernicious blend between the poor of the Scriptures and the proletariat of Marx." The most revealing sentence, however, in terms of the pope's dread of a divided church, was his admission that the Vatican itself was under siege. In Liberation Theology, the cardinal complained, a "critique of the very structure of the Church is developed."[9]

The pope obviously decided that none of these admonitions was taking effect, and that the next step was to single out one of the rebellious theologians. Notified that his teachings were "considered dangerous," Father Leonardo Boff, born in Brazil in 1938 of Italian parents and a former student at Munich of Karl Rahner, was summoned to Rome. In a show of support, two Brazilian cardinals and an archbishop accompanied him. The conclusions of Ratzinger's Sacred Congregation were harsh. Boff's work showed "evidence of Marxist teachings" and "endangers the sound doctrine of faith." He was sentenced to "penitential silence," no longer allowed to write or speak for the liberation movement.

The Vatican, however, misjudged the independence of the Brazilian church, stronghold of the Latin base communities. Ten Brazilian bishops signed a statement protesting Boff's punishment, and Rio de Janeiro and other Brazilian cities awarded him honorary citizenship. Noting that 50 per cent of Brazil's income went to landowners comprising one per cent of the population, Cardinal Paulo Evaristo Arns protested: "To struggle against that is not to promote class struggle, but liberation from merciless oppression."

Cardinal Ratzinger would not be stalled. In another pronouncement from the Sacred Congregation in April 1986, he reiterated that the church "should not be absorbed by preoccupations concerning the temporal order." A few months later, the Brazilian hierarchy crossed the Vatican again by criticizing the government for its delay in land distribution to poor peasants.

Pope John Paul II knew when to make a judicious retreat. In a conciliatory letter to the Brazilian bishops that granted the strength and importance of the base communities, he praised the bishops for adopting an "efficient praxis in favor of social justice and equality. . . ." Even the use of the word "praxis" smacked of the Marxist tone of Liberation Theology. On May 8, 1986, the Vatican removed Boff's punishment of penitential silence.[10]

The overthrow of President Ferdinand E. Marcos of the Philippines in February 1986 undoubtedly forced the pope to adjust his stand against the church's involvement in social justice and Ratzinger's "temporal order." Marcos, a devout Catholic, had long been considered by the Vatican as a bulwark against turmoil and dissent. In fact, Cardinal Jaime Sin of Manila complained that the "nuncio [papal representative] thinks we bishops should shut up and leave Marcos alone." The Bishops' Conference of the Philippines, of course, did just the opposite, branding Marcos's claim of election an "unparalleled" fraud and without "moral basis," and using Radio Veritas, the Catholic station, against Marcos.

Taking to the streets and blocking Marcos's tanks, priests and nuns were an important factor in the avoidance of civil war and the installation of Corazon C. Aquino as president. Much of the clergy had been radicalized by Liberation Theology. Father Balweg led the guerrillas in northern Luzon, and one priest estimated that 60 per cent of the nuns and 40 per cent of the priests in the Bacolod area were Communist sympathizers. "We don't care what ideology people choose as long as they approach it as Christians," Bishop Francisco Claver concluded.

In terms of U.S. constitutional principles, however, the involvement of the Philippine clergy in the selection of a president raises a troublesome issue. If Liberation Theology leads to partisan politics, can it be endorsed without accepting a double standard? The backing of Aquino was an obvious step towards social justice for the church. But was it tarnished by violation of separation of church and state? These questions imply that the United States can force its laws and traditions on other countries. But the unalterable reality is that the Philippines, Brazil, and most Catholic countries have never accepted separation and have no laws defining it. They cannot, consequently, be condemned for a theology that demands the poor and oppressed achieve their liberation by politics as well as religion, and the Catholic clergy in Latin areas cannot be judged by the constitutional standards required of the U.S. clergy.[11]

Liberation Theology, in the long run, calls for a church opposed to autocracy, whether of the Marcos variety or the Vatican's, a church that Father Sobrino calls "relational and not absolute," a church where the "Kingdom of God is greater than the Church." In condemning a hierarchy that acts "as if the Church was an end in itself, as if those possessing ecclesiastical authority stood above and apart from the Church as people of God," Sobrino, of course, attacks the power accrued by the Vatican for centuries.

His "New Church"—"returning the Church to its biblical roots"—corresponds to the model postulated by the radical nuns in the United States. It is a church that shuns the pomp of gilt-encrusted cathedrals, a "Church of the poor most like the Church that is a continuation of Jesus." It is this theme that unites Catholic radicals in Latin America as well as in the United States and many other countries, a theme that seems revolutionary today, but simply harks back to the most basic tradition of the church for social justice. The implications of Liberation Theology, springing from the concept of a democratically controlled church dedicated to the masses, haunt the present autocratic grandeur of the Vatican.[12]

XIII

Sanctuary: "The People Have Become the Church"

SISTER DARLENE NICGORSKI, an American Catholic nun, went on trial in 1985 on criminal charges that could bring a five-year jail term and fines as high as $10,000 on each count. She had been working in a child-care program in Guatemala four years before when government "death squads" harassed her church. Her neighbors were beaten, killed, or listed as missing. Her pastor was shot and killed.

Returning to her home in Arizona, Sister Darlene found that many Guatemalans who had crossed Mexico and escaped across the border were hiding in church-run "sanctuaries," terrified that U.S. immigration agents would ship them back to face arrest and possibly torture and death. Sister Darlene joined the sanctuary movement. Hiding these refugees because the U.S. government would not grant them political asylum, the Reverend John M. Fife of the Southside Presbyterian Church in Tucson explained, "We had people with torture marks on their body, people who were clearly fleeing for their lives, routinely turned down."

Sister Darlene, the Reverend Fife, three Catholic priests, and eleven other church workers were eventually indicted for providing sanctuary and brought to trial in federal court for what the government called a "conspiracy" against the United States. "If I have done anything," retorted Sister Darlene, "I am guilty of following the gospel."

While the sanctuary movement immediately clashes with the Reagan administration's policy on Central American refugees, its deeper significance is its challenge to the Catholic hierarchy, for sanctuary represents the most overt expression of Liberation Theology in the United States. Committed to the struggle against oppression of poor Hispanics, it is a movement that links the teachings of the Bible to a social and political crisis. "If the churches had spoken up in time against Hitler," insists Father William Davis of Pax Christi, an international Catholic peace group, "we might have stopped the Holocaust. Now we must act in time."[1]

Individual responsibility and action are the basis of the movement. *"Basta!* Enough! The blood stops here," announces the Reverend David Chevrier of Chicago's Wellington Avenue Church.

"We are seeing a wonderful thing—people of every faith taking action together on their own whether the hierarchy or institutional church approves or not," explains Father Eugene Brake, a Catholic priest from Washington, D.C. "The people have become the church," concludes Father Davis.

In fact, almost all U.S. bishops have opposed or ignored the sanctuary movement. Cardinal Joseph Bernardin of Chicago and Archbishop John Roach of Minneapolis–St. Paul—both former heads of the U.S. Conference of Catholic Bishops—demanded that the movement should not break immigration laws but concentrate on changing them. Bernardin opposed a public sanctuary set up by Chicago Catholics for a Salvadoran woman and her three children, and labeled sanctuary an illegal "political movement." Embarrassed, to begin with, by this moral refutation of the White House, allied with them on abortion and many other issues, the bishops are especially provoked by aggressive feminism that seeks to radicalize the church. "Women, often Catholic women, are the cutting edge of the movement," observes the Reverend John Steinbruck of the Luther Place Memorial Church in Washington, D.C.[2]

Of the sixteen indicted by the government in Arizona, eleven were women. Sister Julie Sheatzley of the Cincinnati Coalition for Public

Sanctuary insists that the "U.S. government should be indicted on charges of transporting through their deportation tens of thousands of refugees back to harassment, torture and possible death." Sister Darlene accuses the bishops of taking the "legal opinion of corporate lawyers instead of following the Spirit."

No more than ten or twelve Catholic bishops have openly supported sanctuary. In addition to consistent liberals such as Archbishops Raymond G. Hunthausen of Seattle and Rembert G. Weakland of Milwaukee, they come mainly from dioceses with large Hispanic populations. "There are no illegal aliens in the Catholic Church," declares Archbishop Roger M. Mahony of Los Angeles, whose constituency is at least half Hispanic. Speaking of the refugees, an aide to Bishop John J. Fitzpatrick of Brownsville, Texas, states that "we have no choice but to assist them for humanitarian reasons."

Father Anthony Clark, a Catholic priest from Nogales, Arizona, one of the sixteen indicted, calls the Catholic bishops a "bunch of cowards." Although the Presbyterians and Lutherans each donated $100,000 to legal defense for the sanctuary movement, among many Protestant contributions, the U.S. Conference of Catholic Bishops never gave a penny.[3]

It is not so much the immigration law that is being challenged; it is the Reagan administration's interpretation of it. The U.S. Refugee Act of 1980 clearly states that no refugee can be sent back to a country "where his (her) life or freedom would be threatened on account of his (her) race, religion, nationality, membership of a particular social group or political opinion." Applying the act in 1980 to the case of Haitian refugees, U.S. District Court Judge James L. King in Florida ruled that "no asylum claim can be examined without an understanding of the conditions in the applicant's homeland."

The Reagan administration, however, has consistently insisted that almost all those fleeing El Salvador and Guatemala, as a result of what they consider political oppression and the possibility of torture and death, are simply abandoning a depressed economy. They cross the border for jobs. "They are just peasants who are coming to the United States for a welfare card and a Cadillac," asserts Peter Larradee, director of the Immigration and Naturalization Service (INS) processing center at El Centro, California.

The administration's twisted interpretation of the law can be readily seen from admission statistics. In 1985 only one per cent of applications for asylum were approved from Guatemala, and only 3 per cent from El Salvador (rising slightly in the first half of 1986). By contrast, the administration has virtually created an open door to refugees from Communist-dominated countries, admitting 78 per cent of those applying from the Soviet Union in 1983, 44 per cent from Rumania, and 27 per cent from Poland (with partial 1986 figures considerably higher from Rumania and Poland). And the INS director in Florida announced in 1986 that no refugees would be sent back to Nicaragua since they could be persecuted by a government that the White House considers Communist-dominated.[4]

The Reagan policy obviously stems from politics, not from the humanitarian concept of the refugee act. Determined to prop up any civilian or military dictatorship in Central America that will block a Sandinista-type government, the president refuses to acknowledge that any opponents of these regimes can be legitimate refugees. Whether they come from a labor union, a base community, or any affiliation with Liberation Theology or Catholic dissent, they are automatically classified as radical troublemakers rather than as the victims of domestic turmoil. Reagan's sole purpose is to maintain the status quo no matter how destructive it may be of democratic standards. His refugee policy has become an extension of the arming of right-wing governments and CIA penetration that keep U.S. hegemony over most of Central America.

The sanctuary movement, consequently, has volatile political implications. It rises from humanitarian impulses and follows biblical teachings. Every sanctuary worker knows the risks of arrest and jail involved. But its complementary motivation calls for a head-on collision with the government's Central American policy and the need to reverse it. "Sanctuary is a dangerous movement," Father Davis confirms. "It not only confronts the authoritarianism of the Catholic hierarchy, but tears the mask from Reagan's right-wing alliances."

By combining religious fervor with political aims, sanctuary has provided a focus for radicalizing the mainstream churches. In the terminology of the left-wing Students for Democratic Society of the 1960s, sanctuary connotes "participatory democracy," individual involvement that draws people together in communities dedicated to a higher purpose. It appeals to Catholics fed up with the compromises of their hierarchy. Jack Elder, a Catholic layman who heads the diocese-run Casa Oscar Romero in San Benito, Texas, was one of the first sanctuary "conductors"—guiding refugees across the border—to be arrested. The members of St. Anne's, the smallest and poorest Catholic parish in Spokane, Washington, approved making their church a sanctuary by an 83 per cent vote.

Yet the movement remains predominantly Protestant. The first church to commit itself was John Fife's Southside Presbyterian in Tucson, Arizona, in March 1982. Almost all national organizations followed soon after—Methodists, Lutherans, Presbyterians, Church of Christ, and Unitarian-Universalists, among others. "We endorse public sanctuary as an ethical and legitimate response to the persecution of refugees and as a means of alerting the American people to the human cost of U.S. military policies in Central America," the American Friends Service Committee declared in 1983.

While only the reform wing of Judaism, the Union of American Hebrew Congregations, supports sanctuary so far, it was almost as if the mainstream religions had been waiting for a cause that combined religious principles and action. "The ground swell was waiting," Father Davis believes. "It was like a loaded gun ready to go off."[5]

All in all, at least 350 churches and synagogues—the number increases constantly—have joined the movement by 1986. The largest number are in California, forty in San Francisco's Bay area alone. But the movement has spread to local governments as well. At least fifteen city councils, including Chicago, Milwaukee, San Francisco, and St. Paul, have voted to make their territory a sanctuary. And Governor Toney Anaya of New Mexico declared his whole state a sanctuary.

The movement cuts across all political, economic, and ethnic lines. The Seminole Indian nation near Indiantown, Florida, harbors Guatemalan Indians. The Reverend Jesse Jackson's Operation Push in Chicago takes in Salvadoran families. William Clarke, president of a prosperous electrical contracting firm in Massilon, Ohio, convinced fellow parishioners to make the Central Presbyterian Church a sanctuary, arguing that "I'm a Republican, very conservative. I voted for Ronald Reagan. So I'm the last person in the world to be advocating civil disobedience."

The most striking historical parallel to sanctuary is the anti-slavery, or abolitionist, movement before the Civil War. It, too, had its roots in the churches and was driven by a theological fury. Its first leaders were Protestant ministers (the Catholic church was hardly strong enough to enter a national struggle). The Reverend John G. Palfrey of Boston defined abolition as a "mission to lead the way in redemption of a relapsed nation." The abolitionists were determined to redeem the country from the great moral stain of slavery. It was, in effect, a crusade to bring back the idealism of the American Revolution and cleanse the greed of a slaveholding class, and Northern industrialists cooperating with them.

Similarly, the sanctuary movement today sees the refugee deported to a Central American dictatorship as a victim of exploitation. He is being sacrificed to a form of slavery and possible death. He is a pawn of imperialism, a flyspeck in the administration's game of economic and political empire. In an era where almost every individual feels helpless before the threat of nuclear disaster, sanctuary offers a cause that can make a difference. It deals with morality and sin on a national level. It puts the participant at the center of power. It brings religion from the distant prospect of salvation to the here and now.

The parallels between sanctuary and abolition go even further. Sanctuary depends on the "higher law" thesis that was developed by Protestant ministers before the Civil War. When Congress passed the Fugitive Slave Act of 1850, sanctioning the pursuit of an escaped slave in Northern territory by a Southern slave-owner and the use of government arms to bring him home, the Reverend Theodore Parker of Boston demanded that the law be broken and the slave hidden and protected. "When rulers have inverted their functions and enacted wickedness into a law which treads down the inalienable rights of man to such a degree as this," Parker cried, "then I know no ruler but God, no law but natural Justice."[6]

The Reverend Thomas W. Higginson even insisted that the higher law required abolitionists to take up arms against government troops, and organized and led an attack party that stormed the Boston courthouse in an effort to free a captured slave. The rescue failed, but it took 2,000 federal troops to get the slave on a ship to the South. The government never again tried to deport an escaped slave from New England.

Sanctuary workers today, of course, are also breaking a federal law, or at least the administration's interpretation of the law. They must take the same risks today as the abolitionists in 1850. Again, they stake their case on higher law, on their humanitarian mission, on the word of God above law and administration policy.

The risks are not only immediate: the possibility of arrest and jail. They also entail the long-range justification for a religious and philosophic stance that may never be entirely supportable, for only history can prove the abolitionist or sanctuary worker right. Who could say for sure in 1850 that the hiding of an escaped slave would turn out to be a moral and righteous act in the context of the nation's direction a decade or two later? Who could say for sure in 1986 that every refugee given sanctuary was really escaping torture, or simply seeking a welfare card, as the government claimed?

The sanctuary movement builds its moral position by screening those it helps. At best, it can only get about six hundred refugees across the border and hide them each year, checking their backgrounds first if possible. These few rescues must be compared to the 1.2 million aliens arrested in 1985 as "illegal" by the INS—many, of course, being Mexicans who constantly drift back and forth across the border for temporary jobs. Describing the reason his church harbored a Salvadoran woman and raised money for her children still at home, Harvey Cox, the Harvard University theologian, concluded: "We know they need it because their father was killed five years ago by a death squad."

One couple, Brenda Sánchez-Galan and Mauricio Valle, was "conducted" by the Lutheran church from El Salvador to the Casa Romero sanctuary in Texas. Brenda's school had been raided by Salvadoran troops in 1980. She escaped to a Lutheran refugee center and worked there until its doctor was tortured for refusing to hand over the names of "subversive" patients. When the army tortured another woman worker, the Lutherans decided that Brenda and her husband had to be moved to Mexico City, where the Reverend Daniel Long, a Lutheran minister, arranged for underground passage across the U.S. border.

Gonzalo Lara Hartado—a more difficult case to check—had been a policeman and bodyguard for the Salvadoran junta before he rebelled against the killings and fled the country in 1982. When St. Luke's Presbyterian Church in Wayzata, Minnesota, provided sanctuary, the Reverend Richard Lundy, its minister, immediately informed the attorney general. The INS, as a result, had ample time to check whether Hartado was a legitimate political refugee, but it did not arrest him until three years later and after he had given one hundred fifty speeches throughout the community. Almost a thousand people picketed the INS office to protest the arrest. St. Luke's and the National Council of Churches showed their faith in his record by putting up a $50,000 bond, and Hartado applied for legal political asylum.[7]

The fate of political refugees not lucky enough to be rescued by the sanctuary movement but captured by INS agents and sent back to El Salvador was confirmed by an American Civil Liberties Union study in 1984. ACLU documents told how a sixteen-year-old refugee deported to El Salvador was abducted along with his mother and five younger brothers and sisters by the army's Atlacatl Battalion. None have been seen again. Two men deported by the INS in 1982 were picked up by armed civilians at a bus terminal. Five days later, their bodies were found with that of another man on a road near Santa Tecla. Two other deportees were abducted from their homes at night. A professor at the University of El Salvador, seized as he walked home after teaching class, is still missing and presumed dead.

The ACLU study was carried out against heavy obstacles. It first requested lists from the government under the Freedom of Information Act of persons deported from the United States to El Salvador for two years after March 1981. When the government demurred, ACLU had to go to court to eventually secure the names of 8,500 persons. It was an incomplete list, often just a name and no other identifying information, "a mere fraction of the total number of persons persecuted for political reasons since 1979," ACLU complained. Despite the scanty records available, ACLU was able to pin down 112 probable cases of persecution, including 52 political murders, 47 disappearances, and 13 unlawful political arrests. "As to the 7,400 other deportees whose names we obtained, we have no information regarding their welfare or fates," the study concluded.

The U.S. State Department, of course, has tried to prove that captured refugees can be deported without harm, and commissioned the embassy at San Salvador to make its own survey that claimed to cover 482 cases. But ACLU's analysis showed that "only 233 of the persons in that group were ever contacted in any fashion at all." Of that sample, only 120 were interviewed directly, 39 of them by phone.

The State Department's efforts to exonerate itself, ACLU concluded, "can be granted little credence."

Such statistics, however, hardly touch the depth of conflict between the sanctuary movement and the government. A sign at a Phoenix prayer service gives more understanding of the passions involved: "We have conducted 600 Central Americans to safety. We have saved 600 lives while the U.S. government has aided in the deaths of thousands. Who are the real criminals?"[8]

The strength of the sanctuary movement depends not only on its belief in its righteousness under a higher law, but on its acceptance of punishment. To stop the movement, James A. Corbett insists, the government is "basically going to have to put the church in prison." The government still fails to grasp the religious fervor and unity that sanctuary has brought to mainstream religion. When the first "conductor," a Protestant, was arrested a few years ago, bail money for his release of $27,000 was borrowed by a Catholic bishop, John J. Fitzgerald. After interviewing mothers in El Salvador "whose sons and daughters had been murdered by security forces [and] women political prisoners who were pregnant because they had been gang-raped by soldiers who captured them," Sister Maureen Fiedler announced angrily that she would "oppose U.S. foreign policy in Central America with every ounce of energy at my command."

Corbett, a lean, bearded, heavy-muscled Quaker, has transported more than a hundred Salvadorans and Guatemalans across the border. Originally a cattle rancher, he wears a battered cowboy hat and jeans on a typical trip into Mexico to meet a Salvadoran woman. Her husband, long active in a base community, has been abducted, and she may be the next target. He insists she rest a few days in a small hotel used by the movement. Then they set out at night across a terrain of rocky ledges, crawling through barbed wire barriers when they reach the border. They hide one night at a secret shelter in the chilly Sonoran desert, and make an exhausting uphill climb all the next day, finally rendezvousing with a car from Corbett's group that drives them to sanctuary in Tucson.[9]

Two of the first conductors were not as lucky. Stacey Merkt, a Methodist woman, was arrested by INS agents near McAllen, Texas, driving three Salvadorans to San Antonio. Sentenced to a 190-day jail term, she appealed to the U.S. Circuit Court. Jack Elder of the Casa

Romero was arrested while taking three refugees to a bus station in Harlingen, Texas. He served 190 days in "halfway house" detention.

But by going after sixteen indictments in January 1985, a group that included a nun, three Catholic priests, and a Protestant minister, the government obviously intended to make an example of the clergy and show its determination to crush the movement's clerical base. At the trial, moreover, federal Judge Earl Carroll forbade any testimony from the defendants that would bring out their moral and spiritual convictions. The case would have to be decided solely on the grounds of whether they had conspired to break the immigration laws or not.

The government, on the other hand, made no pretense of ethical standards in collecting evidence. It used planted informers with secret taping machines—a technique common in criminal investigations but hardly to be expected in dealing with churches. One undercover agent posed as a sanctuary conductor. Another agent, posing as a volunteer, brought his sound equipment into Bible classes and prayer meetings, and photographed license plates in church parking lots. The national bodies of the Lutheran and Presbyterian churches, joined by individual churches, were so disturbed by these tactics that they brought a countersuit against the government for violation of free exercise of religion on church property.

In a trial that lasted until May 1986, Sister Darlene was convicted on five counts and faced a possible twenty-five years in jail. Two Catholic priests and the Reverend Fife were also convicted along with the lay defendants. Judge Carroll must have decided that enough warning had been given the sanctuary movement in what was obviously intended to be a show of government power against religious dissidents. All of those convicted were put on probation. Three of the eleven defendants were acquitted; charges had previously been dropped against the others.

The opposition of the Catholic hierarchy to sanctuary stems from a calculated and strategic analysis of its own interests. It not only fears that a rebellious movement will erode its authority; it fears to strain its alliance with White House policy and become a partner in civil disobedience. At the same time, its long-range interests require drastic revision of the immigration laws. The Reverend Nicholas DiMarzio, who heads the U.S. Conference of Catholic Bishops' refugee services, told a Senate hearing in 1985 that "in many ways the future of the Catholic Church in the United States is connected to our response to the question of real immigration reform."

The Immigration Reform and Control Act, passed by Congress in 1986, however, mangles the problem of political refugees from Central America and Mexico. It presumes to give relief to illegals who arrived before January 1, 1982, by granting temporary residence as a step towards citizenship. But it ignores the dilemma of many illegals who would consider themselves safer by keeping their status secret than coming out in the open and identifying themselves to the government. Moreover, the bill imposes fines and imprisonment on employers who fail to check the legal status of their workers, setting up a potential witchhunt that could target any Hispanic-looking person, citizen or not, and may discourage many employers from hiring Hispanics altogether.

The interests of the Catholic hierarchy go far beyond the plight of political refugees. All immigrants crossing the U.S. border—an estimated 10,000 Mexicans crossed daily south of San Diego in 1986, 50 per cent more than the year before—work to the advantage of the church. Of an estimated 2.5 to 5 million illegal aliens in the United States, about 70 per cent are believed to be Catholics. The growth of a Hispanic bloc represents Father DiMarzio's "future." With upwardly mobile Irish, Italian, and other ethnic groups mainly limiting their children through birth control to two per family, the expansion of the Catholic constituency depends on Hispanics.

In the fifteen years prior to 1985, the Hispanic population in the United States increased 60 per cent. Population projections show that Hispanics will total 27 million—virtually half of all Catholics here—by the year 2000. Since they tend to cluster in cities, amenable as immigrants to religious authority, and since birth control has hardly limited their fecundity, Hispanics become the portent of renewed power for the church. An immigration bill that legalizes this tide of Mexicans and Central Americans should make the U.S. church a Hispanic church.[10]

The ironies are obvious, but the hierarchy knows how to exploit them. The Vatican may be threatened in South America by a People's Church built on Liberation Theology, and due in part to the poverty generated by the local aristocracy and U.S. exploitation. But poverty and political repression in Central America, by contrast, have driven many of its victims north. The Vatican can hold its base in South America by adapting to Catholic radicalism. It can greatly strengthen its base in the United States by countering the germs of radicalism with a new flood of job-seeking immigrants. The pattern resembles the immigration of the last century. Irish, Italians, and Poles built the church then. Hispanics may be the next building block.

Although Catholics are only a minority in the predominantly Protestant sanctuary movement, they are an important vanguard of dissent. Like the nuns who signed the abortion rights ad, their strategy is daring. It stirs the imagination of mainstream Catholics through its humanitarian ends, bringing hope to the poorest victims of Latin political oppression. The sanctuary movement, moreover, has done more for ecumenism than years of haggling between primates trying to settle the ceremonial formalities and dogmatic differences that have kept Protestantism and Catholicism apart. Sanctuary, above all, challenges the Vatican directly, for it has shifted responsibility from the top to the individual conscience. The growth of the Catholic conscience ensures the decline of Vatican autocracy.

XIV

"The Finest Document"—
The Bishops Against Nuclear War

I

FATHER GEORGE ZABELKA, the Catholic chaplain of the 509th Composite Group, blessed the *Enola Gay* before it dropped the first atomic bomb on Hiroshima. "For the last 1700 years, the Church has not only been making war respectable, it has been inducing people to believe it is an honorable Christian profession," he explained. "We have been brainwashed."

"All I can say today is, 'I was wrong,' " Father Zabelka concluded. "Christ would not be the instrument to unleash such horror on his people. . . ." Returning to the peace shrines at Hiroshima and Nagasaki in 1984, Zabelka recalled that he "fell on my face there after offering flowers at the shrines and praying for forgiveness for myself, my country and my church."

Father Zabelka represented one more step in the growing Catholic protest against nuclear war. Father Daniel Berrigan damaged warhead cones at a Pennsylvania factory in 1980 and received a five- to ten-year jail sentence. Nine priests, nuns, and lay Catholics were convicted for trying to assault nuclear submarines at Groton, Connecticut.

Two nuns were convicted in Denver for forging government passes and forcing their way into the Rocky Flat nuclear weapons plant. As these incidents brought growing pressure on the hierarchy, and a Gallup poll in 1982 showed that 47 per cent of Catholics favored a nuclear freeze, fifty-seven bishops added their support to Pax Christi, the international Catholic peace group.

By 1983, after meeting intermittently on the issue for almost two years, the bishops as a whole were ready for a momentous step: the publication of a pastoral letter on war and peace. It was the most direct intervention by the church in strategic and foreign policy in the nation's history. The Reverend Theodore M. Hesburgh, president of the University of Notre Dame, called it the "finest document that the American Catholic hierarchy has ever produced."[1]

"The Challenge of Peace: God's Promise and Our Response," as the letter was officially known, represented a sharp break with the past. The hierarchy's fervid anti-communism had previously made it support any war or nuclear buildup that might contain the Soviet Union. Most bishops hailed Francisco Franco's rebellion in Spain in 1936 as a crusade against socialism and communism. The Korean and Vietnam wars, with Cardinal Spellman as always a symbol of militancy, became, for the church, spiritual initiatives against the Chinese and Russian threat.

The pastoral letter, however, reshaped the hierarchy's whole approach to peace. Abandoning its support for the Reagan administration's nuclear buildup, the hierarchy weighed the use of nuclear arms against the attainment of peace. Nuclear war and international destruction were judged in moral terms. "We are saying," the letter pronounced, "that good ends (defending one's country, protecting freedom, etc.) cannot justify immoral means (the use of weapons which kill indiscriminately and threaten whole societies)."

The bishops' position was based, to begin with, on Jesus' preaching on peace which had guided the church for at least its first three centuries. But it drew as well on recent Vatican warnings. Pope John XXIII in *Pacem in Terris* in 1963 insisted that "nuclear weapons must be banned." Paul VI in 1976 told the United Nations that the "arms race is one of the greatest curses on the human race; it is to be condemned as a danger, an act of aggression against the poor, and a folly which does not provide the security it promises."[2]

The bishops were not only laying down Christian doctrine; they were willing to put themselves on the line in the heat of congressional debate. Before the House Committee on Foreign Affairs in 1984, they opposed Reagan's money bill both for twenty-one MX missiles and his "Star Wars" project. When the administration's request for $1.5 billion for the MX missiles came up again in 1985, Bishop James W. Malone of Youngstown, Ohio, president of the U.S. Conference of Catholic Bishops, again opposed it, demanding that the money be used for "human needs" and that the poor "should not now be asked to bear the burden of the arms race."

Here were the beginnings of a new type of hierarchy, responsible to an issue that carried the fate of all human beings. Only a few bishops had been involved in the sanctuary movement. Now the bishops as a body were fulfilling their most basic spiritual calling, even though it damaged other alliances with the White House. Moreover, the bishops produced the pastoral letter through a long process of democratic debate that drew on the viewpoints of lay Catholics as well as bishops and priests, and on Protestants and Jews as well as Catholics.

The bishops made it clear that the pastoral letter would not be formulated solely by rulers at the top. "We aren't claiming this is Almighty God handing down the truth from the mountain as with Moses," pointed out Bishop Daniel Reilly of Norwalk, Connecticut. Instead, they were acting as teachers. "We're offering this as a guide to conscience, not the way it was done in the past: 'We know best. This is the answer,' " explained Auxiliary Bishop Thomas Gumbleton of Detroit. "We are trying to engage the whole church in the same process the committee went through."

The bishops, undoubtedly, had to deal with nuclear war after increasing criticism, particularly from women inside and outside the church, that they had harped too long on abortion and similar sexual issues. "What is a woman to think?" asked Sister Joan Chittister, a former president of the Leadership Conference of Women Religious. "That when life is in the hands of a woman, then to destroy it is always morally wrong, never to be condoned, always a grave and unusual evil? But when life is in the hands of men, millions of lives at one time, all at one time, then destruction can be theologized, and some people's needs and lives can be made more important than other people's needs and lives?" Such critiques challenged the bishops to concentrate as much on the destruction of humans on earth as on the fetus in the womb.

Cardinal Joseph Bernardin of Chicago had launched his "seamless garment" thesis—the interdependence of all moral issues—to counter the unsavory publicity that followed Cardinal Bernard Law's claim that abortion ranked number one. Bishop Malone stressed the hierarchy's opposition to a " 'single issue' strategy because only by addressing a broad spectrum of issues can we do justice to the moral tradition we possess as a church. . . ."[3]

As far as abortion was concerned, however, the seamless garment thesis had a striking inconsistency. Other moral issues hardly affected any individual rights. When the bishops opposed capital punishment, the public could be little damaged by the substitution of a life sentence for execution. The ban on euthanasia affected increasingly fewer people as life-prolonging medical technology convinced mainstream Catholics of a patient's right to avoid a painful and lingering death. The pastoral letter on nuclear war affected no one's rights except conceivably those who insisted their security was threatened by limitations on the arms race. In effect, the seamless garment still offered moral choices except in abortion. Here, the bishops would not allow a woman any choice, even if her health or life was at stake. They demanded a total ban, imposing their religious morality on all others.

The pastoral letter, then, can hardly be considered an amplification of the seamless garment thesis. Rather, its significance stems from its risky plunge into military policy and its confrontation not only with the administration but with Catholic hard-liners.

The counterattack against the bishops was led by U.S. Congressman Henry Hyde, a Catholic and staunch ally of the church on abortion, who branded the pastoral letter nothing but unilateral disarmament. Phyllis Schlafly, that persistent gadfly of extremism, brought her pickets to ecclesiastical debates in Washington in 1982 and in Chicago in 1983, with banners proclaiming that "The Kremlin Smiles—Catholic Bishops Meet Today." As stalking horses for the White House, two officials—Secretary of the Navy John F. Lehman, Jr., in a *Wall Street Journal* article, and national security adviser William F. Clark in a letter leaked to *The New York Times*—implied that the bishops were practically tools of the Kremlin. The White House, in fact, used all its influence to manipulate the bishops' debate on the third draft, an intrusion that Archbishop Rembert Weakland of Milwaukee labeled "unwise and impolitic."

Castigating the pastoral letter in the *National Review* as "political opportunism," William Buckley observed that the "bishops are entitled to a presumption of moral attention, but there is no presumption of their enjoying a special knowledge on these matters." Michael Novak, Reagan's ambassador to the United Nations Human Rights Commission, complained that the bishops' "desire to speak like prophets is sometimes only hubris," and lamented that "this is not the faith that nourished me."

The split among the bishops was equally sharp at first. Archbishop Philip Hannan of New Orleans, a chaplain with the 82nd Airborne Division in World War II, raised constant objections during debate and demanded that the whole document be scrapped. Once he shouted at the assemblage: "I don't think you know what you're talking about at all, not having been in the war." After the final vote of approval, he vowed to appeal to Rome.[4]

Cardinal John O'Connor of New York, former chief of chaplains of the armed forces, represented the administration's demands for confrontation and nuclear buildup. He opposed the nomination of William V. Shannon, a history professor at Boston University and former ambassador to Ireland and *New York Times* columnist, to write the draft. Shannon, whom he labeled a liberal, decided not to take the assignment.

During the first draft debate, one participant complained that O'Connor "didn't just want to go back to 'square zero,' he wanted to go back to 'square minus-six.' " After agreeing to sections of the draft, he would insist on returning to them, attempting to water them down. The final draft called for a "halt" to the production of nuclear bombs. O'Connor fought to soften the word to "curb" but was defeated.

The most determined proponents of a strong pastoral letter were Bishop Gumbleton and Archbishop Raymond Hunthausen of Seattle. Gumbleton, once virtually isolated in preaching nonviolence, was president of Pax Christi. He opposed U.S. arms for the "contras" in Nicaragua and spoke out on so many controversial issues that his friends conceded he would never gain further promotion in the church. Hunthausen advocated unilateral disarmament, an extreme position among the bishops. He branded the Trident submarines, carrying nuclear missiles and based near his city, the "Auschwitz of Puget Sound." He risked federal indictment by withholding the half of his income taxes that went to the arms race. Accepting his guilt for the bombing of Hiroshima, he blamed himself for not speaking out "against the evil of nuclear weapons until many years later."[5]

Orthodox on most matters, Archbishop John R. Quinn of San Francisco was a radical on nuclear arms. He even introduced an amendment during debate to ban their use completely, but lost. He asked Catholic hospitals "not to comply with civil defense efforts since compliance might encourage the belief that civil defense was a realistic response to nuclear war." His most extreme position was to urge Catholics in the military to refuse an order—even from the president—to detonate a nuclear weapon, equating the possibility of disaster today with the disaster brought on by the failure of Catholic soldiers, among others, to resist the madness in Nazi Germany.

Quinn may have been compensating for the German church, which largely supported Hitler, and for Pope Pius XII's refusal to condemn Nazi atrocities. But his analysis was hardly realistic. The real responsibility today, as in 1933, had to be borne by mass resistance at the organization level, particularly by religious groups, political parties, and legislatures. The individual soldier, too easily a victim of court martial, could be effective only as part of a public revolt.

Between this clash of polarities at the bishops' debates, Cardinal Bernardin was the principal mediator for consensus. The professorial tinge to his arguments, the comforting appraisal that came from twinkling blue eyes, helped him to get his way almost before his opponents knew it. "When Bernardin makes waves, they're always smooth waves," a colleague noted.

The son of an immigrant Italian stonecutter who died when he was six, Bernardin was the only Catholic boy on his block in Columbia, South Carolina. He recalled that he went to a Baptist Bible school, "especially on the days when they gave out ice cream." After a year as a premedical student, he decided on the priesthood and was ordained in 1952. Twelve years later, he became the youngest auxiliary bishop in the country, helped to rebuild the Chicago diocese demoralized by Cardinal Cody, and was elected president of the U.S. Conference of Catholic Bishops.

As chairman of the committee of five bishops drafting the pastoral letter, Bernardin had to deal with two issues—"deterrence" and "no first use"—that provoked the most violent controversy during debates. Deterrence was the backbone of U.S. policy: amassing a stronger nuclear arsenal than the enemy in order to intimidate it against nuclear attack. Pope John Paul II, in a speech to the United Nations in June 1982, had already deemed it morally acceptable as long as it went with a determined program of disarmament. But deterrence involved many complexities, particularly whether its application could be limited to enemy troops and not civilian populations.

The bishops were generally skeptical of this "limited use" approach. While never conceding that any use of nuclear weapons was moral, they failed to condemn deterrence totally. The final pastoral letter reads: "Deterrence is not an adequate strategy as a long-term basis for peace; it is a traditional strategy justifiable only in conjunction with resolute determination to pursue arms control and disarmament." The bishops, in effect, had followed the Vatican and accepted deterrence for the time being as a necessary evil.

The pastoral letter was equally indecisive in dealing with "first use." Under this concept, the Reagan administration reserved the right to use nuclear weapons first if a Soviet offensive threatened to overwhelm Europe. The bishops would only "urge NATO to move rapidly towards the adoption of a no 'first-use policy'. . . ."[6]

Instead, the bishops put their faith in the principle of "proportionality," which restricted a U.S. response to a Soviet attack with conventional weapons to similar conventional weapons. Admitting that the very possession of nuclear arms could eventually lead to their use, the bishops still clung to the possibility of preventing a nuclear exchange following the start of conventional warfare. Father Bryan Hehir, who wrote the draft of the pastoral letter, conceded that this approach left a "centimeter of ambiguity."

All these compromises may have been necessary to achieve a consensus among the bishops, who approved the final pastoral letter by the remarkable majority of 238 to 9. The letter undoubtedly was a ground-breaking step for the church and opened up moral dimensions that seriously undercut the White House. But its critics saw it falling short of its promise. "A flawed document," charged William V. O'Brien, professor of government at Georgetown University. It failed to answer "its own ultimate question of the moral permissibility of nuclear weapons." Kermit D. Johnson, a major general and former chief of chaplains, insisted that "once the myth of nuclear deterrence is accepted even tentatively, all the rest follows."

"Unfortunately, to the extent that it seems to restore the preeminence of the just-war theory," concludes Gordon C. Zahn, professor emeritus at the University of Massachusetts and former director of Pax Christi USA, the pastoral letter "stumbles and falls short of the prophetic leadership the church and the world need at this critical 'new moment' in time."[7]

Even if such criticisms are valid, the ultimate test of the pastoral letter remains its impact on Catholics. Just after the bishops approved the letter, the House of Representatives voted on a modified nuclear freeze resolution. Catholic Democrats supported it by 82 to 4, and Catholic Republicans opposed it by 23 to 15. These figures, of course, reflect party-line voting, the hawkish stamp of the Protestant South, and other factors. But they still show the start of a Catholic trend against Reagan's nuclear buildup.

Father Andrew Greeley, the sociologist, claims that a more accurate picture of the Catholic shift can be seen in National Opinion Research Center studies. Before the pastoral letter was issued, 32 per cent of the country—the same for Catholics as Protestants—thought that "too much money was being spent on arms." By 1984, Protestant opinion remained unchanged, but Catholic support for the same statement had jumped to 54 per cent. While a 700-person sample could be considered statistically weak, Greeley believed—with no other verification—that the pastoral letter had changed the attitude of some 10 million Catholics. The letter's influence on Protestants has never been measured, but it was recommended to its membership by the National Council of Churches, and the Presbyterian church sent copies to all its 13,000 congregations.

The real problem was that the U.S. Conference of Catholic Bishops failed to follow its immediate breakthrough with a lasting program of lobbying and parish education. The bishops' lobbying against MX missile funds in 1985 started only four days before the vote, and the Senate approved the appropriation by 55 to 45. When 20,000 peace marchers carried a fifteen-mile "ribbon of peace" around the Pentagon and across the bridge to the Lincoln Memorial and up Constitution

Avenue to the White House, Sister Chittister complained that "practically no one noticed." An associate chaplain at a Catholic high school in Wilmington, Delaware, run by the Oblates of St. Francis de Sales, refused to pay his federal taxes for six years and gave the money to peace groups with 10 per cent added. Instead of backing this protest, the school board erased its meaning by paying the chaplain's taxes to the IRS.

A few militant bishops, by contrast, particularly Daniel Reilly and Leroy T. Matthiesen of Amarillo, Texas, attempted to apply the morality of the pastoral letter to the everyday lives of their parishioners. Focusing on those employed at nuclear arms plants, they admitted that such jobs did not entail a mortal sin, but that Catholics holding them should seriously examine their consciences. Matthiesen urged workers involved in the production and stockpiling of nuclear bombs "to resign from such activities and to seek employment in peaceful pursuits," and even offered to support their families until they could find other jobs. Few Catholics, however, were willing to take the risk and accept his offer, and the U.S. Conference of Bishops failed to implement what might have been a telling blow at the arms industry.[8]

Bishop Gumbleton, among others, continued to insist that the pastoral letter be strengthened, and Bishop Maurice Dingman of Des Moines, Iowa, and Auxiliary Bishop Peter Rosazza of Hartford, Connecticut, sought to have it placed on the agenda of the conference in 1985. Seemingly weary of debate, the conference brushed them aside.

It was almost as if the bishops were embarrassed by the furor they had stirred. Although it may have fallen somewhat short of an ideal moral statement, the pastoral letter was a remarkable achievement that gave the American hierarchy worldwide leadership. The pastoral letter enveloped the most fundamental human crisis and tapped a revolutionary energy that had long been absent from the church. The inability of the bishops to exploit this step indicated a failure of nerve. The struggle against nuclear buildup required not just theory but a long, grinding involvement that would jar the hierarchy's alliance with the Fundamentalists and Reagan administration. Once the bishops made their gesture at bringing nuclear arms into harmony with biblical teachings, for most of them, that was enough.

2

A second pastoral from the bishops, "Economic Justice for All: Catholic Social Teaching and the U.S. Economy," was as daring as the nuclear letter. An early draft, released on November 11, 1984, defined the U.S. economic system as "massive and ugly," and challenged capitalism's inherent concentration on wealth which, ironically, had enabled so many Catholics to rise to management and upper-income brackets in recent years. It thrust the church into an area considered far removed from religious expertise, and brought about another confrontation with the Reagan administration whose policies were strongly slanted towards corporate profits and individual gain. Here was added proof of a maturing hierarchy that was willing to grapple with critical issues even at the risk of disturbing much of its own constituency.

Drawing on Liberation Theology to the extent that it labeled discrimination against the poor a "scandal" and called for a "preferential option for the poor," the economics letter inferred the possibility of class conflict which had long been considered intolerable by Pope John Paul II. It was, indeed, a radical document. "No one is justified in keeping for his exclusive use what he does not need when others lack necessities," it declared. "Unequal distribution of income, education, wealth, job opportunities or other economic goods on the basis of race, sex or other arbitrary standards can never be justified."[9]

Such conclusions obviously required some form of redistribution of wealth—a leveling principle that made the Reverend Jerry Falwell attack the bishops for wanting "socialism which is nothing more than shared property." Yet the bishops are disturbingly ambiguous. Do they mean that a millionaire with three homes should give up one of them? Do they mean that an "open admissions" policy at colleges must be instituted across the country? Nor is there any indication of whether the government or private agencies have the responsibility for these changes. In fact, the bishops are almost never specific except in an occasional instance when they urge that "reforms should eliminate or offset the payment of taxes by those below the official poverty line." As a result, the economics letter presents a soaring vision of an egalitarian society with no mechanics for achieving it.

In the second draft in 1985, this vague radicalism was toned down sharply. The drift towards socialism, pinioned by Falwell, was replaced by a weaker admonition that "Catholic support for private ownership does not mean anyone has a right to unlimited accumulation of wealth."

The bishops now stress that the "preferential option for the poor" is "not an adversarial slogan, which pits one group or class against another." They also give added emphasis to the plight of the middle class, particularly to protection of the unions. "We firmly oppose organized efforts, such as those regrettably seen in this country, to use intimidation and threats to break existing unions and to prevent workers from organizing," the bishops declared.[10]

The second draft, consequently, comes much closer to previous Vatican doctrine. In *Quadragesimo Anno* in 1931, Pope Pius XI had already criticized overconcentration of economic power. In *Pacem in Terris* in 1963, John XXIII demanded that food, shelter, and income must be distributed more equitably, and Paul VI in *Populorum Progressio* in 1967 applied these conditions to Third World nations above all. John Paul II in a 1984 speech basically reached the leveling principle of the economics letter when he ruled that the "needs of the poor [should] take priority over the desires of the rich, the rights of the workers over the maximization of profits. . . ."

Even with its ambiguities and more pallid demands in the second, and third and final draft in 1986, the economics letter presented a slashing attack on the gap between wealth and poverty that resembles the beliefs of Liberation Theology. It deplores a poverty rate that has "increased nearly a third" since 1973 and stresses the frightening trend that has given "54 per cent of the total net financial assets [to] two per cent of all families." The bishops are particularly incensed by the high proportion of blacks and Hispanics among 33 million Americans categorized as poor by official standards, and another 20 to 30 million categorized as needy.

The letter, moreover, does not spare President Reagan's priorities, blaming his obsession with the Soviet Union for his disregard of poverty, insisting that the allotment of "so much of the national budget to military purposes has been disastrous for the poor and vulnerable members of our own and other nations."[11]

Remarkably, the debates over the economics letter at three annual meetings of the National Conference of Catholic Bishops were far less bitter than over the nuclear pastoral, and much of the credit was due to the skilled chairmanship of Archbishop Rembert G. Weakland of Milwaukee. He had an intimate knowledge of poverty: his mother could barely support six children growing up in western Pennsylvania after their small family-operated hotel burned down and her husband died shortly after. Weakland still managed an ambitious education, taking a master's degree in piano at the Juilliard School of Music in New York, which became the basis of later studies of the medieval sources of the "Play of Daniel" and his transcribing them for many Pro Musica Antiqua performances. At the age of twenty-two he became a Benedictine monk. Promoted rapidly, he was made primate of the world order and an archbishop at the age of fifty. He lives simply; he gave up his predecessor's mansion for a small apartment dominated by a grand piano. His campaigns against nuclear buildup and for ordination of women quickly brought him into the radical wing of the bishops.

The economics letter, in fact, was tarred as a symbol of growing radicalism in the hierarchy. A group of conservative Catholics, prominent in business, politics, and economics, and calling themselves the Lay Commission on Catholic Social Teaching and the U.S. Economy, issued a critique of the letter the day before the bishops gave it to the press in 1984, and again before the final draft in 1986. Among its members were J. Peter Grace, a Reagan confidant; Clare Boothe Luce, a former congresswoman and ambassador; William Ellinghaus, former president of AT&T; Alexander M. Haig, Jr., President Reagan's first secretary of state; and William E. Simon, secretary of the treasury under Nixon. Since the critique's principal author was Michael Novak, it was dubbed the "Novak Club."

Setting the tenor of the counterattack, Admiral Elmo R. Zumwalt, Jr., a former chief of naval operations, claimed that the bishops totally ignored "that what works most efficiently is that which flows from greed." Simon branded it a "Santa Claus wish-list," contradicting "our deep beliefs in the market system and its capacity for self-correction." What was needed, Simon concluded, was a "larger pie, not a redistribution of the existing one."[12]

The critique was not just a panegyric to capitalism, but an unabashed resurrection of the "trickle down" theory seemingly discredited after its failure during the Depression under President Herbert Hoover. It laid almost total emphasis on the infallibility of the "market system" while virtually glossing over the ravages of American poverty, implying that a "self-correcting" market would rescue increasing thousands of workers dumped into permanent unemployment often after twenty or thirty years with one firm.

The critique's emphasis on greed also required that benefits from the market system should not be shared with others. Foreign aid, according to its analysis, "often helps the poor very little, is often mishandled by the elites and does little to empower the poorest." While these points had occasional validity, they hardly excused the richest nation in the world for shirking all responsibility towards developing economies.

No explanation was given as to how the average worker could apply the virtues of greed to his own advancement, unless the celebration of such green-mailing and takeover heroes as T. Boone Pickens and Ivan Boesky in the last decade established them as the role models for entrepreneurial success. Insisting, above all, that the government should be kept out of the marketplace, the critique blithely ignored government rescue operations which had financed Chrysler, Continental Illinois Bank, and other giants until they regained their competitive strength.

Admittedly, the bishops' letter had some naïve assumptions. But its great contribution was to focus attention on the successes and failures of capitalism and the plight of the poor, and it may have slowed down Reagan's cuts in grants and services. In terms of the hierarchy's own interests, moreover, the bishops' strategy may have been eminently rational. Recognizing that by the turn of the century over half the membership of the church would be Hispanic, and preponderantly poor, the bishops hoped to strengthen their hold on this bloc by emphasizing the problems of poverty and their determination to eradicate them.

Still, courageous as they were in confronting the defects of capitalism, the bishops could never achieve the impact of Liberation Theology in Latin America. Thousands of priests, and even some of the hierarchy, in the Latin church had been aligned with the poor for decades on a daily basis, joining their marches in the streets and helping to build their base communities as a social and political instrument. Above all, Liberation Theology had not shrunk from applying Marxist and socialist solutions to the needs of the Latin poor. It was this pragmatic quality that the Conference of Catholic Bishops avoided. Their rhetoric lacked application. Along with the nuclear pastoral, the economics letter marked a shift in the direction of the church. But both were exploratory documents that could be fulfilled only when the bishops embarked on deep and lasting programs of education that would convince Catholics that national policy had to be changed.

XV

"Epic Change": 1984–1986

T HIS is not a foot in the door, this is an epic change," exulted U.S. Senator Jeremiah Denton, principal sponsor of the Equal Access Act, after its passage by Congress in June 1984. Equal Access allowed students to conduct religious services, prayers, the singing of religious hymns, and readings from the Bible and other religious works on public school property after school hours. It was, indeed, a critical step in President Reagan's campaign to "return God to the classroom," William Safire, *The New York Times* columnist, pointed out.

While the nuclear and economics letters of the bishops applied the highest principles of humanitarianism to critical problems affecting every individual, Equal Access meant that the hierarchy had returned once again to legal enforcement of its special religious interests on the country. Nothing in recent years so well represented the rising power of the Catholic-Fundamentalist alliance. Denton was a Catholic, and pressure for the bill had come from many parishes. He was also a senator from Alabama, speaking for a preponderance of Fundamentalist voters in his state. He was, in addition, a highly conservative Republican and a close ally of the president's. Here was the alliance functioning with remarkable efficiency.

In the *Williamsport* case, testing a parallel situation to Equal Access, the U.S. Catholic Conference had filed a brief which insisted the law did not infringe First Amendment separation but was simply an "accommodation." This was an increasingly important approach for the alliance. The constitution, the bishops claimed, "affirmatively mandates accommodation, not mere tolerance, of all religions and forbids hostility to any."

The U.S. Court of Appeals for the Third Circuit, however, did not see it that way. Religious meetings on school property, it ruled, would be "encouraging religious practice" and segregating students "along religious lines."

The case had started when a group of students in Williamsport, Pennsylvania, began to hold religious meetings after their high school classes ended. The lawyer for the school board thought their prayers and religious songs violated the First Amendment, and John C. Youngman, a school board member, Republican lawyer, and elder of the First Presbyterian Church, challenged the students in federal court. When the court of appeals ruled against them, the case went to the U.S. Supreme Court. But since the Court decided that Youngman did not have legal "standing" to sue in the first place, the Court's decision in March 1986 never dealt with the constitutional issues. Congress had already passed Equal Access, so it remained judicially untested for the time being.[1]

Congress, to be sure, had tried to set up safeguards in Equal Access against First Amendment violations. All religious events had to be held after school hours, and they had to be organized and run by the students themselves. Neither teachers nor school officials could influence the form or content of meetings. Persons from outside the school could not direct these functions nor attend them regularly.

Still, the dangers in a law that Denton had described as more than a foot in the door, were obvious. A dominant student group could try to proselytize students of other religions. "Outsiders"—the Fellowship of Christian Athletes had already gained entry to many school programs—could get around the bill's safeguards by rotating ministers, priests, and athletic stars who attended the meetings. Even worse, hate groups, extremist cults, conceivably the Ku Klux Klan, could call after-school meetings under Equal Access. William Safire thought that the bill permitted "the Atheists Club, the Pot & Booze Society—

not to mention the Ronald Reagan Gay Rights Marching Band—to use school facilities in defiance of local wishes."

All these dangers had been stressed by the Lutherans, the American Jewish Congress, and other mainstream religious groups when they opposed the bill in Congress. But there was a significant split in their ranks. The National Council of Churches approached Equal Access in terms of free speech. The bill would bring "religion up to equality with other kinds of speech," the council claimed. Even the American Civil Liberties Union withdrew its objections once it became convinced that safeguards against compulsory attendance at religious meetings had been made strong enough. The long-standing conflict between the free speech guarantees of the First Amendment and its ban on the establishment of religion had reached a disturbing point of tension.

No safeguards could really eliminate the consequences of religious divisiveness that the court of appeals had warned against in *Williamsport*. When Presbyterian students at Boulder High School in Boulder, Colorado, requested a classroom for after-school prayer, other Protestant groups and Jewish groups opposed the move. Both sides gathered petitions. Parents took up the argument at school board meetings, and the debate became bitter. Eventually, the board decided that the only way to avoid a permanent split was to ban any after-school meetings on the premises that were not directly related to the teaching curriculum.[2]

Although the same pattern of conflict emerged in other school districts, and many boards delayed on Equal Access until the U.S. Supreme Court had decided the constitutional issues, the Catholic-Fundamentalist alliance persisted in trying to push religion into public schools. The primary objective had always been the right to hold prayers in the classroom during school hours.

To implement the campaign for a constitutional amendment, a delegation of bishops visited the White House four times in three weeks during April 1984. Seventy per cent of Catholic children were now enrolled in public schools, and the Knights of Columbus called an amendment "vitally important." Senator Denton, the mastermind of Equal Access, organized a lobby from the Catholic Daughters of America, the Knights, and other groups to pray for the amendment on the Capitol steps.

Always catering to his religious constituency, President Reagan in his State of the Union message on January 25, 1984, told Congress, "If you can begin your day with a member of the clergy standing right here to lead you in prayer, then why can't freedom to acknowledge God be enjoyed again by children in every schoolroom across this land." Coleman McCarthy, the *Washington Post* columnist, observed that Reagan has "turned God into a special interest with himself as its chief Washington lobbyist."

The president, to begin with, was ignoring an obvious difference between Congress and the classroom. No member of Congress had to attend an opening prayer. Children were a captive audience. If they insisted on leaving class during prayer, they could be subject to the taunts of their peers. Young minds, moreover, were far more susceptible to molding and proselytizing than those of adults in Congress.

The prayer lobby also brushed aside previous U.S. Supreme Court decisions. The *Engel* case in 1962 had dealt with a nondenominational prayer developed by the New York State Board of Regents for compulsory use at the opening of each public school day. Although proponents argued in court that a student could remain silent, Justice Hugo Black for the 6 to 1 majority (one vacancy, one justice ill) ruled that prayer was a "religious activity" inconsistent with the Establishment Clause.[3]

The *Schempp* and *Murray* cases, decided by the Court in a single opinion in 1963, dealt with a Pennsylvania state law requiring ten verses of the Bible to be read without comment at the start of public school days. The Court rejected the argument that Bible readings could be considered the study of literature or history, and deemed them an organized and compulsory classroom function and thus unconstitutional. Government must maintain a "strict neutrality, neither aiding nor opposing religion," Justice Tom Clark ruled for the 8 to 1 majority. "The breach of neutrality that today is a trickling stream may all too soon become a raging current and, in the words of Madison, 'it is proper to take alarm at the first experiment on our liberties.' "

Despite the Court, Catholic conservatives and Fundamentalists pressed the issue. It was as though school prayer could remedy all the ills of the country, suddenly halting the current of sexual permissiveness and decline in moral standards that the right-wing alliance thought was at the root of every problem. Prayer could bring children, in fact, the whole country, back to the path of righteousness. The clash over a constitutional amendment, consequently, represented a deeper clash over how society should be run.

When the debate reached the floor of Congress, the anti-amendment groups tried to keep it in a framework of purely religious interpretation. "We didn't want the Fundamentalists to say, 'See, it's the secularists against the religious people,' " observed the Reverend Charles Bergstrom of the Lutheran Council in America. "We wanted to keep this at the level of people who believe in God disagreeing with each other."[4]

The Senate killed the prayer amendment on March 20, 1984, 18 Republicans joining 26 Democrats in a vote falling 11 short of the two-thirds majority needed for passage.

Still, legislatures in West Virginia, Massachusetts, and many other states tried to circumvent this defeat by passing amendments requiring "silent prayer" in the classroom for a minute or so at the start of each public school day. An Alabama statute, challenged by Ishmael Jaffree, a black lawyer with three children at public school, finally reached the Supreme Court. Speaking for a 6 to 3 majority on June 4, 1985, Justice John Paul Stevens warned again of the "myriad, subtle ways in which Establishment Clause values can be eroded," and ruled the Alabama law unconstitutional because it had as its "sole purpose" the fostering of religion in the classroom.

The frequent result of school prayer was religious divisiveness that could affect Fundamentalists as well as sectarians and non-believers. In the scrub-brush country of Oklahoma's "Bible belt," for example, Jo Ann Bell belonged to the Church of the Nazarene in the town of Little Axe, and Lucille McCord to the Church of Christ. Both women and their husbands objected to the school board requirement of organized prayer.

When Bell's children refused to join class prayers at the start of the day, they were kept out of the building until prayers finished, not even allowed in the restroom, "not even if it was raining," Bell recalled. When McCord's son "refused to bow his head in prayer before games," she reported, "he was not allowed to compete in sports" and other students "put upside down crosses on his locker." Bell's minister barred the whole family from church.

After the Bells protested at a school board meeting in 1981, other parents shouted, "Atheists, go home!" Jo Ann Bell related, "We were hit, we were shoved, we were spat upon, we were called atheists and communists by other parents who we thought were our friends."

Driving her young daughter to classes one day, she was attacked in the parking lot by a school employee and dragged from her car. "Except for my husband being there, I would have been killed," she stated. As it was, she had to be hospitalized. Shortly afterwards, the Bells made an out-of-town trip, and their trailer home was destroyed by fire.

Both the Bell and McCord families filed suit in federal court, and the judge ordered a halt to school prayer. But when they received mock obituary notices of their own deaths in the mail, they decided it was time to move from Little Axe. Summing up their stand, Lucille McCord insisted, "Let us believe what we want to, and let everyone else believe what they want to."[5]

Spurred by their success with the Equal Access bill, the Catholic-Fundamentalist alliance concentrated on promoting government funds for parochial school students. It had made some headway already: Minnesota's tuition tax-credit bill, based on the sophistry that government money was not allotted especially to parochial students, had been approved by the Supreme Court in the *Mueller* decision. But tax credits gave only indirect help. President Reagan's secretary of education, William Bennett, wanted a "voucher" plan that would put an average of $600 per child annually directly into the hands of parochial school parents.

The device Bennett proposed in his legislation was to award these vouchers to 4.8 million children already receiving federal assistance in remedial programs under Chapter I of the Education Consolidation and Improvement Act of 1981. In New York City, for example, such programs were taught by public school teachers right on the premises of parochial schools. Although religious symbols had been removed from Chapter I classrooms at St. Brigid's in Manhattan (and many parochial schools), all other rooms displayed crucifixes, and there was a two-story-high cross on the outside of the building. Of course, remedial programs could have been held on public property, as the Board of Education originally requested, but Catholic officials refused.

When the use of public teachers and public money on parochial premises was challenged as a violation of church-state separation in the *Felton* case, the Supreme Court ruled in a 5 to 4 vote on July 1, 1985, that such programs involved a "symbolic union of government and religion" which "inevitably results in the excessive entanglement of church and state."

A parallel *Grand Rapids* case tested the use of Michigan education funds at forty parochial schools. Public school teachers had been sent to parochial institutions to teach remedial and "enrichment" courses. Or in some instances, parochial teachers like Kenneth Zandee at Christian High School were moved overnight to the Grand Rapids public school payroll. The Supreme Court also ruled this type of program unconstitutional since it subsidized the "religious functions of the parochial schools by taking over a substantial portion of their responsibility for teaching secular subjects."

As a result of *Felton*, many school boards had to invoke extraordinary maneuvers to comply with the Court. New York City, for example, puchased seventy vans, which were parked outside parochial schools and served as remedial classrooms, although some students in Chapter I programs were sent to nearby public schools, the logical alternative in the first place. Even this approach met unexpected obstacles. Hasidic girls, members of an ultra–Orthodox Jewish group, went to a Brooklyn public school. Since Hasidic tradition prohibits mixing between sexes and with other faiths, school officials put up a partition to separate them from the rest of the students, who were mainly Hispanic. The Hispanic parents, however, protested this "segregation" and went into federal court to block it. The Board of Education finally agreed to teach the Hasidic children at a "neutral" site.[6]

Secretary Bennett, meanwhile, had his own problems. Members of Congress charged that his "voucher" plan deviously ignored the Supreme Court. "No, we are not trying to run around *Felton*," Bennett protested. U.S. Congressman Augustus F. Hawkins (D-California), chair of the House Education and Labor Committee, labeled the voucher plan "irresponsible." With Bennett's bill stalled in Congress throughout 1986 and eventually withdrawn, the secretary had to find circuitous routes to funnel more money to parochial schools. In a pattern repeated in many areas, St. Peter and St. Paul Catholic School in Boonville, Missouri, had its allotment doubled since 1981. By contrast, the public school allotment was cut 40 per cent.

There were always ways to circumvent legislative and judicial restrictions. Despite a 1970 amendment to the Michigan constitution banning public funds for parochial schools, later modified by a state supreme court decision, almost $13 million in state money went to special education in the 1983–84 school year, $9 million went to transportation, $10 million to auxiliary services, $8.6 million to school meals, and $8.1 million to shared time programs. Parochial schools got a further $11 million in federal money.[7]

In all these efforts to blur the line of separation between church and state, President Reagan became an aggressive catalyst. The *Lynch* case, decided by the U.S. Supreme Court in March 1984, involved a sensitive religious issue. At Christmas time in the heart of the shopping district of Pawtucket, Rhode Island, the city government had placed and maintained with public funds a crèche or nativity scene, consisting of the Christ child and two angels being worshiped by kneeling figures. The Court would have to decide whether a local government had the constitutional power to sponsor what was generally interpreted as a religious symbol.

It hardly seemed a case for White House intervention, but almost certainly on White House orders, Rex E. Lee, the U.S. solicitor general, made a motion for federal intervention on the side of the city of Pawtucket. Such intervention usually requires a case of overriding federal importance, but Lee's explanation was that "religion is part of our heritage."

By a 5 to 4 vote, the Supreme Court agreed. Characterizing a crèche as a "passive symbol," Chief Justice Warren Burger for the majority ruled that it simply depicted the "historical origin of this traditional event long recognized as a national holiday." He added, as if to downgrade its symbolism, "In many respects, the display requires far less ongoing, day-to-day interaction between church and state than religious paintings in public galleries."

In his dissenting opinion, Justice William Brennan argued that a crèche had no "clearly secular purpose," and that the aim of keeping Christ in Christmas was certainly not secular. The most troubling aspect of the Court decision was that it undercut the concept of a pluralistic society, derogating the "belongingness of citizens of other faiths or of no faiths," the Reverend Dean Kelley of the National Council of Churches protested. For Dean Norman Redlich of New York University School of Law, the Pawtucket crèche represented "government support for a central tenet of a religious belief that many Americans do not share."

In the corollary *Scarsdale* case in 1985, the Supreme Court by a 4 to 4 vote (one justice was ill) upheld the approval of a crèche in Scarsdale, New York, by the U.S. Court of Appeals for the Second Circuit. Here, the crèche had been erected and maintained on public property by a private organization, and the issue was access to a public forum for religious speech or symbolism. The crèche cases indicated an increasing trend by the Court towards accommodation in church-state matters.[8]

The efforts by the Catholic hierarchy to influence public policy often showed a duality in its leadership, an adherence to the rigid authoritarianism of the past at the same time as it was struggling to take a progressive stand on nuclear control, the American economic system, and finally, on South African apartheid. While many mainstream Protestant and Jewish groups had long divested themselves of stock holdings in South Africa, it was not till September 1986 that the National Conference of Catholic Bishops, speaking for a church "whose religious and moral teaching is daily contradicted by apartheid," condemned this racist government.

The importance of the move was in strange contrast to the church's hostility to another minority, the homosexuals. Cardinal O'Connor of New York had always been the main Catholic bludgeon against homosexuality, and his vehemence was so sustained it had come to be accepted as an aberration. But suddenly Cardinal Bernardin of Chicago, generally listed in the liberal camp, turned out to be a duplicate of O'Connor.

When a bill that would guarantee the civil rights of homosexuals was introduced into the Chicago City Council in 1986, the political consensus was that it would pass with the votes of at least thirty aldermen. Then Bernardin condemned the bill in as violent a language as ever used by O'Connor. Defections began, and soon Alderman Juan Soliz concluded: "Given the opposition of the archdiocese, I am forced to vote against the ordinance. I don't think any of the Hispanic aldermen can vote for it." The bill was defeated by a vote of 30 to 18.

The issue here is not church teaching itself. Certainly, any religion can set its own sexual standards, contrary as they may be to the changing ethic of society in general and even of its own constituents. Any religion can preach to its members and try to educate the nation at large in its beliefs.

What is really at stake is the line between dogma and civil law. Legislation that guarantees a minority the same rights in jobs or housing as all others is a different matter than the church's position on whether homosexuality is a sin or not. By going beyond its function to preach and educate, by relegating a whole group of citizens to the realm of outcasts, the church is not only negating its own humane mission, but using its power over legislation to force its theology on everyone.

Even more disturbing is the Catholic role in attacking, burning, and bombing abortion clinics. In 1984 there were twenty-four incidents of violence against clinics and in 1985 their number had increased to 224. While there is no way to measure the difference in Catholic and Fundamentalist participation, the Catholic hierarchy, as a highly centralized organization, has proved dismally inactive in condemning this use of violence itself.[9]

After his earlier arrests for breach of peace at clinic demonstrations, the Reverend Edward Markley, a Catholic priest, was charged with assault for forcing his way into a Birmingham, Alabama, clinic, threatening a woman worker alone on the premises and smashing up surgery rooms with a sledgehammer. Markley was sentenced to five years in jail. Instead of condemning this act, Markley's superior, Bishop Joseph Vath, seemed to condone it by stating that "the right to life certainly supersedes the right to property or to privacy." Even Cardinal Bernardin, in one of the rare comments by the leadership, took a similar stance in his explanation that "violence begets violence." The same theme echoes through Fundamentalist writings. Cal Thomas, the Moral Majority's executive vice president and a syndicated columnist, titled his article in the *Los Angeles Times*: "Bombing Abortion Clinics—It's Violent, But Why Not."

The pattern of arrests would indicate that participants—generally recruited from "right-to-life" groups—are not casual adherents to violence but join a planned series of clinic attacks. In 1984, for example, Michael Bray, a member of the ironically named Pro-Life Non-Violent Action Project, was arrested by agents of the U.S. Bureau of Alcohol, Tobacco and Firearms for carrying out the bombings of two Planned Parenthood offices and seven abortion clinics in the Washington, D.C., area. Bray was convicted in U.S. District Court and sentenced to jail for ten years. The conviction was overthrown on a technicality, and he was re-tried and sentenced to six years.

A former Benedictine monk, Joseph Scheidler, in fact, has turned clinic violence into an organized and sophisticated strategy with his published manual "Closed: 99 Ways to Stop Abortion." In describing his techniques during a three-day conference in Florida in 1984, attended by six hundred recruits, Scheidler gave a glimpse of his philosophy when he announced, "I have yet to shed my first tear when I see a charred abortion clinic."

As head of the Pro-Life Action League, and a constant organizer of clinic picket lines and demonstrations, Scheidler was finally arrested in April 1986 for trespassing on the premises of the Delaware Women's Health Center in Wilmington. A few months later, he was named as a defendant in a lawsuit brought by the National Organization for Women, charging him and his associates with a "nationwide criminal conspiracy" under the Sherman Anti-Trust Act to drive abortion clinics out of business. This was the same legal procedure previously used successfully against the Ku Klux Klan. By early 1987, the Scheidler case had still not come to trial in U.S. District Court in Chicago.

The FBI director, William H. Webster, refused to characterize clinic bombings as "terrorism" (as similar attacks on blacks had been characterized by the government during civil rights protests) since the attacks had not been caused by a "definable group or activity." Government agencies eventually became more conscientious about hunting down clinic bombers and arsonists, but the president still had no hesitancy in inviting Scheidler to the White House with an anti-abortion delegation.[10]

The refusal of almost all Catholic bishops to condemn violence against clinic personnel and patients—when they have been so vehement about violence against fetuses—represents a peculiar moral failure. Bishop Vath—and other bishops who never corrected him—undoubtedly realize they are not just talking about property that can be damaged or premises illegally entered. When they condone Catholic and Fundamentalist demonstrations that often erupt into blows and beatings, they are condoning the possibility of serious personal injury to someone whose only fault is believing differently than they do. When they assume that violence begets violence, and shift the blame to the victims of bombing and arson, they are actually condoning the possibility of a target's death.

The reach for power by the Catholic-Fundamentalist alliance has produced a new scapegoat, a dangerous-sounding enemy it calls "secular humanism." Like the red scare of the Joseph McCarthy era, the more elusive and indefinable this opponent, the more threatening it becomes.

Secular humanism is mainly the product of Fundamentalists, but Catholic conservatives have latched on to this device as well. Speaking at a mass in St. Patrick's Cathedral in New York in 1986, Cardinal John Krol of Philadelphia proclaimed that "We should denounce the forces of secular humanism, of the public school establishment. . . . " Any proponent of public education was thus tagged with an ominous nomenclature.

Determined to eradicate what he considers secular humanism's influence on the public schools of Hamburg, New York, James Likoudis, vice president of the International Association of Catholic Laity, concentrates on the danger of sex education. "Prayer was taken out. Why is it different in the case of sex education?" he demands. Phyllis Schlafly, the Catholic head of the Eagle Forum, wants to cleanse public school studies of such diverse topics as nuclear war, human sexuality, and "anti-nationalistic, one-world government or globalism curricula." In her estimation, Holocaust studies amount to "child abuse."

Under right-wing religious pressure, Congress, too, has assailed secular humanism. In an amendment he tacked on to a public school funding bill, U.S. Senator Orrin G. Hatch (R-Utah), a Mormon spokesman, managed to ban any money going to "courses of instruction, the substance of which is secular humanism." The problem is that the act never defines the meaning of secular humanism. But in issuing its regulations, the U.S. Department of Education ruled that a definition depends on the "local educational agency," giving a sizable latitude to school boards controlled by Catholic conservatives or Fundamentalists.[11]

First used officially in a footnote to one of Justice Black's opinions in 1961, secular humanism was defined by *The New York Times* as a philosophical attitude that puts man "at the center of things," that does not include a "belief in theism and a personified God," but "tolerates all religions while accepting none." Rejecting anything that could be described as supernatural or otherworldly, it upholds "human experience and scientific knowledge."

In actuality, however, Fundamentalists and Catholic conservatives have lumped into secular humanism everything from evolution to ecology and the women's movement, whatever conflicts with their own religious tenets. In trying to ban a first-grade reader from the school curricula, a group of parents in Church Hill, Tennessee, took particular offense at one sentence: "Jim cooks while the little girl reads." One father explained that the sentence has already "planted in the first graders' mind that there are no God-given roles for the different sexes."

Organized by the Concerned Women of America, a group that intends to purge secular humanism from the books and curricula of at least two thousand school districts by 1987, the campaign has concentrated on Alabama and Louisiana as well as Tennessee. In Alabama, it was financed by the Reverend Pat Robertson's Freedom Council Foundation. In Louisiana, it forced out of the schools three environmental science textbooks, which supposedly promoted "radical social and political philosophies and practises." A special object of concern was the treatment of the dinosaur in support of the theory of evolution. The works of Homer, Nathaniel Hawthorne, and Ernest Hemingway have been accused of containing secular humanism. All told, by 1982, 56 per cent of schools nationwide that responded to a questionnaire of the National Council of Teachers of English's Committee Against Censorship, reported attacks on their library materials.[12]

The latest strategy in this campaign is to force schools through legislation and court action to give equal class time to "Creation Science"—the biblical teaching on God's creation of man—as schools give to the theory of evolution. In this twisted vision of reality, the scientific basis of evolution, supported by every reputable expert after a century of research, must be wiped out, and evolution treated as nothing more than a principle of faith.

This approach was tried in a Texas case, *Wright* v. *Houston Independent School District*, in 1972. But the federal district court dismissed a request for an injunction against the teaching of evolution, pointing out that if equal time was given "Creationism," it would also have to be given to Christian Science teachings on health and disease and Mormon teachings on racial inequality.

The recent emphasis has been to push through state legislatures a "Balanced Treatment of Creation-Science and Evolution-Science Act." "It is arrogant and naïve for us to assume that we can have control of the national Government if we don't have control of school boards," Garry Jarmin, a conservative political consultant told *Education Week*. Forty-two per cent of the school systems in the South have a policy of teaching creationism alongside evolutionary theory, compared with a national average of about 30 per cent, according to a study by the American Association of School Administrators.[13]

In March 1987, a federal district judge in Mobile, Alabama, gave further impetus to this campaign by banning forty textbooks from public schools on the basis that they promoted the "religion of secular humanism."

The biblical version of creation has thus been transformed into science. Every word of the Bible must be taught in schools as scientific truth. Already this legislation has been passed in Arkansas and Louisiana, and introduced into the legislatures of other states. It was ruled unconstitutional in the *McLean* case in the U.S. District Court in Arkansas, and similarly struck down by the U.S. Court of Appeals for the Fifth Circuit in the *Aguillard* case in Louisiana. *Aguillard* was appealed to the U.S. Supreme Court and declared unconstitutional on June 19, 1987, by a 7 to 2 vote.

As religious extremism tightened its grip on politics, a federal judge from the center of this turmoil—Thomas A. Wiseman, Jr., chief judge of the U.S. District Court of Tennessee's Middle District—warned: "Use of the mechanism of government to enforce momentary majoritarian morality upon which there is no real consensus, creates greater divisiveness in society, disrespect for law, and worse, disrespect for the moral authority of the particular religion." Here was the crux of the danger posed by the Catholic-Fundamentalist alliance: that its reach for power would stamp one religious morality on all others without achieving a consensus of all society. Consensus was essential to the survival of the First Amendment, for the imposition by law of one religious viewpoint could divide society into warring factions, and eventually destroy our cohesiveness and stability.[14]

XVI

Pluralism in Jeopardy

THE EXCOMMUNICATION of Mary Ann Sorrentino on January 21, 1986, by the Providence, Rhode Island, diocese raised troublesome questions involving the meaning of power in the Catholic church today. She had been executive director for nine years of the state's Planned Parenthood office, which provided abortion as well as contraceptive services. It was the first publicly announced excommunication in the country in almost twenty-five years, and to add to the symbolism that the diocese obviously gave her ouster, a church spokesman branded her "Public Enemy No. 1." But what was even more significant was that the papal pro-nuncio in Washington had approved the act.

Here was high drama staged by the Vatican, certainly intended to inflict a lesson on the American church. Pope John Paul II was warning millions of Catholics that no infringement of the church's teaching—whether on abortion, birth control, or anything else—could be excused on the basis of individual conscience. What Sorrentino provided her patients may have been legal under the constitution, but it was illegal for the Vatican. The crackdown had begun. The pope would tolerate no more deviation.

Yet Mary Ann Sorrentino's response raised a different aspect of the meaning of religious power. "I am a Catholic and will always be a Catholic," she announced. "I love this church, and I'm going to work to change it from the inside."

It would seem that Sorrentino was informing the pope that it was not his church alone. She had been born into it forty-three years before, her family bred in it for generations, nourished by its mysteries and its path to salvation, warmed by its images and prayers. She was saying that the church was far more than what the pope commanded it to be, and that she and anyone else labeled a dissenter by the Vatican, still had the right to consider themselves Catholics, and live their lives as they believed the Gospels ordered them, even if denied the rites of the church.[1]

This is the theme that dominates the struggle in the church today. When the Reverend Charles E. Curran, a professor of theology at Catholic University in Washington, D.C., was told by the Vatican in 1986 he could no longer teach theology because of his deviation from accepted thinking, he announced that he would fight his ouster, in the courts if necessary. "I find myself at home in the church, and it's as much my church as anyone else's," he insisted.

Obviously, such a stance would constantly provoke a confrontation with the Vatican. But the attitude of the dissenters was that the church could be gradually changed, at first among the sisterhoods and in a few parishes, eventually in an expanding number of dioceses.

The Vatican persisted in teaching even its youngest constituents the meaning of power. When an eleven-year-old girl announced her support of the right to abortion, she was dismissed from her Catholic school in 1986 by the bishop of Toledo, Ohio, and told not to return until she had repented her error.

What had emerged over the last few decades was a massive rebellion against Vatican authoritarianism and a counteroffensive from Rome to whip dissenters back into line. It was not just prominent figures, such as Sorrentino and Father Curran, who claimed that the church belonged to them as much as to the pope. A *New York Times/ CBS* poll in late 1985 showed that 79 per cent of all Catholics thought they could disagree with the pope on abortion, birth control, and divorce and still qualify as good Catholics. Young Catholics particularly were challenging the pope, only 25 per cent calling him infallible on matters of faith and morals.

On abortion, the most sensitive of all controversial issues, Peter

Hart Research showed that 68 per cent of Catholics supported the U.S. Supreme Court decision legalizing it. Fifty-two per cent in 1985—up from 40 per cent in 1980—agreed that "a woman should be able to get an abortion if she decides she wants one no matter what the reason," according to an ABC News/*Washington Post* poll.

A Gallup poll found that 59 per cent of Catholics considered premarital sex acceptable. Sixty-two per cent favored the option of marriage for the priesthood, and 52 per cent favored ordination of women as priests in the *Times* poll.[2]

This rebellion against Vatican teaching was reflected at the voting booths on two recent election days. In November 1985 the voters of Bristol, Connecticut, a city with a 70 per cent Catholic population, had the chance to decide in a referendum whether or not they wanted to overturn the Supreme Court decision legalizing abortion. Despite the usual influence of parish priests in a working-class city, abortion rights was supported by 56 per cent. In two New Hampshire referendums that year, also in towns with sizable Catholic populations, abortion rights gained 65 and 60 per cent of the vote.

The same pattern was repeated on election day in 1986. In Rhode Island, a state with 67 per cent Catholic population, an anti-abortion referendum was defeated by 65 per cent of the vote. In Massachusetts, which is about half Catholic and where the hierarchy made a special attempt to sway voters, a similar referendum was defeated by 58 per cent. In Oregon, only 12 per cent Catholic, a referendum was defeated by 54 per cent. Only in Arkansas was the vote even close, the anti-abortion referendum losing by a few hundred votes. This would seem to indicate that the Fundamentalist clergy have a stronger grip on their parishioners than the Catholic clergy, and that the Vatican and hierarchy cannot control their constituency on many issues, particularly in geographic areas where they lack Fundamentalist support.

All the evidence from polls and referendums adds up to a phenomenon that is drastically changing the church. Father Andrew Greeley, the sociologist, calls it "selective Catholicism." From National Opinion Research Center studies, he concludes that four-fifths of regular church attenders justify this rebellion against the Vatican "by an appeal to God's love over institutional church authority."[3]

What this means is that four-fifths of American Catholics are guided by their individual consciences. It bears out a split in the church that

particularly affects women, who have refused to accept Vatican dic-
tates on issues concerning their sexuality. Despite the fact that 26 per
cent of American families with children are headed by single parents,
overwhelmingly women, Vatican dogma has taken almost no account
of the changes in marital relationships.

It might be logical to conclude that this rebellious constituency—
a rebellion abetted by Catholic achievements in higher education and
income levels that place the average Catholic family income just behind
Episcopalians, Jews, and Presbyterians—has seriously damaged the
control of the Vatican and the hierarchy. Yet power cannot be measured simplistically. In political terms, the Catholic bishops have gained
enough national influence over legislation by their alliance with the
Fundamentalists and the Reagan administration to make up for most
losses among their own dissenters.[4]

Politics, of course, often depends on a focused campaign. With
their skill at turning out thousands of hard-core lobbyists in Washington and state capitals, the bishops have shown their ability to
influence a few crucial votes on the ERA in Illinois or to pressure the
Chicago City Council against a civil rights bill for homosexuals. The
alliance with the Fundamentalists has given the Catholic hierarchy
the further advantage of huge TV and radio networks to pound away
at issues in which they have a joint interest. Media impact is insep-
arable today from political control, and it is no accident that the
flamboyance and pugnacity of Cardinal O'Connor pushes him far more
often onto the front pages of *The New York Times* than less controversial
Protestant bishops, who are likely to be buried in an inside column.

The Vatican and hierarchy, moreover, have always measured political domination in centuries rather than years. The dissenters in the
American church may be a distasteful annoyance for the time being,
but the bishops know that one power bloc rises up to replace another.
If they are losing their influence among upwardly mobile Irish- and
Italian-Americans, they will soon have a majority bloc of Hispanics
destined to become a compliant base for the church by the year 2000.

Since the fourth and fifth centuries, the Vatican has always depended on an Inquisition mentality to crush dissent, and it is so built
into its psychology that even today punishment and excommunication
remain techniques of control. Any unwelcome force can be met with
a suitable counterforce. After almost two millennia of competition

with monarchs and potentates, the "one, true church," which only admitted Protestant heretics recently to the level of "separated brethren," deals with today's rebellions, not by burnings at the stake but by putting dissenting minds through the same ordeal of fire.

Mary Ann Sorrentino can be dismissed in a simple stroke, but the case of Father Curran becomes more complex. A priest and a distinguished theologian, he already had some experience in challenging the Vatican by organizing seventy-seven other theologians in 1968 in a protest against *Humanae Vitae*, which continued the pope's ban on birth control. The Vatican may have branded Curran's teaching in direct conflict with its doctrine when it ousted him from Catholic University in August 1986 and forbade him to function as a professor of Catholic theology, but his teachings actually correspond to what most American Catholics have long believed and practiced.

On abortion and euthanasia, Curran wrote: "One can be justified in taking truly individual life only for the sake of the life of the mother or for a value commensurate with life itself." Contraception and sterilization, he insisted, "can be good or evil insofar as they are governed by the principles of responsible parenthood and stewardship." Homosexuality "in the context of a loving relationship striving for permanency can in a certain sense be objectively morally acceptable."[5]

Curran argued that the ideas the Vatican outlawed were in the "non-infallible" area of papal doctrine. Although Roman theologians with access to Pope Paul VI had declared that *Humanae Vitae* was not "irreversible," Cardinal Joseph Ratzinger of the Sacred Congregation for the Doctrine of the Faith rejected the difference between non-infallible doctrine and any other. All Catholics must follow to the last detail the "authentic magisterium" laid down by the pope. Here was a pronouncement of special significance, for the pope was determined to bury once and for all the thesis of "selective Catholicism." The conflict involved academic freedom as well as Vatican authority. Although Catholic University operated under a papal charter, Curran insisted that open and unhindered expression of ideas must be maintained. At least seven hundred U.S. and Canadian theologians supported him. But the church was increasingly split: a similar number in the conservative Fellowship of Catholic Scholars, and letters from hundreds of other theologians, backed the Vatican. Curran claimed forty to fifty bishops were with him, but as expected, Bishop James

Malone, president of the National Conference of Catholic Bishops, sided with Rome.

In a further effort to stifle dissent, the Vatican was circulating a "Proposed Schema" that would bind all teachers at Catholic colleges throughout the world to rigid church orthodoxy. Almost all presidents of U.S. Catholic institutions, including the Reverend Theodore M. Hesburgh of Notre Dame, signed a statement against it. The theologian Hans Küng, an early rebel, concluded that, "If it is no longer possible to tell the truth about, for example, *Humanae Vitae*, then we do not know what Catholic theology is taught for."[6]

What it came down to was whether Curran or anyone else had the right to debate ideas from a Catholic platform that were contrary to "authentic magisterium." The pope was determined to enforce unquestioning obedience. Curran represented the onrush of forces that demanded the ascendency of conscience over the official line. A monumental conflict was in the offing.

It was one thing, of course, for the Vatican to deal with a rebellion among theologians and nuns—the nuns who had signed the ad, insisting there were many options on abortion, had still not recanted by the end of 1986. But dissent among American bishops went to the core of Vatican control. No one had really known its extent until Father Terrance Sweeney, a Jesuit, sent a highly sensitive questionnaire to all bishops, and unexpectedly 145 (or almost half) responded. Of these, 24 per cent said they favored the right of a priest to have the choice of marriage or celibacy. Thirty per cent wanted women to have the right of becoming deacons. Twenty per cent approved the recalling of married and resigned priests to the active ministry.

Considering that about 100,000 priests have left the church in the past twenty years, these results were bound to upset the Vatican. In fact, Cardinal Ratzinger, according to Sweeney (or Sweeney's immediate superior in another version), ordered in 1985 that the study be destroyed. Instead, Sweeney refused, released the study to the media, and resigned from the Jesuits.[7]

Archbishop Raymond G. Hunthausen of Seattle would become the highest American prelate in recent times to be the subject of Vatican punishment. Whichever of a long list of his supposed transgressions angered the Vatican most, whether opening his cathedral to a homosexual mass, the use of young women to serve at the altar, or his generous approval of marriage annulments, nothing he did seemed to merit the scope of Vatican wrath. The real issue is why the pope singled him out for extraordinary punishment. After Hunthausen was investigated for years and his case seemingly closed with appropriate warnings, a large part of his responsibilities—morality in health care, liturgical and parish programs, among others—was transferred in 1986 to his auxiliary bishop. Father Richard P. McBrien, head of the University of Notre Dame's theology department, said that, "As a theologian, I don't know of any instance like this before." Rick Anderson, a *Seattle Times* columnist, thought it left Hunthausen "with nothing more to minister than the check-in counter at the Catholic Seamen's Club."

By virtually stripping the archbishop of his authority, the pope was undoubtedly putting all U.S. bishops on notice that no deviance from his policy would be tolerated. Other bishops protested, including Matthew Clark, John Fitzpatrick, Leroy Matthiesen, and Francis P. Murphy, but there was no way of gauging the size of the rebel bloc. Bishop Thomas J. Gumbleton called the punishment "clearly unjust and demeaning." Pax Christi USA warned that it would "increase the polarization within the Catholic church of the U.S."

When all bishops gathered in their National Conference in November 1986, they affirmed their fealty to Rome. Although they sympathized with a censured colleague and "embraced him as a brother," they agreed that the pope's curb on Hunthausen's authority "deserves our respect and confidence."

But the turmoil could not be quieted that easily. Grappling bluntly with the whole issue of dissent, Archbishop Rembert G. Weakland of Milwaukee surmised that, "What could evolve is what happened in Holland, where a large portion of the church gave up on the institution and said why worry about that and went their own way."[8]

Dissent in the hierarchy and among the Catholic constituency may seem to be only an internal problem for the church. Yet it has far larger ramifications. Many of the issues over which dissenters have clashed with Rome—birth control, abortion, and homosexuality, among others—are also issues in American public policy and represent the Vatican's attempts to stamp its morality on that policy. Dissent in the church, as a result, is closely bound to the Vatican's desire to impose its views upon Protestants, Jews, and all Americans, and reveals its threat to the fundamental American principle of separation of church and state.

The separation principle has always been alien to the church, and the Vatican, in large part, has failed to accept it. "To wish the Church to be subject to the civil power in the exercise of her duty is a great folly and a sheer injustice," Pope Leo XIII proclaimed in his encyclical, *Immortale Dei*, in 1885. "Separation, well considered, is only the baneful consequence—as We have often declared, especially in the Encyclical, *Quas Primas*—of laicism, or rather the apostasy of society the [sic] today feigns to alienate itself from God and therefore from the Church," Pius XI stated in *Dilectissima Nobis* in 1933.

Such proclamations can be brushed off as the rhetoric of a half-century or more ago. It was in 1940, too, that Cardinal Spellman referred disparagingly to the "shibboleth of separation of church and state." But these words become more ominous when applied to a specific political struggle. And the Vatican continues to think that they must be applied. The Republic of Ireland, of course, is a predominantly Catholic country, but Prime Minister Garret FitzGerald, a devout Catholic, felt in 1986 that some changes had to be made in the total ban on divorce, which had always been imposed on civil law by the church. He introduced a constitutional amendment, to be voted on by the electorate, aimed at alleviating the suffering of disastrous marriages that still locked both parties together for the rest of their lives.

The amendment had another important purpose. It was meant to prove to the majority of Protestants in Northern Ireland that the republic was not a theocracy disdainful of minority rights, and that its acceptance of other viewpoints could eventually make a union of all Ireland possible.

Although the amendment called for only modest changes, only applicable after a couple had lived apart at least five years, Pope John Paul II refused to accept the slightest relaxation of Catholic dogma, and he and the hierarchy campaigned against it furiously. The amendment, consequently, was turned down by 64 per cent of the voters. Reflecting on the implications for Catholic and Protestant unity, John Hume, the leading Catholic MP politician for Northern Ireland, asked: "Why should Protestants in Northern Ireland be expected to welcome a united Ireland some day if the Republic to the South votes in an election on the word of the Pope?"

Similar intervention by the Vatican and the hierarchy in the political process has long disrupted the American concept of church-state separation. The fear that he would be taking orders from Rome seriously hurt Al Smith's candidacy for president in 1928, and these fears were calmed only by the election of President John F. Kennedy in 1960. Almost without exception, Catholic officeholders have proved their allegiance to the separation principle. The choice between religious beliefs and the Constitution, as Justice William Brennan of the Supreme Court explains it, is clear: "As a Roman Catholic, I might do as a private citizen what a Roman Catholic does, and that is one thing, but to the extent that that conflicts with what I think the Constitution means or requires, then my religious beliefs have to give way."[9]

The Catholic hierarchy, unfortunately, has differed drastically from the Catholic officeholder in its approach. The clearest statement of the separation principle comes from Justice Hugo Black's majority opinion in the *Everson* decision in 1947: "Neither a state nor the Federal Government can set up a church. Neither can pass laws which aid one religion, aid all religions, or prefer one religion over another." Yet the hierarchy has persistently sought to have Catholicism favored over other religions—whether through government funds for parochial schools, or by legislating prayers in public schools—even at the cost of a furious backlash from other faiths.[10]

It is this backlash, this resulting divisiveness, that could threaten the fabric of society. American pluralism—the compact that all groups must respect the rights of others—has flourished in this country only under the protection of the separation principle. When one group tries to force by legislation its morality and beliefs on others, pluralism can be damaged seriously. No matter how strongly the Catholic hierarchy may believe that parochial aid, or any other objective, is morally right and beneficial to the country, it must limit its ambitions to education and persuasion until a consensus has been secured.

The forging of a consensus is never easy. We know its risks from history. The Volstead amendment of 1919, outlawing alcoholic beverages, was the product of a puritanical ethic, mainly in rural Protestant America, convinced that its code of behavior would uplift all others. The amendment turned out to be a disaster. Although Congress and enough state legislatures had passed it, few people respected the law. Breaking the law, whether through bootleggers, speakeasies, or brewing a personal concoction, became a national pastime. Even members of Congress and the White House took part in the game, and this experiment in moral compulsion was repealed just fourteen years later.

The anti-slavery issue started from a moral basis also, stirred by the liberal Protestant clergy of New England. Yet they were only a shrill minority and religion remained peripheral. It was not until an increasing proportion of the country realized that slavery was a complete negation of the promises of the Declaration of Independence that morality and politics became fused. What free and what slave states would be admitted to the Union, whether an industrial economy or agricultural feudalism would decide the nation's direction—these and other decisions were inextricably mixed with the abolition of slavery.

In the end, the moral aspects of slavery were translated into politics only after a consensus had been hammered out in the North and Midwest. This is the lesson for the Catholic hierarchy and the Fundamentalists today. A moral position is difficult to impose. It can be achieved only when the broadest consensus of the population supports it. Even this wrenching process finally split the free and slave states in 1860, and it took the bloodiest of civil wars to hold the Union together and abolish slavery.

The Catholic hierarchy, of course, has as much right as any religion or any other group to forge a national consensus by lobbying and educating the public. But it threatens the separation principle, however, when it assumes it can take preference over other religions by violating the U.S. Tax Code and supporting or attacking political candidates who agree or disagree with its views. This happened when Cardinal Medeiros of Boston attacked two congressional candidates with abortion rights platforms in 1980. And it has happened increasingly over the last decade as bishops and priests, despite official warnings and a federal court suit to stop them, have continued potential violations of the law.

Consensus can never be achieved through a divisive policy that harms other religions. Nor can it be achieved by shutting out all debate among parishioners, a policy invoked by Cardinal O'Connor of New York. When O'Connor in 1984 ruled that no Catholic "in good conscience" could vote for a candidate favoring abortion rights, he was not only using the power of the church to influence an election probably in violation of federal law, but he was dividing the Catholic community as well.

The Catholic voter now had to choose between his civil and religious responsibility. And the Catholic officeholder or candidate was saddled with the stigma that had plagued Al Smith and may plague a Catholic candidate again in 1988—that his public position was dictated by the Vatican, not by the interests of his voters or his own free will. Referring to the separation principle in a speech at the University of Notre Dame, Governor Cuomo reminded the hierarchy, "In fact, Catholic public officials take an oath to preserve the Constitution that guarantees this freedom."

O'Connor produced further divisiveness in 1986 when he sent a directive through his vicar general to all parishes, banning those "whose public position is contrary to and in opposition to the clear, unambiguous teaching of the church" from speaking in church pulpits or at communion breakfasts or any parish meetings. Here was a form of authoritarianism that closed off a parish audience from any dissenting view, whether that of Father Curran or Governor Cuomo.

The forum of debate was also taken away from Protestants, Jews, or representatives of any diverging belief. Protesting the denial of free speech, Cuomo insisted that "we lay people have a right to be heard."

Catholic officeholders and candidates were particularly punished. Assemblyman John C. Dearie of the Bronx, who had worshiped at his parish church for forty-six years, attended its parish school and the University of Notre Dame, and had his children baptized at the same church, complained that his priest had been ordered to ban him from speaking at parish events because Dearie had voted for Medicaid abortion for the poor. Was O'Connor trying to influence the outcome of the next election, Dearie asked? The cardinal called this claim "grossly untrue, deeply insulting and morally libelous," and his ban remained in force at the end of 1986.[11]

Monsignor Harry J. Byrne, chancellor of the New York archdiocese from 1968 to 1970, called the ban a "sort of partial excommunication" that violated the Second Vatican Council's Declaration on Religious Freedom stating that "no one is to be forced to act against his conscience, nor kept from acting according to his conscience privately or publicly." In an article in *America*, the Jesuit magazine, Byrne insisted: "For churchmen to cross the line between, on the one hand, instructing and informing conscience and, on the other hand, trying to force a legislative position on an officeholder by a speaker's ban is a very dangerous political game."

Few mainstream religions have challenged the separation principle by trying to stamp their moral dogma by law on others. Almost all of the Orthodox branch of Judaism opposes abortion, but it still refuses to force its stand on the rest of the country. "We do not feel obligated to impose our view on abortion on others, any more than we demand non-Jews to observe the Sabbath," explains Rabbi Pinchas Stolper, an official of the Union of Orthodox Jewish Congregations and its 1,200 synagogues.[12]

But since Catholic extremists and Fundamentalists insist on turning their morality into law, the crux of the problem is how they can forge a consensus without damaging the balance of pluralism and the rights of other faiths. What, to begin with, makes up a consensus? Would 51 per cent or 55 per cent, as shown by most public opinion polls, be enough? There are no rules to guide us, only the respect that one religion under our pluralistic system must have for others, particularly the respect it must have for the consequences of its acts.

Banning abortion before an overwhelming consensus has been reached is bound to bring divisiveness and turmoil. No religion should so endanger the pluralistic balance. Specifically, since the citizens of dominantly Catholic Rhode Island and Massachusetts turned down recent anti-abortion referendums by 65 and 58 per cent, respectively, it would be destructive for the Catholic church to try to legislate a ban in those states at present. That does not mean that the hierarchy cannot keep working to build a consensus on its side. And if the hierarchy ever produced a convincing majority, and divisiveness seemed minimal, it could logically move to seek legislation to enforce its views.

Sensitive as this process may be, the passage of the Equal Access law by Congress (as described in Chapter XV) shows that a consensus can be hammered out. Most Catholics and Fundamentalists backed the law from the start. But it was only when the National Conference of Churches and the American Civil Liberties Union unexpectedly joined the coalition that Congress recognized a necessary consensus. The law has been in operation only briefly, and many school boards have avoided divisiveness by banning or limiting its application. But unless after-school religious groups embark on proselytizing or other infractions of the law, the chances are that Equal Access can function democratically without upsetting the pluralist balance.

Another problem is the relationship of consensus to the U.S. Supreme Court. The Court does not depend on the weight of public opinion for its interpretation of the Constitution. Yet, if the Court were to overturn its 1973 decision legalizing abortion before the Catholic-Fundamentalist alliance had forged a strong consensus behind it, the country would be torn apart to an extent that could approach the fury of the slavery debate.

Abortion affects everyone, striking at the deepest meaning of every woman's life and the life of the man involved, striking at a woman's control of her childbearing and at the chance to pursue her own work and career, as well as for the chance for a couple to set a desired educational standard for its offspring. Legalized abortion takes nothing from its opponents but the option of preventing or allowing an unborn fetus to develop to term. Banning abortion results in an intrusion into the privacy of people of other beliefs, the Court holds, an intrusion that most religions reject. If the Supreme Court were to overturn abortion rights, everyone would be denied the option of choice and the chance to practice their own religious code.

The prospect of a reversal on abortion by the Supreme Court cannot be dismissed and may, in fact, hang on the death or illness of a single justice during the Reagan administration. In a test of local abortion restrictions in the *Akron* decision in 1983, the vote was 6 to 3. In a not dissimilar test of restrictions under a Pennsylvania law in 1986, Chief Justice Burger switched sides, and the majority was cut to 5 to 4. Speaking for the majority, Justice Harry A. Blackmun decreed that, "Our cases have long recognized that the Constitution embodies a promise that a certain private sphere of individual liberty will be kept largely beyond the reach of government." But it would be hard to predict whether that interpretation would survive a changing Court, and whether a new conservative justice would recognize a "private sphere."[13]

No safeguards can adequately prevent politicization of the Court; the rare Senate rejections of a nomination have generally been based on incompetency rather than political bias. It follows naturally, therefore, that a conservative president would appoint a justice following his own beliefs and reenforcing the Catholic-Fundamentalist alliance. Antonin Scalia, appointed to the Court in 1986, undoubtedly fit Reagan's requirements as a result of his conservative record on the appeals bench.

Beyond the appointment process, the Court may be influenced by political and social forces. In the Dred Scott decision of 1857, depriving Congress of the right to legislate "free soil" territory even when settlers voted for it, the Court provided a prime instance of its susceptibility to the pressure of slavery interests.

The impact of public opinion, as well as legislative and lower-court precedents, must have had some bearing on the Court's 1973 decision legalizing abortion. The groundwork was laid by the *Griswold* case in 1965, when the Court overturned by a 7 to 2 vote one of the last state laws against birth control, concluding that, "The present case, then, concerns a relationship lying within the zone of privacy created by several fundamental constitutional guarantees." The passage of liberalizing state abortion laws in the next few years, climaxed by the sweeping New York State law of 1970, and a ground swell of public opinion involving the most prestigious medical, legal, and professional societies, undoubtedly supported the thinking of the Court when it extended the "zone of privacy" to abortion.

The national mood of conservatism, certainly since 1980 and even before, has markedly affected the Court's interpretation of the Establishment Clause and the traditional wall of separation. In fact, in the *Mueller* decision in 1983, upholding a Minnesota law giving parents tax credits for children at parochial and private schools, the five-member majority denigrated the clause's importance. "At this point in the 20th century we are quite far removed from the dangers that prompted the Framers to include the Establishment Clause in the Bill of Rights," Justice William Rehnquist, named Chief Justice in 1986, asserted in quoting a previous decision. "The risk of significant religious or denomination control over our democratic processes—or even of deep political division along religious lines—is remote. . . ."

In light of the furious divisions along religious lines already set off by the abortion issue, and the bombings and burnings of clinics, Rehnquist's conclusion for the majority seems strangely unrealistic. Even less explosive issues, such as divorce reform and parochiaid, have produced bitter clashes in state legislatures and during referendums. Referring to the Court's vacillations over the First Amendment's religion clauses, Justice Blackmun in 1986 warned a group of judges that, "This is an area where we have not done well. And where I think the Court is tending, tending to the right, pulling down a little bit, a couple of bricks off a so-called wall between church and state."[14]

If the Catholic-Fundamentalist alliance has already been reflected in the Court's weakening support for the separation principle, the threat will persist as long as the White House backs extremism. The threat encompasses not just abortion rights but a whole range of First Amendment and morality issues. The Court still remains as susceptible to outside pressures as it was in the Dred Scott era. And these pressures have been intensified by the emergence of the Reverend Pat Robertson's presidential candidacy.

Robertson's virtual candidacy, aimed at galvanizing all elements of extremism into a unified campaign, brings the possibility that a theocracy—or something close to it—will dominate the democratic process. The direction of the Court and the country, consequently, may be influenced not just by another Reagan justice before 1989, and future nominations by an equally conservative president, but by the impact of Robertson's campaign. Even if his chances of winning the Republican nomination in 1988 or 1992 are slim, his chances of becoming a power broker in the party, with increasing control over judicial appointments, cannot be underestimated.

The alternative of a Democratic administration after the next election may do less than expected to blunt the extremist threat. The Catholic-Fundamentalist alliance is not a temporary phenomenon. It has launched a permanent revolution to reconstruct America in its image and harness the country to its rigid morality. American pluralism has been put in constant jeopardy. The alliance can build on its successes: the defeat of ERA, most notably. It can herald its partial gains: a parochial aid bill at the state level, affirmed by the Supreme Court. It has its losses as well: the survival of abortion rights, clinging by a one-vote margin in the Court. The total record adds up to a harbinger of what an unshakable belief in its God-given mandate can bring to a movement.

No scorecard can measure this ultimate source of power: the conviction that a religiously controlled state must eventually triumph. It may be easy to dismiss Archbishop Hughes's contention—"Everybody should know that we have for our mission to convert the world—including the inhabitants of the United States"—as the fantasy of more than a century ago. But it is harder to ignore a best-selling Mormon work of 1967, *Prophecy: Key to the Future*, which devotes two chapters to the Mormon takeover of the United States, and proclaims the vision of a Latter-day Saints theocracy after a "series of internal wars" and the "complete collapse of the national and state governments in the United States."[15]

At the very moment when Catholic-Fundamentalist power approaches its peak, however, it is quixotic that an incipient rebellion in Catholicism challenges Vatican authoritarianism. A new church may be in the offing, a divided church with a radical wing that may be Roman in name only, but soon resemble the independent status carved out by the church in Holland. The clash of these two contradictory forces could determine the religious design of America. It will not be a quick decision, and its results may not be evident for decades. Meanwhile, radical Catholicism, aligned with mainstream Protestantism and Judaism, remains the best hope for holding extremism in check, and preserving American pluralism and the separation principle against its enemies.

ACKNOWLEDGMENTS

It almost seems gratuitous to try to express again my debt to my wife, Joan Summers Lader. Taking time from her own career, she has always been able to produce an essential piece of research, check facts, read chapters and edit them shrewdly, and still produce a setting of love and dedication that has made my work possible for twenty-five years.

It is equally difficult to define the contribution of my agent, Roberta Pryor. I have been with her predecessor agencies for almost forty years and with Roberta herself for at least twenty. Her wisdom, cheerfulness, and devotion have always sustained me, and I cannot conceive of undergoing the trials of authorship without her help.

While I naturally take full responsibility for all the material in this book, I want to acknowledge the labors of my editor at Macmillan, Ned Chase; my publisher, Hill Black; and their assistant, Dominick Anfuso. I have had the special privilege of legal guidance from three brilliant constitutional lawyers: Marshall Beil, Ephraim London, and Leo Pfeffer. Pfeffer's writing and court cases, particularly in the First Amendment area, have given him a deserved reputation.

Two noted, Catholic theologians, Marjorie and Dan Maguire, have kindly cooperated in advising me on the dogma and practices of the church.

It has been my joy to carry out most of the documentary research for this book, and many previous books, in the Frederick Lewis Allen Room of the New York Public Library. This remarkable room, which gives a writer the facilities to work in total concentration, is just one of the glories of the public library. I am indebted to Vartan Gregorian, its head, and to many staff members, particularly David Beasley. The friendship of other Allen Room writers, such as Susan Brownmiller, Robert Caro, John Demaray, and Jonathan Kandell, has helped to lighten the load. Paul Schmidt of the research room at the Jefferson

Market Library and the staffs of the Union Theological Library and the New York University Library have always been unfailing in their advice.

Albert J. Menendez of Americans United for Separation of Church and State has been a superb research support and friend, and Robert L. Maddox, the executive director, has made the copious files of the organization available for frequent use. Edith Tiger of the National Emergency Civil Liberties Committee and Mort Yarmon of the American Jewish Committee have given generously of their professional skills.

While this book is obviously the product of my own work and research in family planning, abortion rights, and First Amendment doctrine, going back thirty-five years to my biography of Margaret Sanger, I am indebted to many organizations for allowing me to use their documents and interview their staffs. Some of these consultants are credited in the Notes, but I want to offer my thanks especially to: Janet Benshoof and Alan Reitman of the American Civil Liberties Union; Eve Paul of the Planned Parenthood Federation of America; Stanley Henshaw, Jeannie Rosoff, and Deirdre Wulf of the Alan Guttmacher Institute; Eleanor Smeal and Noreen Connell of the National Organization for Women; Alice Mehling and Ruth P. Smith of the Society for the Right to Die; and Florence Flast of the Committee for Public Education and Religious Liberty.

It could be too easily assumed that this book is slanted against the Catholic church. Admittedly, when the church and Fundamentalists have transgressed the crucial "wall of separation" between church and state, I have been harsh indeed. Still, I hope I have been objective in presenting facts and interpreting them. Objectivity, of course, is an indefinable target. My book *Abortion*, in 1966, was an obvious plea for the right of abortion, but I like to think that its objectivity was given some credence when it was cited eight times by the U.S. Supreme Court in its 1973 decision legalizing abortion.

Objectivity, in the case of this book, has an added complication. There are today in the United States actually two Catholic churches— a radical wing increasingly alienated from the autocratic structure of the Vatican and the hierarchy. While the bishops have occasionally taken positions on controversial issues, particularly in their nuclear and economics letters, that seem to me in accord with high public interest, I have found that the radical wing represents the best moral aspirations of the church and a bedrock defense of First Amendment principles and constitutional doctrine.

If my advocacy of the radical wing should smack of partiality to some observers, I believe I shall be proved more objective over the next twenty or forty years as this still small band transforms the American church to the standards that the Gospels set forth. I am deeply grateful to many of these radicals, particularly the nuns, not just for their help to me, but for their courage and moral leadership for the country.

One organization, Catholics for a Free Choice, stands out above all, and Frances Kissling, its head, deserves a special tribute. I also want to thank a group of nuns whose aid has been essential: Sisters Maureen Fiedler, Lora Ann Quinonez, Ann Patrick Ware, and especially the late Marjorie Tuite, whose energy, gift for friendship, and organizational achievements will always remain a beacon to her faith. It seems no exaggeration to predict that Sister Marjorie will some day become a model that the whole church will want to follow.

NOTES

To keep the notes manageable, I have followed the practice of occasionally grouping sources for two or more paragraphs under one note number. Titles of books are given in full only when first cited in each chapter.

For the most frequently used newspaper and magazine sources, as well as for organizations used repeatedly, I have adopted a shortened form listed under "Abbreviations and Acronyms."

Since this book concentrates on events of the last ten years, with most participants available, I have drawn largely on personal interviews. These are named in appropriate paragraphs in the Notes, except in the few cases which requested anonymity.

ABBREVIATIONS AND ACRONYMS

ACLU	American Civil Liberties Union
ARM	Abortion Rights Mobilization
Cath. Al.	*Catholic Almanac*
CBN	Christian Broadcasting Network
C & S	*Church & State*
FPP	*Family Planning Perspectives*
IRS	Internal Revenue Service
NCC	National Council of Churches
NCCB	National Council of Catholic Bishops
NCR	*National Catholic Reporter*
NORC	National Opinion Research Center
NOW	National Organization for Women
NYT	*New York Times*
Pap. Encyc.	*Papal Encyclicals*
PEARL	Committee for Public Education and Religious Liberty

PP   Planned Parenthood Federation of America
USCC United States Catholic Conference
WP   *Washington Post*

I *Designs for Power*

1. U.S. Department of Commerce, Bureau of Census, *Historical Statistics of the United States* (Washington, D.C., 1975).

2. *NYT*, Aug. 3, 1984, p. 1.

3. Jefferson letter of Jan. 1, 1802, to Danbury, Ct., Baptist Association; quoted in 16 *Jefferson Works* 281 (Monticello ed., 1903); also quoted in *Reynolds* v. *United States*, 98 U.S. 145 (1878).

4. Description of Town Hall meeting and involvement of Archbishop Hayes from interviews with Morris Ernst, Anne Kenndey, Juliet Rublee, and Margaret Sanger, quoted in Lawrence Lader, *Margaret Sanger and the Fight for Birth Control* (Garden City, N.Y.: Doubleday, 1955), pp. 171–78; also *NYT*, *New York Tribune*, Nov. 15, 1921, p. 1; *New York Post*, Nov. 16, 1921, p. 1.

5. This and preceding paragraph from *United States Diplomatic Relations with the Vatican in International and Constitutional Law* (New York: American Jewish Congress, 1984), pp. 10–11, 28; Robert A. Graham, *Vatican Diplomacy* (Princeton, N.J.: *Princeton University Press*, 1959), p. 182; *Americans United for Separation of Church and State* v. *Reagan*, E. Dist., Pa., No. 84-4476, Complaint, pp. 28–29

6. John Cooney, *The American Pope* (New York: Times Books, 1984), p. 65; Robert I. Gannon, *The Cardinal Spellman Story* (Garden City, N.Y.: Doubleday, 1962), p. 155; Cordell Hull, *Memoirs*, Vol. 1 (New York: Macmillan, 1948), p. 713; *NYT*, July 29, 1939.

7. Interview with John Cooney; Cooney, *Pope*, p. 213.

8. Interview with Dean Kelley.

9. Draper testimony before U.S. Senate Foreign Relations Committee, Jan. 27, 1984.

10. Interview with Dean Kelley.

11. Editorial, "U.S. Ambassador to the Vatican," *Journal of Church & State*, Spring 1984, pp. 197–207.

12. Interview with Albert J. Menendez; *Americans United for Separation of Church and State* v. *Reagan*, U.S. Dist. Ct., E. Dist., Pa., No. 84-4476, Complaint (1984); *American Baptist Churches* v. *Reagan*, S. Ct. 86-113 (1986). William A. Wilson resigned as ambassador to the Vatican on May 20, 1986, following revelations of unauthorized dealings with Libya.

13. Mary Hanna, *Catholics and American Politics* (Cambridge, Mass.: Harvard University Press, 1979), p. 214.

14. *WP*, Sept. 16, 1984, p. A 6.

15. *C & S*, Sept. 1965, p. 3.

16. *WP*, Sept. 16, 1984, p. A 6.

17. John Cogley, *Catholic America* (New York: Dial, 1977), p. 271; Joe Klein, "Abortion and the Archbishop," *New York Magazine*, Oct. 1, 1984, pp. 36–43. For this and preceding paragraph, interview with Daniel Callahan.

II *The Upward Leap: 1900–1960*

1. Archbishop Hughes quoted in Ray Allen Billington, *The Protestant Crusade* (Chicago: Quadrangle, 1964), p. 291.

2. G. H. Haynes, "A Know-Nothing Legislature," *American Historical Association Reports*, 1896; Madeleine H. Rice, *American Catholic Opinion in the Slavery Controversy* (New York: Columbia University Press, 1944).

3. Edward M. Levine, *The Irish and Irish Politicians* (Notre Dame, Ind.: University of Notre Dame Press, 1966), p. 120; U.S. Department of Commerce, Bureau of Census, *Historical Statistics of the United States* (Washington, D.C., 1975).

4. Stephen Steinberg, *The Academic Melting Pot* (New York: McGraw-Hill, 1974), pp. 84, 91; John D. Donovan, "The American Catholic Hierarchy," *American Catholic Sociological Review*, 19 (1958): 98–112.

5. Matthew Josephson, *Alfred E. Smith* (Boston: Houghton Mifflin, 1969), p. 365.

6. For this and preceding paragraph: Gustavus Myers, *History of Bigotry in the United States* (New York: Random House, 1943), p. 318; Albert J. Menendez, *Religion at the Polls* (Philadelphia: Westminster, 1977), pp. 41, 45, 49–53; Josephson, *Smith*, pp. 380, 391.

7. George Q. Flynn, *Roosevelt and Romanism* (Westport, Ct.: Greenwood, 1976), p. 37; National Catholic Welfare Conference *Newsletter*, May 15, 1937.

8. For this and preceding paragraph: Thomas A. Bailey, *Man in the Street* (New York: Macmillan, 1948), p. 208; Harold L. Ickes, *The Secret Diary of Harold L. Ickes* (New York: Simon & Schuster, 1953), Vol. II, pp. 389–90, 605; Vol. III, p. 217; Flynn, *Roosevelt*, p. 40.

9. James Hennessy, *American Catholics* (New York: Oxford University Press, 1981), p. 272; Flynn, *Roosevelt*, p. 34.

10. John Cooney, *The American Pope* (New York: Times Books, 1984), pp. 116, 177; Joseph Lash, *Eleanor: The Years Alone* (New York: Norton, 1971), pp. 157, 158. For "shibboleth": Federal Council of Churches *Bulletin*, New York, May 1940, p. 4.

11. For this and preceding paragraph: Lash, *Eleanor*, pp. 159–60.

12. Warren Moscow, *Last of the Bigtime Bosses* (New York: Stein & Day, 1971), p. 122.

13. For this and preceding paragraph: Eleanor Roosevelt column, "My Day," Aug. 24, 1949; Irwin Ross, "Cardinal Spellman," *New York Post*, Sept. 18, 1957; *NYT*, July 23, 26, 28, 1949, p. 1; Aug. 6, 1949, p. 1.

14. For this and two preceding paragraphs: Interviews with Ephraim London and Leo Pfeffer. *NYT*, Jan. 8, 1951, p. 1. *Joseph Burstyn, Inc.* v. *Wilson*, 343 U.S. 495 (1952).

15. For this and two preceding paragraphs: Gerald F. Fogarty, *The Vatican and the American Hierarchy from 1870 to 1954* (Stuttgart: Anton Hierjeman, 1982), pp. 334–35, 339; Jean-Guy Vaillancourt, *Papal Power* (Berkeley: University of California Press, 1980), p. 199; Joseph La Palombara, *Interest Groups in Italian Politics* (Princeton, N.J.: Princeton University Press, 1964), p. 354; Cooney, *Pope*, pp. 158–59. For U.S. law on foreign allegiance: Sec. 401 (B) (D) *The United Statutes at Large*, 1929 to 1941, Vol. 54, Part I, p. 1157, Sec. 335 (b) in part.

16. Claudia Carlen, ed., *The Papal Encyclicals* (Raleigh, N.C.: McGrath, 1981). *Rerum* in 1878–1903, pp. 243–44; *Quadragesimo* in 1903–1939, pp. 428–30.

17. For ACTU in this and four preceding paragraphs: Interviews with Frank Donner, Albert Fitzgerald, James Matles, and Charles O. Rice. Higgins quotation: John M. Freeman, *No Friend of Labor* (New York: Fulfillment, 1948), p. 3. Quill quotation: A. H. Raskin, "Quill," *NYT Magazine*, March 5, 1950, p. 11. Douglas P. Seaton, *Catholics and Radicals* (Lewisburg, Pa.: Bucknell University Press, 1981), pp. 102, 109, 146, 205.

18. For this and preceding paragraph: Andrew Greeley, *The American Catholic* (New York: Basic Books, 1977), p. 74; Steinberg, *Melting Pot*, pp. 100, 102, 170; Norval D. Glenn and Ruth Hyland, "Religious Preference and Worldly Success," *American Sociological Review*, Feb. 1967, p. 75.

19. For this and preceding paragraph: Kennedy quotation from *NYT*, July 18, 1963, p. 8. Peale quotation: Robert Booth Fowler, *Religion and Politics in America* (Metuchen, N.J.: Scarecrow, 1985), p. 60; *NYT*, Sept. 8, 1960, pp. 1, 18; Sept. 13, p. 1.

20. Theodore H. White, *The Making of the President, 1960* (New York: Atheneum, 1961), pp. 260, 391–93.

21. For this and preceding paragraph: archbishop's intervention from Roger Van Allen, *The Commonweal and American Catholicism* (Philadelphia: Fortress, 1974); also letter of Ambassador Theodore Moscosco, *NYT*, Sept. 23, 1984, Sec. 4, p. 22. *Baptist Standard* from Cooney, *Pope*, p. 271.

22. For interpretation of 1960 election, interview with Albert J. Menendez. Also Fowler, *Religion*, p. 62.

III *Catholic Schools: The Church's "Essential Instrument"*

1. For Hollings, *NCR*, Dec. 16, 1983, p. 3. Knights: *C & S*, Oct. 1983, p. 19. Erlenborn: James L. Adams, *The Growing Church Lobby in Washington* (Grand Rapids, Mich.: Erdmans, 1970), p. 192.
2. Pope John Paul II in *Florida Catholic*, St. Petersburg diocese supplement, Feb. 23, 1984, p. B. *Rappresentanti* in *Pap. Encyc.* 1903–1939, p. 365.
3. For this and three preceding paragraphs: *Emerson* v. *Board of Education*, 330 U.S. 1 (1947). Grant: *NYT*, Dec. 30, 1875, p. 1; also *Congressional Record* 4, 1875, p. 175. Blaine: Anson Phelps Stokes and Leo Pfeffer, *Church and State in the United States* (New York: Harper & Row, 1 vol., 1964), p. 352.
4. James Bryant Conant, *Education and Liberty* (Cambridge, Mass.: Harvard University Press, 1953), p. 81.
5. *Abington School District* v. *Schempp*, 374 U.S. 203 (1963).
6. For this and preceding paragraph: Felicia A. Foy, ed., *Catholic Almanac 1986* (Huntington, Ind.: Our Sunday Visitor, 1986), p. 518; *WP*, March 27, 1985, p. A 18; *NYT*, Sept. 6, 1984, p. B 3.
7. *Harvard Education Review* 17, 1947, p. 73.
8. *C & S*, Feb. 1983, pp. 9–10.
9. *McCollum* v. *Board of Education*, 333 U.S. 203 (1948).
10. *Zorach* v. *Clauson*, 343 U.S. 306 (1952). For this and preceding paragraph, interviews with Florence Flast and Leo Pfeffer. Robert F. Drinan, *Religion, the Courts and Public Policy* (New York: McGraw-Hill, 1963), pp. 87, 89. Leo Pfeffer, *Church, State and Freedom* (Boston: Beacon, 1953), pp. 418, 432.
11. Interviews with Edd Doerr and Martin A. Larson.
12. Rockefeller from John Cooney, *The American Pope* (New York: Times Books, 1984), pp. 312–13. The Blaine amendment campaign is largely based on interviews with Edd Doerr and on his book, *The Conspiracy That Failed* (Washington, D.C.: Americans United for Separation of Church and State, 1968), pp. 34, 42, 128, 143–46, 154–55, 167.
13. Rockland County, N.Y., *Journal-News*, June 1, 1967; *The Nation*, Oct. 23, 1967, p. 389; *Newsweek*, Nov. 6, 1967, p. 61.
14. *NYT*, Oct. 31, 1967, p. 1.
15. *NYT*, Nov. 8, 1967, p. 1.
16. For Greeley and Collins in this and preceding paragraph: Andrew Greeley, *An Ugly Little Secret* (Kansas City, Kans.: Sheed, Andrews & McMeel, 1977), p. 38; *NCR*, Feb. 29, 1967.
17. For this and two preceding paragraphs: Cavanaugh in *New York Herald Tribune*, Feb. 20, 1958; Ryan in Mary Perkins Ryan, *Are Parochial Schools the Answer?* (New York: Holt, Rinehart & Winston, 1964), pp. 51, 158; Callahan in Daniel Callahan, *Federal Aid and Catholic Schools* (Baltimore: Helicon, 1964), p. 77.
18. For this and two preceding paragraphs: *Board of Education* v. *Allen*, 392 U.S. 236 (1968); *Tilton* v. *Richardson*, 403 U.S. 672 (1971); *Earley* v. *DiCenso* and *Lemon* v. *Kurtzman*, 403 U.S. 602 (1971).
19. For this and six preceding paragraphs: Interviews with Florence Flast and Leo Pfeffer. *PEARL* v. *Nyquist*, 413 U.S. 756 (1973); *Meek* v. *Pittenger*, 421 U.S. 349 (1975).
20. *U.S. News & World Report*, March 5, 1984, p. 42.
21. White House meeting: *C & S*, April 1983, p. 6; Flagship: Dr. Robert L. Maddox letter, Jan. 1985. Bennett: *PEARL Newsletter*, May 1985, p. 2.
22. Interview with Stanley Geller. *C & S*, April, 1983, pp. 6–8.
23. This and four preceding paragraphs: Interview with Marc D. Stern. *Mueller* v. *Allen*, 103

S. Ct. 3062 (1983). *C & S*, June 1985, p. 4. Leo Pfeffer, *Religion, State and the Burger Court* (Buffalo, N.Y.: Prometheus, 1984), pp. 44–45.

IV *Birth Control*

1. NORC study: Andrew M. Greeley, *American Catholic Schools in a Declining Church* (Kansas City, Kans.: Sheed & Ward, 1976), p. 129. Suenens: F. V. Joannes, ed., *The Bitter Pill* (Boston: Pilgrim, 1970), p. 20.

2. This and preceding paragraph: *Humanae* in *Pap. Encyc.* 1958–1981, p. 223. Former priest: James Kavanaugh, *A Modern Priest Looks at His Out-dated Church* (New York: Trident, 1967), p. 135. Interview with Sheldon Segal.

3. This and preceding paragraph: Hellegers in Peter Hebblethwaite, *The Runaway Church* (London: Collins, 1975), p. 213. Tong in Joannes, *Bitter Pill*, p. 344.

4. This and preceding paragraph: Cavanagh in Robert B. Kaiser, "Long Road to Birth Control," *NCR*, May 3, 1985, pp. 9–12. *Casti* in *Pap. Encyc.* 1903–1939, p. 404.

5. Saint Jerome: Elizabeth Clark and Herbert Richardson, *Women and Religion* (New York: Harper & Row, 1977), pp. 56, 66, 81. See also Rosemary Ruether, ed., *Religion and Sexism* (New York: Simon & Schuster, 1974), pp. 90, 106, 157–59.

6. This and preceding paragraph: Onanism (Gen. 38:8–10) in Anthony Kosnik, *Human Sexuality* (New York: Paulist, 1977), p. 220. See also John T. Noonan, Jr., *Contraception* (Cambridge, Mass.: Harvard University Press, 1965), pp. 33–35, Lord Acton, *Correspondence*, Vol. 1 (London: Longmans, Green, 1917), p. 103.

7. This and two preceding paragraphs: *Cath. Al.* 1986, p. 186; *NCR*, May 3, 1985, pp. 10, 12.

8. This and preceding paragraph: Doepfner, Leger, and Maximos IV in NCR, *ibid.*, pp. 9–11. Saes in Joannes, *Bitter Pill*, p. 103. See also Malachi Martin, *Decline and Fall of the Roman Church* (New York: Putnam, 1981), p. 217.

9. This and three preceding paragraphs: Interviews with Frances Kissling and William V. Shannon. NORC studies in Andrew M. Greeley, *American Catholics Since the Council* (Chicago: Thomas More, 1985), pp. 54–55, 61, 88, 114, 216. Also Greeley, *Catholic Schools*, pp. 127, 129, 145. For Bishop Shannon: *NCR*, June 4, 1969; and William H. Shannon, *The Lively Debate* (New York: Sheed & Ward, 1970), p. 214.

10. *NCR*, Aug. 31, 1984, p. 4; May 3, 1985, p. 12. *NYT*, May 15, 1985, p. A 10. Interview with Leonard Swidler.

11. United Nations Population Conference based on interviews with Paul Micou, David Poindexter, Sheldon Segal, Steve Viederman, and Deirdre Wulf. For White House amendment: Amendment to Document E/Conf. 76/5, Aug. 8, 1984. See also Deirdre Wulf and Peters D. Willson, "Consensus and Controversies," *International Family Planning Perspectives*, Sept. 1984, pp. 81–85. For Clausen: *Population Today*, Population Reference Bureau, Oct. 1984, p. 8. For *L'Osservatore: Religious News Service*, Aug. 15, 1984.

12. This and preceding paragraph: Farley: *NCR*, March 21, 1986, p. 22. Father Shannon: *NCR*, April 11, 1986, p. 19. *Gaudium*: Art. 62, Par. 9 in Walter M. Abbott, ed., *The Documents of Vatican II* (New York: America Press, 1966), p. 270.

13. *NCR*, April 4, 1986, p. 6; March 21, p. 12.

14. The most comprehensive study of teenage pregnancy: Elise F. Jones et al., "Teen-age Pregnancies in Developed Countries," *FPP*, March/April 1985, pp. 53–63. Also *NYT*, Feb. 10, 1986, p. A 14; March 15, 1985, p. A 26 editorial. Interview with Stanley Henshaw.

15. Chastity: *Christianity Today*, Nov. 11, 1983, p. 27. Scheidler: *C & S*, April 1985, p. 18, quoting Jeffrey Hart column. Schlafly: *NYT*, Jan. 9, 1986, p. C 10. Fundamentalist parents, schools: *Christianity Today*, Nov. 11, 1983, p. 27.

16. This and three preceding paragraphs: Suffolk and Erie counties in *NYT*, April 26, 1984, II, p. 2. New York archdiocese and O'Connor in New York *Post*, Sept. 22, 1986, p. 3; *NYT*,

Oct. 16, 1986, p. B 12. Law in Boston *Herald*, May 12, 1986, p. 1. Roach and Gallagher in *NYT*, Oct. 12, 1986, p. 53. Interview with James Franklin.

17. This and preceding paragraph: St. Paul study in Laura E. Edwards et al., "Adolescent Pregnancy Prevention Services in High School Clinics," *FPP*, Jan. 1980, p. 6. Four high schools: Jan./Feb. 1986, p. 44. Johns Hopkins: Laurie S. Zabin et al., "Evaluation of Pregnancy Prevention Programs for Urban Teen-agers," *FPP*, May/June 1986, p. 119. Gallup: *NYT*, Nov. 1, 1985, p. B 5. Harris: *Planned Parenthood Review*, Winter 1986, pp. 22–23. Gordon: "Cross Currents" on Channel 13, New York, June 6, 1985. Interview with Susan Newcomer. House Rep.: *FPP*, March/April 1986, p. 85.

18. This and two preceding paragraphs: The Second Vatican Council statement on sex education in "Declaration on Christian Education," *Documents of Vatican Council*, III, par. 1. Ironically, the church's official stamp of approval was removed from Father Kawiak's pamphlet by Bishop Matthew Clark of Rochester, N.Y., in Dec. 1986 (*NCR*, Dec. 12, 1986, p. 3). Interviews with Robert Harrington, Matthew Kawiak, and Thomas Lynch. See also Robert Harrington, "Why Schools Should Teach Children About Sex," *McCall's*, Oct. 1981, p. 182; and "A Joint Pastoral Statement on Education in Human Sexuality" by New Jersey's bishops, Dec. 9, 1980, p. 5.

19. Adolescent Family Life Act is numbered P.L. 97-35 § 300Z (b) (1) and (2); and analyzed in Patricia Donovan, "AFLA and the Promotion of Religious Doctrine," *FPP*, Sept./Oct. 1984, p. 222. For congressional debate, see *Congressional Record*, S 6324, June 17, 1981. Hart in *C & S*, April 1985, p. 18. Polls in *NYT*, March 8, 1985, p. A 35; May 16, p. C 9.

20. This and four preceding paragraphs: Interviews with Janet Benshoof and Lynn Paltrow, ACLU. See ACLU testimony before subcommittee of House Energy and Commerce Committee, April 27, 1984; and *NYT*, July 16, 1984, p. A 20.

V   *Abortion: Cutting Edge of the Religious Right*

1. *Roe* v. *Wade*, 410 U.S. 113 (1973). Cardinal Law: *NYT*, Sept. 6, 1984, p. B 13.

2. Hogan: *WP*, Oct. 29, 1970. Shaneman: *Washington Star*, May 21, 1973. Seattle archdiocese: Letters and documents in ARM files, New York. *Pastoral Plan*: *Origins*, Dec. 4, 1975, p. 370.

3. Bishop Head letter and other documents in ARM files. See also New York *Village Voice*, Nov. 28, 1977; *NCR*, Jan. 27, 1978. Interview with university scholar requesting anonymity, whose research uncovered some of these documents. U.S. Tax Code prohibiting direct political intervention by tax-exempt religious groups: 26 U.S.C. Sec. 501-c-3.

4. No. 1 priority: *NCR*, Feb. 10, 1984, p. 20. Holocaust: Joe Klein, *New York Magazine*, Oct. 1, 1984, pp. 36–43. Brickner: *Jewish Week and American Examiner*, April 20, 1984, p. 22. "Good conscience": *NYT*, June 25, 1984, IV:13. Cuomo: *NYT*, Aug. 3, 1984, p. B 2.

5. Interviews with three chaplains who served with O'Connor and requested anonymity, and with Joe Klein and Paul O'Dwyer. Gumbleton: *NCR*, April 22, 1983, p. 44.

6. Interview with Martha Mann. See also *NYT*, July 14, 1984, p. 10; June 25, p. B 3; Dec. 27, p. B 3.

7. Interviews with James Nash, William V. Shannon, and two Boston theologians requesting anonymity. See also *NYT*, March 24, 1984, p. 1.

8. Interviews with Karen Jacobson, Mitchell Lynch, Boston political aide, and Washington reporter. See also *NCR*, Feb. 3, 1984, p. 1.

9. See U.S. Tax Code, *op. cit.* Documents relating to cited violations of U.S. Code by the Catholic church in ARM files. See also *NCR*, July 2, 1980.

10. Interviews with William P. Homans, Jr., Pamela Lowry, and a Boston Protestant minister. Documents relating to Cardinal Medeiros in ARM files. See also Boston *Globe*, Sept. 11, 1980.

11. Pennsylvania and Virginia documents in ARM files. Bishop Welsh, Archbishop Hickey: *WP*, Dec. 12, 1982; July 11, 1984. NCCB: *NYT*, Aug. 9, 1984, p. 1. IRS documents on *Christian Century* case in ARM files. In holding the NCCB and USCC in "contempt of court" and fining them $100,000 a day on May 8, 1986, federal Judge Robert L. Carter said the Catholic bishops have "made a travesty of the court process."

12. Ferraro: *NYT*, Sept. 10, 1984, pp. 1, B 9. Catholics for a Free Choice ad: *NYT*, Oct. 7, 1984, p. E 7. Interviews with Maureen Fiedler, Frances Kissling, and Marjorie R. Maguire. See also *NCR*, Oct. 19, 1984, p. 12; Feb. 8, 1985, pp. 12, 17.

13. Catholic position on fetal life: Roger J. Huser, *Criminal Abortion in Canon Law* (Washington, D.C.: Catholic University of America Press, Canon Law Studies No. 162, 1942), pp. 62, 75–78, 103–5. John T. Noonan, Jr., *Contraception* (Cambridge, Mass.: Harvard University Press, 1965), pp. 88, 91, 232. See also personal letters from Huser and Noonan to author in Lader, *Abortion* (Indianapolis: Bobbs-Merrill, 1966), p. 185, fn 9. Kennedy: *NYT*, Sept. 11, 1984, p. 26. Siegman: *NYT*, Let., Oct. 23, 1984. *Tablet:* July 28, 1984. Bernardin: *NCR*, April 6, 1984, p. 26.

14. Cuomo speech from Governor's office, Albany, N.Y., pp. 5, 6, 14; Bishop Sullivan, p. 15. Interview with Ilene Margolin. Catholic opinion: *FPP*, Sept./Oct. 1984, p. 233. Underground abortion: Lader, *Abortion*, p. 2.

15. Early statistics on Catholic underground abortion: Lader, "First Exclusive Survey of Non-Hospital Abortion," *Look*, Jan. 21, 1969, p. 3.

VI *Catholic Medicine*

1. Interview with Abraham Stone, in Lawrence Lader, *Margaret Sanger and the Fight for Birth Control* (Garden City, N.Y.: Doubleday, 1955), p. 338.

2. This and preceding paragraph: Theological Society in *NCR*, June 12, 1973, pp. 3–4. Connecticut law: Interview with Eve Paul.

3. Kings County case from conversations with Louis M. Hellman, M.D. See also *NYT*, May 3, 1958, p. 21; July 24, p. 24; Aug. 4, p. 23; Aug. 6, p. 27; Sept. 18, p. 21. Interview with Mary Calderone, M.D.

4. Miles City, Mont., *Star*, Dec. 16, 1972, p. 1; July 22, 1980, p. 1. Missoula, Mont., *Missoulian*, Dec. 13, 1972, p. 1. *NCR*, Jan. 5, 1973.

5. This and preceding paragraph: Hague Hospital from ARM files, New York. See also Hudson County, N.J., *Dispatch*, March 17, 1977; Jersey *Journal*, March 17, 1977; Newark, N.J., *Star Ledger*, March 18, 1977. New York Medical College: Interview with Joseph E. Davis, M.D. See also *NYT*, March 10, 1984, p. 1; March 12, p. B 3; March 19, p. B 4.

6. This and preceding paragraph: Catholic hospitals in *Cath. Al.* 1985, p. 443; *Obstetrics-Gynecology News*, Jan. 15, 1972. Hoban in Leo Pfeffer, *Creeds in Competition* (New York: Harper & Bros., 1958), p. 118. Upjohn in *WP*, July 10, 1980.

7. Hill-Burton funding in Robert Drinan, *Religion, the Courts and Public Policy* (New York: McGraw-Hill, 1963), p. 37; and U.S. Department of Health and Human Services, *Directory of Facilities Obligated to Provide Uncompensated Services as of January 1, 1985* (Rockville, Md.: Public Health Service pub. no. HRP 0906422). Interviews with Blake Crawford, Leonard Krystynak, and Charlotte Muller. Creed case: *Simkins* v. *Moses Cone Memorial Hospital*, 323 F. 2d 959 (4th Cir. 1963). Oregon case: *Barbara Ann Chrisman* v. *Sisters of St. Joseph of Peace*, U.S. Ct. of Appeals, 9th Cir. 1974, No. 72-3087. Analysis of public status of religious hospitals from interviews with Marshall Beil and Charles O. Porter.

8. Other cases bearing on public status issue: *Taylor* v. *St. Vincent's Hospital*, 369 F. Supp. 948, 950 (D. Mont. 1973); *Shulman* v. *Washington Hospital Center*, 319 F. Supp. 252 (D.C. 1970) at 255; *O'Neill* v. *Grayson County War Memorial Hospital*, 472 F. 2d. 1140 (6th Cir. 1973); *Atkins* v. *Mercy Medical Center*, 364 F. Supp. 799 (D. Idaho 1973).

9. This and three preceding paragraphs: Glanville Williams, *The Sanctity of Life and the Criminal Law* (New York: Knopf, 1968), pp. 60–61. Archbishop Mahony: *NYT*, Dec. 8, 1986, p. B 14. *Casti* in *Pap. Encyc.* 1903–1939, p. 404. Cardinal O'Boyle in Earl Raab, ed., *Religious Conflict in America* (Garden City, N.Y.: Doubleday Anchor, 1964), p. 19.

10. This and four preceding paragraphs: *Ethical and Religious Directives for Catholic Health Facilities*, U.S. Catholic Conference, 1971, Pt. 24, p. 7; Pt. 13, p. 5. Ectopic: P. A. Finney, *Moral Problems in Medical Practice* (St. Louis: B. Herder, 1922), p. 135; Williams, *Sanctity*, p. 98; Joseph

Fletcher, *Morals and Medicine* Boston: Beacon, 1960), pp. 146–47, 157. Interview with William Ober, M.D.

11. Artificial insemination: Williams, *Sanctity*, p. 141. Transplants: Charles McFadden, *Medical Ethics* (Philadelphia: Davis, 1949), pp. 265–66. See also Patricia Donovan, "New Reproductive Technologies," *FPP*, March/April 1986, pp. 57–60. An estimated 300,000 children are believed to have been conceived through AID, at a rate of 10,000 to 20,000 per year. Twenty-eight states consider the child the legal offspring of the couple; the child is in legal limbo in 22 states.

12. In vitro procedures: *Science*, Oct. 14, 1983, p. 129; and Deane Wells, *The Reproduction Revolution* (New York: Oxford University Press, 1984), p. 33. Religious views: *Christian Century*, Aug. 16, 1978, p. 757; *America*, Aug. 19, 1978, p. 75; *NYT*, July 27, 1978, p. A 16; *Time*, July 31, 1978, p. 69.

13. Vatican position: *NCR*, Nov. 21, 1986, p. 2. N.J. bishops: *NYT*, DEC. 4, 1986, p. B 12. Tendler: *NYT*, March 12, 1987, P. B 10. Battani: *NYT*, April 17, 1986, p. A 26. No state law explicitly prohibits embryo transfer or surrogate parenthood, which is estimated to account for several hundred children in the U.S. each year. A few laws propose limitations: Michigan's would bar the freezing of an embryo, thus preventing the kind of dilemma that followed the Rios deaths.

14. This and two preceding paragraphs: Vatican on euthanasia in *NYT*, June 27, 1980, p. A 12. Quinlan decision: Supreme Court of New Jersey, *In re Quinlan*, 70 N.J. 10, 355 A. 2d 647 (1976). The National Conference of Catholic Bishops Committee for Pro-Life Activities states that "life-sustaining treatment should not be withdrawn from a pregnant woman if continued treatment may benefit her unborn child." Analysis of "right to die" issue from interviews with Alice V. Mehling, Ruth P. Smith, and Fenella Rouse.

15. This and five preceding paragraphs: Catholic positions in Connecticut, Virginia, and other states cited from files of Society for the Right to Die, New York. See also John J. Paris and Richard A. McCormick, "Living Will Legislation, Reconsidered," *America*, Sept. 5, 1981, pp. 86–89. Father Barry: *National Catholic Register*, Aug. 25, 1985. Denver archdiocese: *Our Sunday Visitor*, June 2, 1985.

16. Conroy: *In the Matter of Claire C. Conroy*, No. A-18, New Jersey Supreme Court, Jan. 17, 1985. Brophy: *NYT*, Oct. 24, 1986, p. B 9. Farrell: *NYT*, June 24, 1986, p. B 1. N.J. bishops: *NCR*, Oct. 31, 1986, p. 3.

17. John M. O'Lane, M.D., "Sterilization and Contraceptive Services in Catholic Hospitals," *American Journal of Obstetrics and Gynecology*, Feb. 15, 1979, pp. 355–57. Sisters of Mercy: Chicago *Sun-Times*, Oct. 3, 1983. Burghardt: Let., *NYT*, April 8, 1980, p. 15. Greeley, *American Catholics Since the Council* (Chicago: Thomas More, 1985), p. 213.

VII   *The Vatican Grip on Marriage, Divorce, and the Family*

1. Canon 1108: *Code of Canon Law* (Washington, D.C.: Canon Law Society of America, 1983). Canon 1109: *Canon Law Digest* (New York: Bruce, 1969), p. 637, S.C. Doct. Fid., May 16, 1967). Hooft: *America*, Sept. 28, 1963, pp. 354–56.

2. St. John's University: 34 Misc. 2d 319, Sup. Ct., Special Term, Part 1, June 5, 1962; 17 A.M. 2d 632, July 2, 1962; 12 NY 2d 802, 235 NYS 2d 834, Dec. 6, 1962. See also *NYT*, June 7, 1962, p. 37; Dec. 7, 1962, p. 43.

3. Analysis of canon law on marriage in *Cath. Al.* 1985, p. 241. See also *NYT*, Feb. 7, 1985, Sec. C.

4. This and three preceding paragraphs: *Casti* in *Pap. Encyc.* 1903–1939, p. 404; *Sertum*, 1939–1958, p. 27. John J. Kane, *Marriage and the Family* (New York: Dryden, 1952), p. 152. Students: A. J. Prince, *Attitude of College Students Towards Intermarriage and Family* (New York: Crowell, 1969); Iris Tan Mink, "An Investigation of Marriage." University of California at Los Angeles; Ph.D. dissertation, 1971, p. 26. Larry Bumpass, "Trend of Interfaith Marriages in the U.S.," *Social Biology*, 17(1970): 253–59. Hanusch: *NYT*, April 11, 1985. Intermarriage stability: John L. Thomas, *The American Catholic Family* (Englewood Cliffs, N.J.: Prentice-Hall, 1956), p. 227;

H. T. Christensen and K. E. Barber, "Interfaith vs. Intrafaith in Indiana, *Journal of Marriage and the Family* 29: 460–69; Albert I. Gordon, *Intermarriage* (Boston: Beacon, 1964), p. 117.

5. Vatican pressure: Thomas, *American Catholic*, p. 162; Kane, *Marriage*, p. 152. Episcopal: *Christian Century*, Oct. 19, 1949. Disciples: Gordon, *Intermarriage*, p. 131.

6. This and preceding paragraph: *Commonweal*, March 5, 1965, p. 714. *Christian Century*, April 10, 1963, p. 455. Kane in Gordon, *Intermarriage*, p. 151. Sincere promise: NCCB statement, Nov. 16, 1970, from letter of Pope Paul VI, March 31, 1970, *Implementation of the Apostolic Letter Matrimonia Mixta*, in *Cath. Al.* 1985, p. 243. Andrew Greeley, *The Hesitant Pilgrim* (New York: Sheed & Ward, 1966), p. 26.

7. Unmarried: *FPP*, Jan./Feb. 1985, p. 36; Andrew Greeley et al., *America*, Sept. 27, 1980, p. 155. Contraception: *FPP*, Jan./Feb. 1985, p. 10. Elaine Sciolino, "American Catholics," *NYT Magazine*, Nov. 4, 1984, p. 70. Divorce: *Casti*, p. 404. Pope Pius XII in Leo Pfeffer, *Church, State and Freedom* (Boston: Beacon, 1953; rev. 1967), p. 258. Pope Paul VI: Interview with Carla Ravaiolo; Francis X. Murphy, *The Papacy Today* (New York: Macmillan, 1981), p. 127.

8. New York divorce reform based on interviews with Leo Pfeffer, Philip Schaeffer, and Jerome L. Wilson. See also *NYT*, Feb. 2, 1966, p. 1; Feb. 16, p. 1; Feb. 20, p. 34; Feb. 26, p. 1; April 14, p. 21; April 28, p.1.

9. Baltimore: *WP*, April 5, 1982, p. A 1. Nullity: John L. McKenzie, *The Roman Catholic Church* (New York: Holt, Rinehart & Winston, 1969), p. 177. Annulments: St. Petersburg, Fla., *Independent*, June 30, 1984; *Cath. Al.* 1986, p. 243. Theriault: *NCR*, Dec. 27, 1985, p. 14.

10. Catholic divorce: *Cath. Al.* 1985, pp. 243–44. NORC: *NYT*, March 21, 1985, p. A 30. Exodus: Andrew M. Greeley, *Crisis in the Church* (Chicago: Thomas More, 1979), p. 59; Greeley et al., *America*, Sept. 27, 1980, p. 155.

11. Goldman: 331 Mass. 647, 121 N.E. 2d 843 (1954); cert. denied, 348 U.S. 942 (1955). Interview with Leo Pfeffer. *Religious News Service*, April 26, 1955. *Ellis* v. *McCoy*, 332 Mass. 254 (1955). *Matter of Gally*, 329 Mass. 143 (1952). Yoswein: *NYT*, March 17, 1966, p. 52; March 23, p. 34; Aug. 14, 1967, p. 30. New York *Herald Tribune*, April 10, 1966, p. 22.

12. Burke: *NYT*, July 2, 1971, p. 35; Aug. 3, 1967, p. 1. Dickens: 407 U.S. 917 (1972), dismissing appeal from 281 N.E. 2d 153. Interviews with Clare Berman, Ira Levin, and David Tobis. Mary K. Benet, *The Politics of Adoption* (New York: Free Press, 1976), pp. 28–29. Barbara Joe, *Public Policies Towards Adoption* (Washington, D.C.: Urban Institute, 1979), p. 4.

13. ACLU case: (originally *Sugarman*) 385 Fed Sub. 1013; *Wilder* v. *Bernstein*, 499 Fed sub. 980. Interviews with Mary Lee Allen, Marcia Lowry, and Ellen Segal. Cardinal O'Connor: *NYT*, Jan. 24, 1987, p. B 1. Fiorenza: Sciolino, "American Catholics," p. 70.

VIII *Money, Power, and the Media*

1. John M. Farley, *History of St. Patrick's Cathedral* (New York: Society for the Propagation of the Faith, 1908), pp. xii, 122. *Life of Archbishop Hughes* (Philadelphia: T. B. Patterson Bros., 1864), p. 20. *St. Patrick's Cathedral* (pamphlet), Archdiocese of New York, 1942, pp. 23, 29.

2. O'Connell: *Commonweal*, June 3, 1983, p. 335. Ginder: *Our Sunday Visitor*, Vol. XLIX, No. 4 (May 22, 1960).

3. Of the major dioceses in the United States, only Chicago and New York supplied the author with financial statements (Los Angeles, for example, gave a highly restricted report). Martin A. Larson and C. Stanley Lowell, *The Religious Empire* (Washington, D.C.: Robert B. Luce, 1976), pp. 4, 204. Association of Laity: Pittsburgh *Post-Gazette*, Jan. 12, 1972. Nash: address to Congregational ministers, May 10, 1979. Religious properties are not specifically identified on the New York City tax rolls, and a single property may be listed under different categories (St. Patrick's Cathedral, for example, is Block 1286 1 2; 21 0; 30 1; and 53 3).

4. John Heinerman and Anson Shupe, *The Mormon Corporate Empire* (Boston: Beacon, 1986), pp. 4, 116, 125. Robert Gottlieb and Peter Wiley, *American Saints: The Rise of Mormon Power* (New York: Putnam's, 1984), pp. 5, 80, 96–97, 105–7. Larson and Lowell, *Religious*, pp. 160–64. Interviews with Alice Pottmyer and Martin A. Larson.

5. This and six preceding paragraphs: Schuller in *NYT*, Sept. 11, 1981, p. A 16; *Christianity Today*, Jan. 21, 1983, p. 22. Knights: *NYT*, Dec. 18, 1953, p. 1. Christian Brothers: *De La Salle Institute* v. *United States*, Civil Action No. 7499, U.S. Dist. Ct., No. Dist., Cal. *Diffenderfer* v. *Central Baptist Church of Miami*, 404 U.S. 412 (1972). Interviews with Dean M. Kelley and Leo Pfeffer. Dean M. Kelley, *Why Churches Should Not Pay Taxes* (New York: Harper & Row, 1977), pp. 13, 143, 148. D. B. Robertson, *Should Churches Be Taxed?* (Philadelphia: Westminster, 1968), p. 22. Nash: Congregational address, May 10, 1979.

6. Nash: Congregational address, May 10, 1979. Kelley, *Why Churches*, p. 60. Christian Echoes: *C. E. National Ministry Inc.* v. *United States*, 470 F 2d 849 (10th Cir. 1972). Kauper: Dallin H. Oaks, ed., *The Wall Between Church and State* (Chicago: University of Chicago Press, 1963), p. 109.

7. *Walz* v. *Tax Commission*, 397 U.S. 664 (1970).

8. Maher, Hawkes: *NCR*, Jan. 7, 1986, p. 7; Sept. 11, 1985, p. 3. Cody: Chicago *Sun-Times*, July 26, 1975, p. 3; *NYT*, Sept. 15, 1981, p. A 28; Sept. 13, A 30; Sept. 21, p. A 9; Oct. 3, p. A 19; Sept. 20, 1985, p. A 20. *America*, Sept. 2, 1972. Charles W. Dahm with Robert Ghelard, *Power and Authority in the Catholic Church* (Notre Dame, Ind.: University of Notre Dame Press, 1981), p. 160. Interview with Martin Larson.

9. Krol: Interviews with Babette Joseph, Kathryn Kolbert, Franklin Littell, John McNamee, and Leonard Swidler. With Reagan: *NYT*, Sept. 10, 1984, p. B 9. Lobby cardinals: Andrew M. Greeley, *The Making of the Popes* (Kansas City, Kans.: Andrews & McMeel, 1979), p. 196. Sindona: *Philadelphia Magazine*, March 1983, p. 102. Cicognani: Gary MacEoin, *The Inner Elite* (Kansas City, Kans.: Sheed, Andrews & McMeel, 1978), p. 21. Leahy: *NCR*, Oct. 25, 1985, p. 1. Detroit: MacEoin, *Inner*, pp. 22–23. AIDS: *NCR*, July 4, 1986, p. 12.

10. United Way: "The Priests of Berks County Want You to Know," *Newsletters* No. 1, No. 2, 1981, mailed by St. Peter's Church, St. Margaret's Church, Reading, Pa. Reading *Times*, Reading *Eagle*, March 21, 18, 1981. Interview with Marguerite Gilpatric.

11. This and four preceding paragraphs: *Hail Mary* in *NYT*, Sept. 26, 1985, p. C 17; *NCR*, Nov. 24, 1985, p. 2; *C & S*, Dec. 1985, p. 16; *NYT*, Feb. 10, 1986, p. A 11. Durang: *C & S*, Sept. 1985, p. 8. Interview with Roz Udow. *Censorship News No.* 12, National Coalition Against Censorship, New York, Jan. 1983. Gastonia: Charlotte, N.C., *Observer*, May 9, 1981, p. 1.

12. Island Trees: 457 U.S. 853 (1982). *Are You a Secular Humanist?* (pamphlet), Colorado Education Association, March 1982, p. 3. *Censorship News*, Feb. 1980, p. 4. *Coda*, Sept./Oct. 1985, p. 3. Falwell: Peggy L. Shriver, *The Bible Vote* (New York: Pilgrim, 1981), p. 16.

13. Harry John: Interviews with Albert J. Menendez and Everett Parker. For tax returns, grants: The Foundation Center, New York. See also *NCR*, Dec. 9, 1983, p. 1; May 30, 1986, p. 4, ; Aug. 29, 1986, p. 1; Sept. 19, 1986, p. 4.

14. This and four preceding paragraphs: Gulf Coast in *Wall Street Journal*, Oct. 8, 1986, p. 1. Interviews with Fred Eiland, William Fore, Richard Hirsch, and Maurine Perritone. For tax returns, grants: The Foundation Center. See also *Employment, Estate and Gift Taxes* (Chicago: Commerce Clearing House, 1983), Vol. II, Sec 7605(c). Angelica: *NCR*, Oct. 7, 1983, p. 1.

15. This and five preceding paragraphs: Interview with Ben Armstrong. Bakker, Scott: *Christianity Today*, Jan. 21, 1983, p. 24; *NYT*, Dec. 24, 1985, p. A 8; *C & S*, Jan. 1986, p. 3. CBN, Trinity: *Christianity Today*, Aug. 6, 1982, p. 44; *NYT*, Jan. 16, 1986, p. C 21. Justice Department petition on KSL before FCC, Washington, D.C., Sept. 3, 1974.

16. This and six preceding paragraphs: The FCC has not required financial statements from religious stations since 1981. As of Oct. 1986, Pat Robertson had filed a statement with the Federal Election Commission showing $547,000 raised for political candidates and $542,000 expended. This may or may not include money raised by CBN, which is tax-exempt. Although the author agreed to be interviewed for a CBN program, CBN officials refused to return any phone calls relating to broadcast coverage and finances. See also *Christianity Today*, Aug. 6, 1982, p. 44; *C & S*, Dec. 1985, p. 8; *NYT*, June 23, 1986, p. A 9; Dec. 10, p. B 11; *U.S. News*, April 23, 1984, p. 68; *Christian Century*, Jan. 7/14, 1981, p. 29; Dick Dabney, "God's Own Network," *Harper's*, Aug. 1980, p. 33.

17. Humbard in Peter G. Horsfield, *Religious Television* (New York: Longman, 1984), p. 32; Jeffrey K. Hadden and Charles E. Swann, *Prime-Time Preachers* (Reading, Mass.: Addison-Wesley, 1981), p. 2. Dunn: Hadden, *Prime-Time*, p. 145. Annenberg: *U.S. News*, April 23, 1984, p. 68. Episcopal Church: Shriver, *Bible*, p. 113. Robertson: *Psychology Today*, April 1983, p. 21.

IX *Catholics and Fundamentalists Against the ERA*

1. Houston: *Ms.*, Nov. 1977, pp. 60–62, 107. Tanner: *Ensign*, Jan. 1974, p. 7. Kimball: *Miami Herald*, April 20, 1980, p. 1. Interviews with Alice Pottmyer and Catherine East.

2. Interviews with Maureen Fiedler, Mary Jean Collins, and Monica McFadden. Lou Harris from Haima Jellinek. Schlafly: Carol Felsenthal, *The Sweetheart of the Silent Majority* (Garden City, N.Y.: Doubleday, 1981), pp. xi, 25, 118, 245, 273.

3. Interviews with Marjorie Tuite, Mary Daly, Betsy Dunn, Jennifer Jackman, and Fiedler. Young: *Ms.*, July/August 1982, pp. 42–45. Jepsen: *Congressional Record*, June 17, 1981, S 6324, 6327, 6334. Christian Cause: *NCR*, July 30, 1982. Welsh: *WP*, Dec. 12, 1982, p. B 8. Interview with Sonia Johnson.

4. Trade-offs: Jackman interview. Oklahoma and Florida insurance: Interviews with Twiss Butler, Eleanor Smeal, Dunn, and Jackman; NOW ad in *NYT*, June 3, 1982; and NOW research files, Washington, D.C.

5. Mormons: Interviews with Jackman and Johnson; Sacramento, Calif., *Bee*, April 19, 1980, p. 1; *Miami Herald*, April 19, 1980, p. 1.

6. Illinois: Interviews with Katherine Bonk, Collins, Fiedler, and Jackman. See also *NYT*, June 19, 1980, p. 18; June 23, 1982, p. 12; June 26, p. 9.

7. For Schlafly, I have drawn particularly on Felsenthal, *Sweetheart*, pp. xviii, 108, 110, 146, 158, 167, 169, 196, 248, 289. *Schlafly Report*, Jan., 1981. Birch: Janet K. Boles, *Politics of the ERA* (New York: Longman, 1979), p. 67. Walker: *NCR*, July 16, 1982, p. 1, and East interview. Harassment: *Time*, May 4, 1981, p. 29. Donors: *Ms.*, Sept. 1982, p. 42; *New Republic*, April 30, 1977, p. 14; *NCR*, July 16, 1982, p. 1.

8. Fundamentalist Crusade: *NYT*, Sept. 29, 1979, p. 46. Sensenbrenner: National Women's Political Caucus memo, Feb. 7, 1985.

9. Welsh, Congress: *WP*, Dec. 12, 1982, p. B 8; *Ms.*, Sept. 1982, p. 42. Emerson: Elizabeth Alexander and Maureen Fiedler, "ERA and Abortion," *America*, April 12, 1980, p. 314. Iowa: Collins and McFadden interviews. Alan Crawford, *Thunder on the Right* (New York: Pantheon, 1980), p. 274.

10. Maine: Guttmacher Institute *Washington Memo*, Nov. 18, 1984, p. 4. New York: Interview with Noreen Connell; *NYT*, Aug. 3, 1984, p. 1; Family Planning Advocates *Albany Memo*, Aug. 1984, p. 12. Phyllis Schlafly, *The Power of the Positive Woman* (New Rochelle, N.Y.: Arlington House, 1977) in Felsenthal, *Sweetheart*, p. 112.

X *Politics and Money at the Vatican*

1. John Milton, *Complete Poems and Major Prose*, ed. Merritt Hughes (New York: Odyssey, 1957), p. 738. Galileo: *NYT*, Nov. 11, 1979, p. 5. Interviews with Tatina Drudi and Carla Ravaioli.

2. The analysis of Pope Pius XII is based largely on documents supplied by Charles R. Allen, Jr., and on interviews with him. This and six preceding paragraphs: Scavizzi, Lwów, "propaganda," Tisserant in Deborah E. Lipstadt, "Moral Bystanders," *Society*, March/April 1983, pp. 21–26. Christmas 1942, in Lipstadt, "Moral Bystanders," and Gerhart M. Riegner, "The Holocaust and Vatican Diplomacy," *Reform Judaism*, Fall 1984, pp. 12–13, 30.

3. This and four preceding paragraphs: Mediocre in *Christian Century*, April 22, 1964, p. 507. Morley: Lipstadt quoting John Morley, *Vatican Diplomacy and the Jews During the Holocaust, 1939–1943* (New York: Ktav, 1980). SS escape: Charles R. Allen, Jr., "The Vatican and the Nazis," *Reform Judaism*, Spring/Summer 1983, pp. 4–5. Barbie, Rauff: Allen, "Barbie's Escape," *JTA*

Daily News Bulletin, Feb. 16, 1983, pp. 1–2. Ustachi: William Bole, "Who Helped Nazis Escape to America?" *Present Tense*, Summer 1986, pp. 6–10. Dragonovic known as Krunoslav also.

4. Graham in Bole, *ibid*, p. 5. La Vista in Allen, *Reform*, p. 5.

5. Pius X: Interview with Arthur Hertzberg. John Paul II: *NYT*, April 14, 1986, p. 1.

6. For editing of Vietnam analysis, I am indebted to Donald Luce. Kennedy, Spellman, Martin: John Cooney, *The American Pope* (New York: Times Books, 1984), pp. 241, 306. Ottaviani: C. Stanley Lowell, *Report from Vietnam* (Washington, D.C.: Americans United for Separation of Church and State, 1972), p. 28.

7. Paul VI, Spellman: Cooney, *Pope*, pp. 292, 306.

8. This and five preceding paragraphs: Bishop appointments, Indonesia, Hunthausen, Lehrman in *NCR*, Nov. 7, 1986, p. 15; May 24, 1985, p. 10; Dec. 6, 1985, p. 2; May 23, 1986, p. 8. Netherlands, Hunthausen: *NYT*, May 23, 1985, p. A 13; Nov. 28, 1985, p. A 16; Sept. 5, 1986, p. A 10. Ratzinger, Küng: E. J. Dionne, Jr., "Pope's Guardian of Orthodoxy," *NYT Magazine*, Nov. 24, 1985, p. 41; *NCR*, June 21, 1985.

9. *C & S*, Sept. 1985, pp. 13–16. Paul Hoffmann, *O Vatican!* (New York: Congdon & Weed, 1984), pp. 229–42.

10. The analysis of Vatican finances is based largely on documents supplied by Umberto Venturini and Lee Seldes, and on interviews with them. $20 billion: Malachi Martin, *Rich Church, Poor Church* (New York: Putnam's, 1984), pp. 14, 49, 72. Marcinkus, Sindona contributions, drugs: *NCR*, Feb. 28, 1975, p. 3; April 4, 1986, p. 4.

11. Frankel, Kenney, Bordoni in *Trial Record*, U.S. Dist. Ct., N.Y., Feb. 13–15, 1980, pp. 2637, 2639, 3048–49. "Colossal losses": Carlo Bordoni in *Il Mondo*, Feb. 13, 1978, "Ten Years with Sindona." Sindona banks: Seldes letter in *Barron's*, April 1, 1980. Christian Democratic: Tana De Zulueta, *Sunday Times* (London), Jan. 6, 1980. Videotaped witnesses: Seldes letter.

12. Calvi and Marcinkus, Latin America, "letters of comfort": Larry Gurwin, "Death of a Banker," *Institutional Investor*, Oct. 1982, pp. 105–27. Opus Dei: *C & S*, Sept. 1985, pp. 13–16. Pazienza: *NYT*, Sept. 15, 1985, p. E 3; Dec. 13, p. A 3. Andreatta: Rupert Cornwell, *God's Banker* (New York: Dodd, Mead, 1983), pp. 228, 232. Arrest Warrant: *NCR*, March 6, 1987, p. 1.

13. Interview with Ettore Massina.

14. Cameroon: *NYT*, Aug. 13, 1985, p. A 3; Aug. 16, p. A 4. *NCR*, Feb. 7, 1986, p. 2. African bonds: *NCR*, April 4, 1986, p. 18.

XI *Radical Nuns and Troublesome Priests*

1. Gramick, Gartner: *NCR*, Feb. 8, 1985, p. 18; March 18, p. 23. Rausch: address, Religious Newswriters Association, Chicago, May 17, 1977. Kopp: Ann Patrick Ware, ed., *Midwives of the Future* (Kansas City, Mo.: Leaven, 1985), p. 206. John Paul II: *C & S*, April 1985), p. 7. Nuns ad: *NYT*, Oct. 7, 1984, p. E 7. Riesman: Ware, *Midwives*, p. 80.

2. Interviews with Maureen Fiedler and Ann Patrick Ware. *Gaudium*: art. 62, par. 9 in Walter M. Abbott, ed., *The Documents of Vatican II* (New York: America Press, 1966), p. 270. King march: Ware, *Midwives*, p. 211.

3. Willinger: John Gregory Dunne, *Delano* (New York: Farrar, Straus & Giroux, 1967), pp. 50, 83. Chavez: Mark Day, *Forty Acres* (New York: Praeger, 1971), p. 58.

4. Interview with Leonard Swidler. Congar, McKenzie, Fiorenza: Leonard and Arlene Swidler, *Women Priests* (New York: Paulist Press, 1977), pp. 8, 213, 120.

5. Interviews with Ada Maria Isasi-Diaz and Kristen Wenzel. McDonnell, Dominican: Ware, *Midwives*, pp. 202, 152. Degrees: *Newsweek*, Feb. 4, 1985, p. 63.

6. Letters from Diane Christian. Nun recruitment: *Cath. Al.*, 1986, pp. 436, 441. Rothluebber: *NCR*, March 1, 1985, p. 16. Fina: *Out of Order* (TV script, Documentary Research, Inc., Buffalo, N.Y.), pp. 1, 8, 10. Cullom, Gramick: *New Woman, New Church*, July 1984, p. 3. Morancy, Violet: *NYT*, May 6, 1984, p. 29; Jan. 14, 1985, p. C 12. Arlene Violet was defeated for reelection as state attorney general in Nov. 1986.

7. Interviews with Fiedler, Frances Kissling, and Marjorie Maguire. Hatch: Religious News Service, June 1, 1982. May: *Time*, Feb. 4, 1985, p. 62. For dismissal, see Canon Law Nos. 696, 698, 1398; *Probe*, Jan./Feb. 1985, p. 5. Quinn: Jane O'Reilly, "On the Vatican 24," *Vogue*, April 1985, p. 182. Traxler: *NCR*, Feb. 1, 1985, p. 5.

8. Theological Society: David Anderson, UPI, Feb. 2, 1985. Gramick, Carr, Vaughan, abortion: *NCR*, Aug. 15, 1986, pp. 6, 20; Oct. 19, 1984, p. 2; May 3, 1985, p. 3; April 5, 1985, pp. 19–20; Feb. 22, 1985, p. 17.

9. Solidarity ad: Kissling interview. Statements by Barbara Ferraro and Patricia Hussey at "Ethical Issues in Reproductive Health: Religious Perspectives" (conference sponsored by Catholics for a Free Choice, Washington, D.C., Dec. 5–6, 1986). Hussey: *NCR*, Aug. 15, 1986, p. 20; *NYT*, March 2, 1986, p. 31. Loretto, Traxler: *NCR*, July 4, 1985, p. 15; Aug. 15, 1986, p. 20. Interview with Eugene Brake.

10. Interviews with Fiedler, Lora Ann Quinonez, and Marjorie Tuite. Statements at Free Choice conference by Ferraro and Marilyn Thie. Vatican powerless: *Probe*, Jan./Feb. 1985, p. 3. Ashe: Ware, *Midwives*, p. 222.

11. Ordination: *NYT/CBS* poll, Nov. 1985; *NCR*, June 20, 1986, p. 3. *Pastoral on Equality* (Priests for Equality, West Hyattsville, Md., Dec. 8, 1984, p. 2). Priests' marriage: Malachi Martin, *The Final Conclave* (New York: Stein & Day, 1978), pp. 75–77. Andrew M. Greeley, *American Catholics Since the Council* (Chicago: Thomas More, 1985), p. 115. Eder, Henriques, Koop: James F. Colaianni, *Married Priests and Married Nuns* (New York: Ace, 1968), pp. 25, 26, 125, 150.

12. Interview with John Cooney. Shorter, Nugent, Simon: *NCR*, Feb. 7, 1986, p. 7; Oct. 4, 1985, p. 18; May 10, 1986, p. 15. Lesbian nuns: *NYT*, April 12, 1985, p. A 12. McNichols: *NYT Book Review*, Nov. 25, 1984, p. 30. Gordon: *NCR*, March 6, 1987, p. 20.

13. Pedophilia: *NCR*, June 7, 1985, pp. 1, 4–5; Aug. 2, p. 1; Jan. 17, 1986, p. 3. *NYT*, May 4, 1986, p. 26. Gauthe, Portland: *NCR*, June 7, 1985, pp. 4–21. Lafayette: *NYT*, May 4, 1986, p. 26. New Ways: *NCR*, April 4, 1986, p. 13.

14. Homosexuality: *Principles to Guide Confessors in Questions of Homosexuality* (Washington, D.C.: NCCB, 1973), p. 3. McNeil: *NYT*, July 14, 1984, p. 10. Georgetown: *NYT*, Oct. 31, 1984, p. E 6; July 31, 1985, p. E 4; *NCR*, Oct. 28, 1983, p. 17. Ratzinger: *NCR*, Nov. 14, 1986, p. 1. Dignity: *NYT*, March 9, 1987, p. B 3.

15. Interview with Martha Mann. O'Connor: *NYT*, May 8, 1985, p. 1; May 9, p. A 30; May 20, B 5; March 17, 1986, p. B 3. Hunt: *NCR*, March 15, 1985, p. 36.

XII *Liberation Theology: Challenge to the Vatican*

1. Interview with Sonia Mindlin. John Paul II: *Newsweek*, Feb. 11, 1985, p. 36. Walter J. Broderick, *Camilo Torres* (Garden City, N.Y.: Doubleday, 1975), pp. 161, 195, 318.

2. This and five preceding paragraphs: Interview with Jerry Persha, Maryknoll, N.Y. Population: Interview with Sheldon Segal. Jean Luis Segundo, *Liberation of Theology* (Maryknoll, N.Y.: Orbis Books, 1976), p. 190. Wealth: Philip Berryman, *Religious Roots of Rebellion* (Maryknoll, N.Y.: Orbis Books, 1984), p. 44. Arrupe: Redmond Mullin, *The Wealth of Christians* (Maryknoll, N.Y.: Orbis Books, 1983), p. 213. Gustavo Gutiérrez, *Theology of Liberation* (Maryknoll, N.Y.: Orbis Books, 1973), p. 113. Patience: Alvaro Barreiro, *Basic Ecclesial Communities* (Maryknoll, N.Y.: Orbis Books, 1982). p. 50. Boff: Jon Sobrino, *Christology at the Crossroads* (Maryknoll, N.Y.: Orbis Books, 1984), p. xi. Primacy: Hugo Assmann, *Theology for a Nomad Church* (Maryknoll, N.Y.: Orbis Books, 1976), p. 59.

3. Interview with Avery Dulles. Gutiérrez: Dennis McCann, *Christian Realism and Liberation Theology* (Maryknoll, N.Y.: Orbis Books, 1981), p. 159; Michael Novak, ed., *Liberation South, Liberation North* (Washington, D.C.: American Enterprise Institute, 1981), p. 59; Arthur F. McGovern, *Marxism: An American Christian Perspective* (Maryknoll, N.Y.: Orbis Books, 1980), p. 199. Vidales: *Christian Century*, May 29, 1985, p. 553. Boff: *NYT*, Feb. 16, 1985. *Theology of Liberation*, p. 190. Supreme norm: *America*, Sept. 22, 1984, p. 138. Sobrino: *Christology*, p.

36. Cámara: Penny Lernoux, *Cry of the People* (Garden City, N.Y.: Doubleday, 1980), p. 411; John Eagleson, ed., *Christians and Socialism* (Maryknoll, N.Y.: Orbis Books, 1975), p. 153; International Documentation and Communication Center, *Church at the Crossroads* (Rome, 1978), p. 175; Lernoux, *Cry*, p. 201.

4. *Rerum: Pap. Encyc.* 1878–1903, p. 241; *Quadragesimo*, 1903–1939, p. 415; *Divini*, 1903–1939, p. 537; *Populorum*, 1958–1981, p. 183; *Laborem*, 1958–1981, p. 297. *Gaudium et Spes*, The Pastoral Constitution on the Church in the Modern World, in Walter M. Abbott, ed., *The Documents of Vatican II* (New York: America Press, 1966).

5. Interview with William Davis. Silva: Eagleson, *Christians*, pp. 41, 47, 238. Trujillo, DeRance: The Foundation Center, New York; Lernoux, *Cry*, p. 306; Daniel H. Levine, ed., *Churches and Politics in Latin America* (Beverly Hills, Calif.: Sage, 1979), p. 62; Gustavo Gutiérrez, *The Power of the Poor in History* (Maryknoll, N.Y.: Orbis Books, 1983), p. ix.

6. John Paul II: Levine, *Churches*, p. 63; John Eagleson and Philip Scharper, eds., *Puebla and Beyond* (Maryknoll, N.Y.: Orbis Books, 1979), p. 32; National Catholic News Service, July 17, 31, 1980. Virginia M. Bouvier, *Alliance or Compliance* (Syracuse, N.Y.: Syracuse Universiy, Maxwell School of Citizenship and Public Affairs, Foreign and Comparative Studies, Latin American Series No. 3, 1983), p. 75; IDOC, *Church*, p. 122. James Brockman, *The World Remains: A Life of Oscar Romero* (Maryknoll, N.Y.: Orbis Books, 1982), pp. 148, 173, 201, 212.

7. Communities: Mindlin and Persha interviews. Boff: *NYT*, March 21, 1985, p. A 18. Cox: *NCR*, Dec. 6, 1985, p. 9. See also Barreiro, *Basic*, pp. 9, 13, 58.

8. Cardenal: *NYT*, Dec. 11, 1984, p. A 3. Obando: Stephen Kinzer, "Nicaragua's Combative Archbishop," *NYT Magazine*, Nov. 18, 1984, p. 75; *NCR*, Jan. 31, 1986, p. 9; Feb. 7, p. 2. Reagan: *America*, Nov. 10, 1984, p. 294; Renny Golden, Michael McConnell, *Sanctuary: The New Underground Railroad* (Maryknoll, N.Y.: Orbis Books, 1986), p. 85. Denton: *C & S*, Dec. 1983, p. 15; *NCR*, Dec. 30, 1983, p. 1.

9. Interview with Eugene Brake. Obando: *NYT*, Aug. 1, 1984, p. A 6; July 10, p. A 10; Kinzer, p. 102. Callahan: *NCR*, Feb. 14, 1986, p. 7. Ratzinger: *Nation*, June 2, 1984, p. 657; *Newsweek*, Feb. 11, 1985, p. 36; *NYT*, Sept. 2, 1984, p. 8; Sept. 4, p. 1

10. Boff: *Christian Century*, May 29, 1985, p. 553; *NYT*, May 9, 1985, p. 21; April 6, 1986, p. 1; July 7, p. A 3; *NCR*, March 29, 1985, p. 21; May 2, 1986, p. 4.

11. Sin: *NCR*, March 7, 1986, p. 23; *NYT*, Feb. 15, 1986, p. 1; March 28, p. 9; Feb. 27, p. A 17. Guerrillas: *NYT*, Feb. 28, 1986, p. A 13; March 2, p. 14; *NCR*, March 28, 1986, p. 9.

12. Interview with Marjorie Tuite. Jon Sobrino, *The True Church and the Poor* (Maryknoll, N.Y.: Orbis Books, 1985), pp. 202, 216, 223, 78, 122.

XIII Sanctuary: "The People Have Become the Church"

1. Interview with William Davis. Fife: *NYT*, May 6, 1986, p. A 20. Nicgorski: Renny Golden and Michael McConnell, *Sanctuary: The New Underground Railroad* (Maryknoll, N.Y.: Orbis Books, 1986), p. 78.

2. Interviews with Eugene Brake, Davis, John Steinbruck. Chevrier: Golden, *Sanctuary*, p. 49. Bernardin: *NCR*, Dec. 18, 1986, p. 4.

3. Interview with Maureen Fiedler. Sheatzley: Golden, *Sanctuary*, p. 79. Nicgorski: *NCR*, May 16, 1986, p. 5. Mahony, Fitzpatrick: *NYT*, June 15, 1986, p. 10. June 28, 1984, p. A 10. Clark: *NCR*, May 9, 1986, p. 1.

4. Interview with Lora Ann Quinonez and Ada Maria Isasi-Diaz. Haitians: U.S. Dist. Ct., S.D., Fla., 2 July 1980, No. 79-2086-Civ. JKL, 503 F. Supp. 442 (1980), p. 442 ff., in *Refugee Center* v. *Civiletti*, Larradee: Gary MacEoin and Nivita Riley, *No Promised Land* (Boston: Oxfam America, 1982), p. 57. Asylum: Golden, *Sanctuary*, p. 203; *NYT*, Dec. 29, 1985, p. E 14; April 17, 1986, p. 1.

5. Interview with Davis. Golden, *Sanctuary*, pp. 132, 30.

6. Clarke: Golden, *Sanctuary*, p. 132. Palfrey, Parker: Lawrence Lader, *The Bold Brahmins: New England's War Against Slavery* (New York: Dutton, 1961), pp. 110, 143–45.

7. Cox: *NYT*, March 3, 1986, p. A 15. Sánchez-Galan: Golden, *Sanctuary*, pp. 64–66. Hartado: Allan Nairn, "Assault on Sanctuary," *Progressive*, Aug. 1985, p. 20.

8. Statements by Morton M. Halperin, Wade J. Henderson, Carol L. Wolchok, ACLU Washington office, before House Judiciary Committee, Subcommittee on Immigration, Nov. 7, 1985. *The Fates of Salvadorans Expelled from the United States* (Washington, D.C.: ACLU, Political Asylum Project, Sept. 5, 1984). Golden, *Sanctuary*, p. 70.

9. Corbett: *NCR*, Jan. 25, 1985, p. 26; David Quammen, "Keepers of the Flame," *Esquire*, June 1985, p. 253. Fiedler: Ann Patrick Ware, ed., *Midwives of the Future* (Kansas City, Mo.: Leaven, 1985), pp. 37–52.

10. This and three preceding paragraphs: Interviews with Stanley Henshaw and Edith Tiger. DiMarzio: *C & S*, Sept. 1985, p. 3. Immigration statistics: *NYT*, June 26, 1986, p. D 22; Oct. 19, p. A 26. Immigration Act: HR 3810 (1986).

XIV   "The Finest Document"—The Bishops Against Nuclear War

1. Zabelka: *NCR*, Nov. 15, 1985, pp. 9–10. Gallup: *U.S. News*, May 16, 1983, p. 33. Hesburgh: Philip J. Murnion, ed., *Catholics and Nuclear War* (New York: Crossroad, 1983), p. vii.

2. Pastoral Letter Pt. 332 in James Castelli, *The Bishops and the Bomb* (Garden City, N.Y.: Doubleday, 1983), p. 97. *Pacem: Pap. Encyc.* 1958–1981, p. 119. Paul VI: Philip Lawler, *The Ultimate Weapon* (Chicago: Regnery, 1984), p. 116.

3. Interview with James Castelli. Malone: *NYT*, March 16, 1985, p. 1; March 17, p. 37. Reilly, Gumbleton: *Time*, Nov. 29, 1982, p. 68. Chittister: Robert F. Drinan, *Beyond the Nuclear Freeze* (New York: Seabury, 1983), p. 112. Malone: *NYT*, Nov. 13, 1984, p. A 22.

4. Interview with Marjorie Tuite. Schlafly: *New Republic*, May 30, 1983, p. 15. Lehman, Weakland: *Newsweek*, May 16, 1983, p. 26. Buckley, Novak, Hannan: *Time*, Nov. 8, 1982, p. 16; May 16, 1983, p. 65.

5. O'Connor, Hunthausen: Castelli, *Bishops*, pp. 97, 27; Francis Schaeffer, Vladimir Bukovsky, and James Hitchcock, *Who Is for Peace?* (Nashville, Tenn.: Nelson, 1983), p. 90.

6. Quinn: Lawler, *Ultimate*, p. 20; *Christian Century*, May 25, 1983, p. 520. Bernardin: *Time*, Nov. 29, 1982, p. 68. Pastoral: Castelli, *Bishops*, pp. 190, 192.

7. Hehir: *New Republic*, May 30, 1983, p. 15. O'Brien: Judith A. Dwyer, *The Catholic Bishops and Nuclear War* (Washington, D.C.: Georgetown University Press, 1984), pp. 40–42. Zahn: Murnion, *Catholics*, p. 130.

8. Greeley: *NCR*, April 12, 1985, p. 11. Chittister: *NCR*, Sept. 13, 1985, p. 13. Matthiesen: *America*, May 21, 1983, p. 393; Lawler, *Ultimate*, p. 20.

9. "Economic Justice for All: Catholic Social Teaching and the U.S. Economy" (National Catholic News Service, Washington, D.C., in *Origins*, 1st draft, Nov. 15, 1984; 2nd draft, Oct. 10, 1985). See Part 2, Pt. VII B; Part 1, Pt. II C, p. 339, and Pt. II B, p. 339 in 1st dr.; Chap. II, Pt. 77, p. 226 in 2nd dr.

10. Falwell: *Christian Century*, Dec. 19, 1984, p. 1200. *Origins*, 2nd draft, II, Pt. 197 d, p. 277; II, Pt. 90, p. 267.

11. *Pap. Encyc.*: Quadragesimo, 1903–1939, pp. 415–41; *Pacem*, 1958–1981, pp. 108–27; *Populorum*, 1958–1981, pp. 183–99. *Origins*, 2nd draft, II, Pt. 95, p. 268; II, Pt. 170, p. 274; II, Pt. 181, p. 275; I, Pt. 20, p. 260; I, Pt. 17, p. 259; IV, Pt. 308, p. 287.

12. Zumwalt: *NYT Magazine*, Aug. 12, 1984, p. 25. Simon: *Christian Century*, Dec. 19, 1984; p. 1200; *Business Week*, Nov. 12, 1984, p. 104.

XV   "Epic Change": 1984–1986

1. Interviews with Barbara McSweeney, Leo Pfeffer, and Marc Stern. Denton, Safire: *NYT*, June 26, 1984, p. A 1; July 30, p. A 21. *Bender v. Williamsport Area School District*, 741 F. 2d 538 (3d Cir.), *Vacated*, 54 U.S.L.W. 4307 (1986). USCC: *C & S*, May 1986, p. 5.

2. Interviews with Hyman Bookbinder and Dean M. Kelley. Safire: *NYT*, July 30, 1984, p. A 21. NCC: *NYT*, May 2, 1984, p. A 26 citing April 27 letter.

3. Interview with Howard Kohr. *Engel* v. *Vitale*, 370 U.S. 421 (1962). Denton: *NCR*, April 27, 1984, p. 2. President: *C & S*, March 1984, p. 10. McCarthy: *WP*, Feb. 12, 1984.

4. *Abington School District* v. *Schempp*, 374 U.S. 203 (1963); *Murray* v. *Curlett, ibid.* Bergstrom: *C & S*, April 1984, p. 6.

5. Interview with Albert J. Menendez. *Wallace* v. *Jaffree*, 105 S. Ct. 2479 (1985). Bell, McCord: *NCR*, March 16, 1984, p. 22; *C & S*, Nov. 1983, pp. 4–5.

6. Interviews with Florence Flast and Stanley Geller. *Mueller* v. *Allen*, 403 U.S. 388 (1983). *Aguilar* v. *Felton*, 105 S. Ct. 3232 (1985). *Grand Rapids School District of the City of Grand Rapids* v. *Ball*, 105 S. Ct. 3216 (1985). Vans, Hasidic: *NYT*, April 22, 1986, p. B 1; Oct. 21, p. B 5.

7. Bennett, Boonville, Michigan: *C & S*, April 1986, p. 4; March, p. 4; Jan. p. 12.

8. Interview with Marshall Beil. *Lynch* v. *Donnelly, McCreary*, 465 U.S. 688, 686 (1984). *Village of Scarsdale* v. *McCreary*, 105 S. Ct. 1859 (1985). Kelley, Redlich: *NYT*, Dec. 21, 1984, p. A 10; March 26, p. A 19.

9. Interview with Barbara Radford. South Africa: *NYT*, Sept. 12, 1986, p. A 9. Chicago: *C & S*, Sept. 1986, p. 18.

10. Vath: *NYT*, Jan. 20, 1985, p. 24. Bernardin: *NCR*, Feb. 22, 1985, p. 17. Thomas: *Washington Memo* (Guttmacher Institute), Dec. 5, 1984, p. 2. Scheidler: Patricia Donovan, "The Holy War," *FPP*, Jan./Feb. 1985, pp. 5–9. Webster: *Washington Times*, Dec. 5, 1984, p. A 4. Enough dynamite was placed at the Manhattan clinic of New York PP in Dec. 1986 to have blown out the front of the building and injured or killed many of the occupants if the charge had ignited.

11. Interview with Edith Tiger. Krol: *C & S*, March 1986, p. 7. Likoudis: *Wall Street Journal*, Aug. 6, 1985, p. 1. Schlafly: *Midstream*, Dec. 1985, p. 9. Hatch amendment: 20 U.S.C. § 4059. 50 Fed. Reg. 21194 (1985), to be codified at 34 C.F.R. § 280, 40 (d). In a lawsuit filed in 1986 in the U.S. District Court in Manhattan, the National Emergency Civil Liberties Committee challenged the constitutionality of the Hatch amendment on behalf of such scholars as Isaac Asimov, the author, and B. F. Skinner, the Harvard psychologist. The suit claimed that Hatch violates the Establishment Clause of the First Amendment by removing from schools ideas considered inconsistent with a particular religion.

12. Black footnote: *Torcasso* v. *Watkins*, 367 U.S. 488 (1961), fn 11. Humanism: *NYT*, Feb. 28, 1986, p. A 19. Church Hill, Robertson, Teachers: *NYT*, Feb. 28, 1986, p. A 19; Sept. 16, p. C 1.

13. *Wright* v. *Houston Independent School District*, 366 F. Supp. 1208 (S.D. Tex., 1972). Jarmin: *NYT*, Nov. 4, 1986, p. C 11.

14. *McLean* v. *Arkansas Board of Education*, 529 F. Supp. 1255 (E.D. Ark., 1982). *Aguillard* v. *Edwards*, 765 F. 2d 1251, rehearing denied, _____ F. 2d _____ (5th Cir., 1985). In Oct. 1986, a federal district judge in Tennessee ruled that the school district had violated the civil rights of seven Fundamentalist families by requiring their children to read about such subjects as evolution, feminism, and humanism and awarded them $50,000 to send their children elsewhere.

XVI *Pluralism in Jeopardy*

1. Statements by Mary Ann Sorrentino at "Ethical Issues in Reproductive Health: Religious Perspectives" (conference sponsored by Catholics for a Free Choice, Washington, D.C., Dec. 5–6, 1986). New Haven, Ct., *Advocate*, March 5, 1986, p. 10. Sorrentino resigned from PP in 1987.

2. Curran: *NYT*, Aug. 19, 1986, p. 1. *NYT*/CBS: *NYT*, Aug. 24, 1986, p. E 7. Infallible: Andrew M. Greeley, *American Catholics Since the Council* (Chicago: Thomas More, 1985), p. 54. Abortion: ABC/*Post* in Guttmacher Institute, *Washington Memo*, Feb. 13, 1985, p. 2. Gallup: *NYT*, Aug. 21, 1986, p. A 14.

3. Interview with Jeannie I. Rosoff. Greeley: *American Catholics*, p. 71.

4. Interview with Joseph O'Rourke.

5. Charles E. Curran, *Politics, Medicine and Christian Ethics* (Philadelphia: Fortress, 1973), pp. 131, 217. *NYT*, Aug. 20, 1986, p. A 10.

6. Ratzinger, theologians: *NYT*, Aug. 19, 1986, p. 1; *NCR*, Aug. 29, 1986, p. 32; Oct. 10, p. 22. Schema, Küng: *NYT*, Oct. 8, 1986, p. 1; Sept. 5, p. 25. Interview with Frances Kissling.

7. Sweeney: *NCR*, Aug. 29, 1986, p. 32; Nov. 21, p. 25.

8. McBrien, Anderson: *NCR*, Sept. 12, 1986, p. 5; Sept. 19, p. 25. Gumbleton, Christi: *NCR*, Oct. 3, 1986, p. 31. NCCB, Weakland: *NYT*, Nov. 13, 1986, p. 1; Oct. 9, p. A 22.

9. *Dei: Pap. Encyc.* 1878–1903, p. 114, Sec. 33; *Delectissimi:* 1903–1939, p. 492, Sec. 6. Spellman: *Bulletin*, Federal Council of Churches, N.Y., May 1940, p. 4. Ireland: *C & S*, Sept. 1986, p. 7. Brennan: *NYT Magazine*, Oct. 5, 1986, p. 79. On Spellman, the Federal Council of Churches commented: "Separation of church and state is no shibboleth; it is one of the priceless treasures of American history, of as much importance today as it ever was." The Federal Council was predecessor of the National Council of Churches.

10. Black: *Everson* v. *Board of Education*, 330 U.S. 1 (1947).

11. For attacks by Cardinal Medeiros and Msgr. Leo Battista on congressional candidates, see Boston *Globe*, Sept. 11, 1980, and other evidence in ARM files, New York. *ARM, Inc.* v. *Secretary of the Treasury*, 544 F. Supp. 471 (S.D.N.Y., 1982) is the lawsuit charging Catholic bishops with violations in U.S. Dist. Ct. So. Dist., New York. O'Connor, Dearie: *NYT*, Sept. 5, 1986, p. 1; Sept. 9, p. B 1, Sept. 11, p. 1.

12. Byrne: *America*, Dec. 6, 1986, p. 356. Stolper: *NYT*, Sept. 13, 1986, p. 31.

13. Equal Acess: Interview with Dean M. Kelley. *City of Akron* v. *Akron Center for Reproductive Health, Inc.*, 462 U.S. 416 (1983). *Thornburgh* v. *American College of Obstetrics and Gynecology*, 106 S. Ct. 2169 (1986).

14. *Griswold* v. *Connecticut*, 381 U.S. 479 (1965). *Mueller* v. *Allen*, 463 U.S. 388 (1983), quoting Justice Lewis F. Powell in *Wolman* v. *Walter*, 433 U.S. 229 (1977). Blackmun: *NYT*, Dec. 14, 1986, p. E 24.

15. Hughes: Ray Allen Billington, *The Protestant Crusade* (Chicago: Quadrangle, 1964), p. 291. Mormon: Duane S. Crowther, *Prophecy: Key to the Future* (Salt Lake City: Bookcraft, 1967), pp. 65–66.

SUPPLEMENTARY BIBLIOGRAPHY

This is a limited list of books that have proved valuable. It does *not* include those already in the footnotes.

Antieau, C. J., P. M. Carroll, and T. C. Burke. *Religion Under the State Constitutions.* New York: Central Book Co., 1965.

Barrett, Patricia. *Religious Liberty and the American Presidency.* New York: Herder and Herder, 1963.

Blanshard, Paul. *American Freedom and Catholic Power.* Boston: Beacon, 1949.

Bronder, Saul E. *Social Justice and Church Authority.* Philadelphia: Temple University Press, 1982.

Buhlmann, Walbert. *God's Chosen Peoples.* Maryknoll, N.Y.: Orbis Books, 1982.

Byers, David M., ed., *Justice in the Marketplace: Collected Statements of the Vatican and the U.S. Catholic Bishops on Economic Policy.* Washington, D.C.: U.S. Catholic Conference, 1985.

Carroll, Jackson W., Douglas W. Johnson, and Martin E. Marty. *Religion in America.* New York: Harper and Row, 1979.

Charles, Rodger, and Orostan Maclaren. *The Social Teaching of Vatican II.* San Francisco: Ignatius Press, 1982.

Comblin, Joseph. *The Church and the National Security State.* Maryknoll, N.Y.: Orbis Books, 1979

Curran, Charles E. *American Catholic-Social Ethics.* Notre Dame, Ind.: University of Notre Dame Press, 1982.

————. *Directions in Catholic Social Ethics.* Notre Dame, Ind.: University of Notre Dame Press, 1985.

Ellis, John Tracy. *American Catholicism.* Chicago: University of Chicago Press, 1956.

Enos, Don, et al. *Displaced Persons in El Salvador.* Washington, D.C.: Bureau for Latin America and the Caribbean, Agency for International Development, 1984.

Falconi, Carlo. *Pope John and the Ecumenical Council.* Cleveland: World Publishing, 1964.

Fletcher, Joseph. *Humanhood: Essays in Biomedical Ethics.* Buffalo: Prometheus Books, 1979.

Gibellini, Rosino, ed. *Frontiers of Theology in Latin America.* Maryknoll, N.Y.: Orbis Books, 1979.

Gilkey, Langdon. *Society and the Sacred.* New York: Crossroad Publishing, 1981.

Gudorf, Christine E. *Catholic Social Teaching on Liberation Themes.* Lanham, Md.: University Press of America, 1980.

262 *Supplementary Bibliography*

Gutiérrez, Gustavo. *Power of the Poor in History.* Maryknoll, N.Y.: Orbis Books, 1983.
———. *We Drink from Our Own Wells.* Maryknoll, N.Y.: Orbis Books, 1984.
Hennelly, Alfred T. *Theologies in Conflict.* Maryknoll, N.Y.: Orbis Books, 1979.
Herberg, Will. *Protestant, Catholic, Jew.* Garden City, N.Y.: Doubleday, 1955.
Hitchcock, James. *The Decline and Fall of Radical Catholicism.* New York: Herder and
Herder, 1971.
Howe, Mark DeWolfe. *The Garden and the Wilderness.* Chicago: University of Chicago
Press, 1965.
Hughes, Emmet J. *The Church and the Liberal Society.* Princeton, N.J.: Princeton
University Press, 1944.
Kaiser, Robert B. *The Politics of Sex and Religion.* Kansas City, Mo.: Leaven Press,
1985.
Katz, Wilber G. *Religion and the American Constitution.* Evanston, Ill.: Northwestern
University Press, 1964.
Konvitz, Milton R. *Fundamental Liberties of a Free People.* Ithaca, N.Y.: Cornell Uni-
versity Press, 1957.
Küng, Hans. *Structures of the Church.* Notre Dame, Ind.: University of Notre Dame
Press, 1964.
Kurland, Philip B. *Church and State: The Supreme Court and the First Amendment.*
Chicago: University of Chicago Press, 1975.
LaNoue, George R. *Public Funds for Parochial School.* New York: National Council of
Churches of Christ, 1963.
McMillan, Joseph. *Catholic Principles and Our Political Parties.* New York: Vantage
Press, 1971.
Mecham, John L. *Church and State in Latin America.* Chapel Hill, N.C.: University
of North Carolina Press, 1966.
Morgan, Richard E. *The Supreme Court and Religion.* New York: Free Press, 1972.
Murray, John Courtney, ed. *Freedom and Man.* New York: P. J. Kenedy, 1965.
Nash, Ronald. *Freedom, Justice, and the State.* Lanham, Md.: University Press of
America, 1980.
O'Brien, David J. *Renewal of American Catholicism.* New York: Oxford University
Press, 1972.
Pfeffer, Leo. *God, Caesar, and the Constitution.* Boston: Beacon, 1975.
Quade, Quentin L., ed. *The Pope and Revolution.* Washington, D.C.: Ethics and Public
Policy Center, 1983.
Ryan, John A., and F. J. Boland. *Catholic Principles of Politics.* New York: Macmillan,
1940.
Shields, Currin V. *Democracy and Catholicism in America.* New York: McGraw-Hill,
1958.
Sizer, Theodore R., ed. *Religion and Public Education.* Boston: Houghton Mifflin, 1967.
Smith, Brian H. *Church and Politics in Chile.* Princeton, N.J.: Princeton University
Press, 1982.
Stuhlmueller, Carroll, ed. *Women and Priesthood.* Collegeville, Minn.: Liturgical Press,
1978.
Tracy, David, Hans Küng, and Johann B. Metz, eds. *Towards Vatican III.* New York:
Seabury Press, 1978.
Wakin, Edward, and Joseph F. Scheuer. *The De-Romanization of the American Catholic
Church.* New York: Macmillan, 1966.

INDEX